# THE
# FIRST OF THE BOURBONS
## Vol. II.

### Large Paper Edition

This edition is limited to one thousand copies, of which this is Number 139.

# The First of the Bourbons. BY CATHERINE CHARLOTTE, LADY JACKSON

*IN TWO VOLUMES*
*VOLUME II.*

**WILDSIDE PRESS**

# CONTENTS OF VOL. II.

### CHAPTER I.
PAGE

The Huguenots, Being Dissatisfied with Henri, Hold Aloof from His Army. — Conference at Chauny. — D'Aubigné's Prediction. — Gabrielle's Reply. — Rosny Endeavours to Dissuade the King from Declaring War against Spain. — Council of War Favours Henri's Project. — Philip Enraged at the Béarnais's Presumption. — Sancy and the Marquise. — Henri at Franche-Comté. — His Daring Valour. — Proposals to Mayenne. — Bad News from the North. — Absolution Granted by Clement VIII. — Prince Henri of Condé Taken from the Huguenots . . . 1

### CHAPTER II.

The Pontifical Absolution Being Granted after Three Years' Consideration, Mayenne, with a Safe Conscience, Can Bend the Knee to the Béarnais. — Jeannin Employed to Negotiate Terms. — The King's Concessions Regarded as Excessive. — Gabrielle Supposed to Have Interceded for Mayenne. — The Swiss Request Henri to Evacuate the Neutral Territory of Franche-Comté. — Great Losses in Fortresses, Troops, and General Officers. — Cruelty of the Spaniards. — Cambray taken. — Calais Threatened. — Guise Family Declared Innocent of Complicity in the Assassination of Henri III. — Guise's Conquest of Provence. — Marseilles Snatched from Philip's Grasp . . 15

### CHAPTER III.

Elizabeth, Requested to Send Her Fleet to the Coasts of France, Refuses. — Consents When too Late. — Spaniards Take Calais. — La Fère Surrenders. — Impoverished Treasury. — King Anxious to Place Rosny in the Financial Council.— Great Opposition Encountered. — A Perilous Journey. — King's Emotion. — Proposal to Revive Feudalism. — King's Indignation with Montpensier. — Explains to Him How He May Repair His Error. — Montpensier Penitent. — Rosny Refuses to Attempt to Conciliate Opposing Members of the Council. — Disappointed, He Determines to Leave the Court. — Death of His Brother a Pretext. — Bouillon Ambassador, Rosny Refuses to Accompany Him. — Gabrielle Approves Rosny's Conduct. — He Is Appointed Director of the Council . . . . . . . . . . 36

## CHAPTER IV.

Assembly of Notables Convoked at Rouen. — Rosny Enters on His Duties as Superintendent of Finance. — Great Opposition from Members of the Council. — Obtains 500,000 Crowns for the King's Use. — Arrival of Legate in Paris. — Little Prince Henri of Condé Sent to Meet Him. — Clement VIII. Anxious for the Cessation of War. — Henri Not Unwilling, yet Prepares for War. — Henri's Harangue to the Notables. — Gabrielle Surprised to Hear the King Speak of Putting Himself *en Tutelle*. — The Notables Dismissed. — Birth of a Daughter. — Her Royal Christening at Rouen. — The Edict of 1577 in Favour of Huguenots Registered . . . . 56

## CHAPTER V.

Unsatisfactory Result of the Discussions of the Notables. — Astrologers Prophesy Evil Things. — Court Festivities and Efforts to be Mirthful. — A Last Appeal to Madame Catherine. — Rosny Entreats to be Excused from Making It. — The King Will Accept No Excuses. — The Visit to Fontainebleau. — The Princess, Indignant That He Should Meddle in the Affairs of Persons above Him, Calls Him a Sycophant and Complains to the King, Who at First Receives Rosny Coldly. — Reconciliation. — A Grand Christening. — Amiens Taken by Surprise. — Great Consternation . . . . . . . 70

## CHAPTER VI.

Raising Money to Carry on the Siege of Amiens. — Parliament, Refractory, Refuses to Register the King's Edicts. — Rosny's Successful Efforts to Equip the Army after

Some Delay. — Elizabeth Refuses to Take Calais. — Huguenots Again Rally Round Henri. — "Charmante Gabrielle." — Successful Siege. — Henri's Imprudence. — Amiens Capitulates, 19th of September. — *Te Deum* Chanted. — Tomb of Porto-Carrero. — Death of Saint-Luc. — Entry into Paris. — The Grand-mastership of the Artillery. — D'Estrées Reappointed. — Rosny's Ill-feeling towards Gabrielle . . . . . . . . 89

CHAPTER VII.

Renewal of Peace Negotiations. — Elizabeth and the United Provinces Withdraw. — Henri Marches on Brittany. — Huguenots Press Their Claims. — A Bribe to Gabrielle from Mercœur, Who Offers His Only Child and Heiress in Marriage to César Monsieur. — The Offer Accepted. — César Made Duke and Peer, and Presented with the Duchy of Vendôme. — Magnificent Betrothal. — Rosny Greatly Mortified. — Movement to Nantes. — Famous Edict Signed There. — Visit to Rennes. — Chenonceaux Exchanged with the Queen for Moulins. — Peace Signed by the King and the Archduke. — Death of Philip II. . 108

CHAPTER VIII.

Rosny Remarks That the King, Notwithstanding the *Fêtes* Given in His Honour, is Frequently Silent and Meditative. — He is Troubled about the Succession to the Crown. — He is Recommended to Marry Again, but None of the Princesses of Europe Possess the Qualities Personal or Mental Which Form His Ideal of a Wife. — Only in His Mistress Does He Find Perfection. — Rosny, Astounded, Remonstrates with the King. — A Council Discusses the Marriage Question. — Opinions Vary, and Marguerite is Consulted. — Grand Christening of Gabrielle's Second Son. — Rosny Indignant. — A Terrible Scene. — Gabrielle Faints, and Becomes Ill and Unhappy. — Marriage of Madame Catherine. — A Worthy Archbishop. — Festivities. — Departure for Lorraine . . . . . 123

CHAPTER IX.

Henri Now Determines to Delay No Longer the Verification of the Edict of Nantes. — Henri's Address to the Remonstrances of the Deputies. — Edict Registered 15th February, 1599. — Parliament of Rouen's Resistance. —

King's Divorce Applied for. — Secret Negotiation of Rosny, Villeroy, and Others with Tuscany. — Henri Shrinks from a Medici, but Rosny Is Enamoured of Marie's Dowry of 600,000 Crowns. — Signs and Wonders. — Gabrielle Depressed. — King Seeks to Reassure and Console Her. — Their Parting. — Gabrielle Seized with Strange Pains at Zameti's. — Her Death; Magnificent Funeral. — King's Grief. — Court Mourning. — Duke of Tuscany Suspected. — The Divorce Granted . . . 145

## CHAPTER X.

Parties of Pleasure, Banquets, and the Chase Again Occupy the King. — The Withered Heart is Revivified. — An *Intrigante* of the Court Sells Him Her Smiles for 300,000 Crowns and a Promise of Marriage. — Heaven Comes to Henri's Rescue. — A Scene with Rosny. — Secret Negotiations of His Ministers to Marry Him. — His Excitement on Learning That the Contract is Signed by Them. — Divorce Obtained. — Clement Also Annuls Catherine's Marriage. — Charles Emanuel of Savoy Visits France. — Rosny Buys D'Estrées's Post of Grand Master. — The New Cannon, etc., Shown to Duke of Savoy. — Plots, Intrigues, and Attempts to Assassinate. — War against Savoy Declared . . . . . . . 162

## CHAPTER XI.

The Dispute between Du Perron and Du Plessis-Mornay Occurs While Awaiting the Duke's Decision. — Biron's Treachery. — Rosny's Marvellous Exertions in This War. — The King Inactive. — Under the Spell of His New Mistress. — Clement VIII. Offers His Mediation. — The Grand Master's Reception of the Legate. — Marriage Negotiation Concluded. — Bellegarde Desires to Represent the King. — The Ceremony at Florence. — The State Galleys. — Arrival at Lyons. — Success of the Campaign Attributed to Rosny and Lesdiguières. — A Wet and Cold Journey. — Legate and Rosny Settle the Peace. — Biron's Treason. — Appointing the Queen's Household. — A Warning to the King. — Dinner at the Arsenal. — The Two Medals . . . . . . . 186

## CHAPTER XII.

The Peace of Lyons Regarded as a Lasting One. — An Insult to the French at Valladolid. — Satisfaction Obtained. — The Grand Seignior and the Venetian States Congratulate the King on His Marriage. — Henri Being at Calais, Elizabeth Repairs to Dover, Desiring to See Him. — He Fears to Give Umbrage to Spain, Should He Cross the Channel. — Rosny Visits London; Is Received by the Queen at Greenwich. — She Explains to Him Her Plan for Curbing the Ambition of Austria. — Rosny Enchanted with Her Wisdom and Prudence. — King Returns to Paris. — The Double *Ménage*. — Maria Furious. — Birth of a Dauphin. — Taken through Paris in His Cradle. — La Rivière's Prediction. — Vague Words. — Queen's Ballet. — The Muses and the Virtues . . 204

## CHAPTER XIII.

Festivities at Court. — Plots and Intrigues among the Discontented. — Biron Complains of the King's Ingratitude, and Resumes His Intrigues with Spain and Savoy on Returning to His Government of Burgundy. — He Is Betrayed by His Confidant. — The King Promises Pardon if He Confesses His Treason and Abstains from It in Future. — Haughtily Declares Himself Innocent. — He is Arrested, also Comte d'Auvergne. — Confronted with La Fin. — Strange Scene. — Sentence of Death. — Execution. — Congratulations. — Duc de Bouillon Retires to Geneva and Germany. — Visit of Maurice le Savant to Paris. — Henri Confesses Himself Still a Protestant. — Death of Queen Elizabeth . . . . 222

## CHAPTER XIV.

The Landgrave of Hesse Takes Leave of the King. — Henri Sets Out for Metz. — He Is Received with Enthusiasm. — The Despotic Lieutenants Dismissed. — The King Spends His Birthday with His Sister, at Nancy, Where He Receives the News of the Birth of a Daughter, to the Great Disappointment of the Queen, Who Had Expected a Son, as Prophesied by a Nun. — Henri Attempts to Console Her. — The Marquise Bribed to Obtain the King's Consent to Galigai's Marriage with Concini. — Is Invited to the Queen's Ballet. — Consent Obtained. — The Queen Furiously Jealous. — England Expected to Fall Again into the Toils of Rome. — Disappointment. — An Embassy to the English Court . . 239

## CONTENTS

### CHAPTER XV.

Rosny's Special Embassy to James I. — Misunderstanding between the English and French Admirals. — Arrival at Dover. — No Lodgings; No Coaches. — Governor Weymmes. — From Dover to Canterbury. — Well Received by the Refugees. — The Cathedral. — Bad Treatment at Next Stage, Rochester. — Arrival at Gravesend. — The King's Barges in Waiting. — The Landing at the Tower. — Salute from the Tower Guns. — Arundel House. — Midnight Brawl between Frenchmen and Englishmen. — One of the Latter Killed. — The Assailant Sentenced by Rosny to Death. — Gives up the Prisoner to the Lord Mayor. — Presented to James. — Dinner at Greenwich. — The Grand Project. — James Interested. — Rosny's Return . . . . . . . . 249

### CHAPTER XVI.

The Marquis's Return to France. — Finds the King Occupied with the Question of the Recall of the Jesuits. — The Council Request That Rosny May Join Them. — He Attends at the King's Desire. — Refuses to Take the Lead in the Matter. — Desires to Consult the King. — Discusses with Him the Disadvantages of Recalling so Dangerous a Set of Priests as the Brotherhood of Jesus. — The King's Reason for Allowing Their Return. — Mariana's Treatise on Royalty. — Father Cotton in Paris. — La Flèche Given to Them. — The Pyramid. — Death of Madame Catherine. — The Legate. — Calvin and Luther. — Concessions to Protestants. — Charenton . . . 264

### CHAPTER XVII.

Henri Surrounded by Traitors. — Nicolas de Hoste Drowned While Escaping. — D'Auvergne Resumes His Intrigues with Spain. — The Marquise Aims at Supplanting the Queen. — She Vows Vengeance on Her Rival. — Scene with the King. — The Marriage Promise Laid at Her Majesty's Feet. — A Brief Space of Tenderness. — Domestic War Renewed with Vigour. — The Marquise Promised an Asylum in Spain. — Henri Entreats Her to Return to Him. — Disdainful Refusal. — A New Mistress Taken. — Arrest of D'Auvergne. — D'Entragues

# LIST OF ILLUSTRATIONS

## VOLUME II.

|  | PAGE |
|---|---|
| MARIE DE' MEDICI | *Frontispiece* |
| CATHERINE DE' MEDICI | 31 |
| PRINCE HENRI OF CONDÉ | 63 |
| CATHERINE HENRIETTE D'ENTRAGUES | 162 |
| CONCINO-CONCINI, MARQUIS D'ANCRE | 212 |
| ELIZABETH OF ENGLAND | 238 |
| DUC DE SULLY | 317 |
| MADAME ROYALE, DAUGHTER OF HENRI IV. | 338 |

# THE
# FIRST OF THE BOURBONS

---

## CHAPTER I.

The Huguenots, Being Dissatisfied with Henri, Hold Aloof from His Army. — Conference at Chauny. — D'Aubigné's Prediction. — Gabrielle's Reply. — Rosny Endeavours to Dissuade the King from Declaring War against Spain. — Council of War Favours Henri's Project. — Philip Enraged at the Béarnais's Presumption. — Sancy and the Marquise. — Henri at Franche-Comté. — His Daring Valour. — Proposals to Mayenne. — Bad News from the North. — Absolution Granted by Clement VIII. — Prince Henri of Condé Taken from the Huguenots.

CHASTEL'S crime to some extent rendered a service to the Huguenots, who, not without reason, had been latterly much dissatisfied with the king. Of the political and religious disabilities they laboured under, none had been removed or even mitigated. Henri feared to offend the Pope, and further to imperil his anxiously expected plenary absolution, should he still show a leaning towards his former coreligionists. They now held aloof from his army —

"the benefits of his conquests," they said, "being all reserved for Catholics." Another campaign was at hand; something, therefore, must be done for them. The assassin's knife, perchance, pricked the king's conscience as well as his lips, and suggested the revival of the edict of 1577, which so much favoured the Protestants that they were declared by it eligible, equally with the Catholics, for appointments to all offices of the state.* Zealous Catholics were still strongly opposed to it; but the king's wishes (his commands had then but little weight) obtained the support of the first president, Achille de Harlay, with that of the more moderate of the members of the Paris Parliament, and the edict was registered.

The Huguenots, however, were not satisfied with it. They would have preferred L'Hôpital's edict of 1562, granted when Catherine de' Medici believed for a time that Protestantism was likely to gain the upper hand in France, and she, too, if it should prove so, was prepared to say her prayers in French with the rest. But this edict, like all others in their favour, was either never registered or never put in force. Something more definite, more to be relied on, was therefore needed, and as the king had abandoned "the religion," the

---

* When this edict was obtained from Henri III., it was said that he must at heart be himself a Protestant to make such concessions to the people of "the religion." It was, however, revoked almost immediately after its publication.

Huguenots proposed to appoint a protector — some Protestant prince, meaning the Duc de Bouillon, who was anxious to assume that character.

Henri, greatly annoyed, declared that he alone was the protector of his subjects, and would tolerate no other. A discussion took place respecting it between Henri and his former friend and negotiator, Du Plessis-Mornay — now rather slighted by the new convert as inconveniently austere. Nothing satisfactory resulted from this conference, which took place at Chauny, whither Gabrielle accompanied the king. On arriving he perceived another of the now neglected stanch friends of his youth — Agrippa d'Aubigné — standing amongst other Huguenot officers and nobles who were there to receive him.

"Ah!" he exclaimed gaily, "*voilà Monseigneur d'Aubigné*," and held out his hand to him.

After a few words of pleasant greeting, he "honoured him with the command to hand the *belle marquise* from her coach," which at that moment drove up. On alighting, she was desired by the king to unmask and salute his old and faithful friend. He then showed D'Aubigné his wounded lip.

"Sire," said the zealous Huguenot, "you have yet renounced God only with your lips, and He is satisfied with piercing them; but should you ever in your heart deny Him, He then will pierce your heart."

"This is an admirable speech, M. d'Aubigné," rejoined Gabrielle; "but is it not an unseasonable one?"

"Perhaps so, madame," he replied, "but it is a true one." It was certainly prophetic.

The recent attempt on his life, of which, in some quarters, Philip was believed to be cognisant and to have approved, confirmed the king in his desire to realise the idea which for some time past he had cherished of striking a powerful blow against Spain, — of defying face to face the enemy who had pursued him from youth to manhood, and who was the cause of all the troubles and misery that had fallen on suffering France. He was strong enough, he thought, to measure his strength against him, and to render him blow for blow. His friend, the Baron de Rosny, to whom he disclosed his project, strongly advised him to defer seeking vengeance more direct until the utter extinction of the League was accomplished. That achieved, he would be better prepared for offensive war; but until then, he considered it injudicious, even dangerous, to urge Philip to some desperate effort against him.

In a council of war it was decided otherwise. Biron, imagining that his greatness and glory depended on the continuance of war, was entirely of the king's opinion. The Duc de Bouillon promised the conquest of Luxembourg, and most of the council and nobles of the court inclined to the idea of putting an end to civil war by engaging in a foreign one. Some few there were of a contrary opinion, who saw that the most desperate valour on the part of the king and his generals would not fully compensate for the insufficiency of troops and the want of money.* However, success was declared infallible, and a formal declaration of war against Philip II. was made on the 17th of January.

Philip had been less energetic of late, and was supposed to be growing weary of war, perhaps owing to increasing years and much bodily suffering. But, whatever the cause, Henri's declaration effectually roused him. His indignation and rage were boundless at the audacity of "the Béarnais," as he derisively named him, in venturing to defy him, "the King of the Spains and the Indies."

The Protestant colonel, Nicolas de Sancy, was anxious that the king should invade the neutral territory of Franche-Comté. He believed that the great influence of Gabrielle — which he knew to his cost was all-powerful with the king — might induce him to attempt it, if she could be prevailed on to mention it to him, by suggesting to her the suitability of Franche-Comté as an appanage with the title of Duke of Burgundy for her son, César Monsieur, whom the king had lately legitimised.

* Henri's Council of Finance, which had been nearly a year established, does not appear to have been more liberal in supplying him with cash than was the superintendent with his treasurers.

Sancy was considered a brave officer, but he was one of those who made offensive jokes at the expense of the marquise, and circulated ridiculous and slanderous stories concerning her and the king.

He could not, therefore, address her himself, but persuaded a lady of the court to pour this tale into her ears. The result does not appear to have been wholly satisfactory, as Sancy himself urged the king to take possession of Franche-Comté, assuring him that the Swiss, with whom he believed he had some influence, would not oppose it. He seems to have been actuated by the expectation of being called upon to effect this arrangement with the cantons, and of being appointed governor.

But already several small towns of Franche-Comté were taken by the Lorraine troops, who had passed into the service of France. Philip immediately ordered the Constable of Castile, Fernando Velasco, to march with 10,000 men to the defence of the Comté, and the Comte de Fuentés to fall at the same time on Picardy, both officers being strictly enjoined to omit not to punish the audacity of Henri of Bourbon and his partisans with the utmost rigour. The Archduke Ernest, Governor of the Netherlands, died early in February, leaving Fuentés acting-governor. Henri believed that hostilities, owing to that event, would be retarded in the North during 1595. He therefore determined on setting out for Burgundy, following Biron, whom he had named governor of the duchy, and who was on his way thither with 5,000 men.

Mayenne was endeavouring at all hazards to maintain his authority there, though Velasco refused to render him assistance. "His mission," he said, "was solely to protect La Franche-Comté." The decapitation, by Mayenne's order, of one of the principal men of the municipality of Dijon inspired no terror in the Burgundians, but deep resentment, and when Biron arrived a sanguinary encounter was taking place in the streets of Dijon between the inhabitants and Mayenne's soldiers, similar scenes having occurred at Beaune and other towns. As his Spanish friends would not aid him to retain possession of Burgundy, Mayenne refused to give it up to them, but doubtless would have gladly recognised Henri IV. had he then confirmed him in the governorship of the province. This he would not do, and Mayenne, driven to despair, was about to seek refuge in Savoy. But the king — from a feeling of pity for his greatly humiliated enemy, and still more because of the certitude that, in concert with Philip, the late pretender to the crown would still find means of prolonging the war and its attendant troubles in France — secretly offered him a safe-conduct to Châlons, where he could remain in full security until terms of peace could be arranged between them. The offer was gladly accepted, as it released Mayenne from the burdensome yoke he had allowed Spain to impose on him.

For two successive months the king overran and ravaged La Franche-Comté, yet was not able to draw Velasco into giving battle. No regular engagement did, in fact, take place, but two very vigorous skirmishes, the second especially recalling what were termed "the king's heroic follies, or errors, of the Journée d'Aumale." But these last instances of his heroism could not be called errors. They were daring deeds of valour in an unexpected position of such extreme danger that few probably would not have done as he was urgently entreated to do (a fleet Arab horse being brought to him), "mount and fly."

A hundred or two of his cavalry were making a reconnoissance, when suddenly the vanguard of the Spanish army appeared, marching directly upon them, the main body following. Instantly they fled in great confusion, and Maréchal de Biron, who strove to rally them, was wounded and carried along with them in their precipitate flight. They met the king, and he, more successful than Biron, put a stop to this *sauve qui peut*, and rallying many of the fugitives around him, instead of retreating with them as they expected, turned with his party of cavaliers to meet the advancing foe. Remonstrances ensued, for the king had no helmet, or armour beyond his gorget, and his few brave cavaliers were scarcely better equipped for defying a powerful army. "Gentlemen," he exclaimed, "no advice; but do as you see I am going to do;" then charging impetuously, he rushed into the midst of the enemy's squadrons, which opened to receive him, and overthrew three or four, each more numerous than his own.

The resolute, uncovered countenance and reckless daring of this modern god of war seemed to have utterly scared or paralysed the enemy, all of whom recognised in his prodigious feats of valour that the great soldier, "Henri of Navarre," was before them. Other detachments of his army arriving — the Protestant Duc de La Trémouille and his Huguenots ably supporting him on this occasion — the fight for a short time became more general, ending in the retreat of the Spaniards and the restoration of Burgundy to the king.*

When writing to his sister after this famous combat, so unequal in numbers, and in which, as in similar encounters, he received no wound, Henri speaks in glowing terms of the bravery of those who were with him, and of the mercy of God towards himself. "Many times before," he tells her, "he had fought for victory, but at Fontaine-Française he fought for life, and was very near leaving her his heir."

The king might have further extended his conquests had not the Swiss prayed him to withdraw his troops and restore La Franche-

* Mathieu; *Mémoires de Sully.*

Comté to the neutrality it had always enjoyed. He at once complied. Sancy had been too confident of the indifference of the cantons to the conquest of that frontier country, whose neutrality was again recognised by both France and Spain.

The news from the North, awaiting the king on arriving at Lyons to arrange terms with the last Leaguer chiefs, greatly damped the satisfaction he had felt with the success of his campaign in the Southeast. Fuentés had ravaged Picardy, taken many towns, and committed, in pursuance of his instructions, the most frightful atrocities. Unhappily, the generals left to conduct the campaign were so much at variance with each other that the misfortunes which had occurred were chiefly due to their quarrels and mutual jealousy.

The distinguished General d'Humières was killed at the siege of Ham, and Admiral Villars, one of the bravest and most active of officers, met with a terrible fate at Doullens, which the Spaniards were besieging, by relying on Bouillon's promise to assist him. Bouillon failed to keep his promise, and Villars, after a desperate struggle, was taken prisoner and horribly mutilated. "The Spaniards were inveterate against him for surrendering Rouen and joining the Royalists. He had but a short enjoyment of his new honours."*

* L'Estoile; *Mémoires de Sully.*

However, to crown the king's success, and to console him for his reverses, Clement VIII., after "mature consideration," determined to absolve the *hérétique relaps*, and to hail him as Most Christian King. It was evident to him, no doubt, that if withheld much longer the absolution would be as lightly regarded as his confirmation of Henri's right to the throne, which by long lingering he had hoped might eventually be sought from him. His holiness announced his intention to the sacred college of cardinals, whose views on the subject he had ascertained to be generally favourable to the royal penitent. Cardinal Colonna alone raised an objection, but was silenced on Clement's declaring his resolution taken.

The 17th of September was named for the public celebration of the event. It was a great day in Rome for "God's vicegerent." A splendid throne was arranged under the portico of the church of Saint-Peter, and there in solemn state, surrounded by the dignitaries of the Roman Church, arrayed in their most sumptuous vestments, sat the holy father, Clement VIII. Kneeling before him and reverently kissing his feet were the king's ecclesiastical representatives, Ossat and Du Perron. To the latter was assigned the reading of the king's confession of crime in following the heresy of Calvin, and his prayer for pardon and absolution.

The absolution granted by the bishops who had presumed to entrench on the sovereign pontiff's prerogative was first annulled, and the prayer of the penitent, on certain conditions, promised. The king's agents having sworn that those conditions should be religiously observed, the choir then chanted the *Miserere*, and at the end of each verse the holy father, being armed with a small switch or wand, inflicted a light blow on the shoulder alternately on each of the king's representatives, kneeling at his feet. Clement then read aloud the formula of absolution, announcing that he received Henri IV. into the bosom of the Church as Very Christian King of France.

The signal given, the bells of the holy city pealed forth in joyous volleys, to which trumpets and drums and the roar of Saint-Angelo's cannon responded, the pious thousands, assembled in the square of Saint-Peter to witness this rare ceremony, adding their loud acclamations to the general uproar. Having again kissed the Pope's feet, his holiness raised both Ossat and Du Perron and embraced them. He had opened, he told them, the gates of the Church militant to the Most Christian King; it now remained with him, by faith and good works, to open the gates of the Church triumphant.

Though there were thanksgivings and rejoicings throughout the land, and the king's agents were recompensed for their zealous services by the highest ecclesiastical dignities, they were yet far from having satisfied the king or any person of intelligence who had at heart the dignity and independence of the crown and the nation. Their submission to the formality of the Pope's correction with the rod was regarded as most humiliating, and no less so the conditions that he should accept and publish the edicts of the Council of Trent, contrary to the rights and liberties of the Gallican Church; that he should reëstablish the Jesuits, and exclude the Protestants from all offices and dignities; that he should even strive to the utmost entirely to exterminate them, and to compel them to make restitution of all that during the long course of religious warfare the Catholics had been deprived of.

He was directed to take the Holy Virgin for his mediatress and patroness, and many puerile practices were enjoined on the great soldier-king as penances. But, according to Rosny, he complied with the conditions imposed on him only so far as he deemed it right to do, rejecting the rest.

That he withdrew, as required, the young Prince Henri of Condé from Saint-Jean d'Angely and the protection of the Protestants to bring him up as a Catholic, contrary to the declared will of the child's father — or, rather, reputed father — was a great blow to the friends of that zealous Huguenot prince. The little Prince Henri was, however, the then presumptive heir to the French throne; but the king's readiness to fulfil the wishes of the Pope being first displayed in a matter so deeply affecting the Huguenots, they, with the sensitiveness natural to their position, were inclined to think that the order depriving them of the guardianship of a prince, looked upon as a future Protestant leader, was but the first step towards a return to the intolerance and persecution of the preceding reigns.

## CHAPTER II.

The Pontifical Absolution Being Granted after Three Years' Consideration, Mayenne, with a Safe Conscience, Can Bend the Knee to the Béarnais. — Jeannin Employed to Negotiate Terms. — The King's Concessions Regarded as Excessive. — Gabrielle Supposed to Have Interceded for Mayenne. — The Swiss Request Henri to Evacuate the Neutral Territory of Franche-Comté. — Great Losses in Fortresses, Troops, and General Officers. — Cruelty of the Spaniards. — Cambray taken. — Calais Threatened. — Guise Family Declared Innocent of Complicity in the Assassination of Henri III. — Guise's Conquest of Provence. — Marseilles Snatched from Philip's Grasp.

IT had been affirmed more than once in the course of the past two years that the League had received its death-blow. Either it was the result of some heroic feat of arms on the part of the king, or of having been laughed into contempt and extinction by the satirists of the "*Ménippée*" and other wits of the day. Yet so long as Spain could be depended on to furnish even diminished supplies of money and men to the chief of the League and the dispirited remnant of the faction, it contrived to linger on and occassionally to show signs of revival.*

* The Leaguers Villeroy and Jeannin — Mayenne's secretaries of state, whom Henri, in the vain endeavour to reconcile all parties, sought to attach to his own interests in the same capacity

When, however, war was declared by Henri IV. against Philip II., and intercepted letters made known to the Duc de Mayenne that the Spaniard Feria had informed his sovereign that the lieutenant-general of the kingdom — of whom he spoke with the utmost contempt — had alone, and for his own ends, thwarted the accomplishment of that sovereign's views on France, then conviction dawned on the mind of the duke that not only his long-cherished scheme of putting the crown on his own head, but even that minor one of snatching a province or two from the heritage of the Béarnais, had utterly and hopelessly collapsed. Ignominiously expelled from Burgundy, he was on the point of seeking refuge at the court of the intriguing Charles Emanuel of Savoy, when Henri, with his accustomed magnanimity, allowed him to repair to a safer asylum at Châlons. Though glad, indeed, to avail himself of it, the chief of the League could not yet bring himself to bow the knee to the prince to whom, but recently, he had sent his agents, Villeroy and Jeannin, with some inadmissible proposal of truce, expecting to treat with him on equal terms, as one sovereign with another.

Ardent zeal for the maintenance of the Roman Catholic faith was the principle always put forward

---

—acknowledged that the League and its wars, from their beginning to their end, were carried on solely by means of the doubloons and the troops of Philip of Spain. — *Mémoires de Sully; Mémoires de Villeroy.*

by Mayenne to conceal from Philip II. his designs on the crown, and to veil from the king the real motive of his opposition to him. But while Henri's renunciation of Protestantism and subsequent coronation, followed by the subjection of Paris, led to the voluntary surrender of several towns until then in arms against him, and the willing submission of the inhabitants, no less inflamed by religious zeal than Mayenne, those events served rather to increase than to abate one jot of the lieutenant-general's hostile feeling towards him.

Solemnly he had sworn that nothing short of the sovereign pontiff's concession of plenary absolution to the relapsed heretic would induce him to acknowledge the Huguenot Henri of Navarre King of France. At the same time, in concert with Philip II., the fanatics of the Vatican, the Jesuits, and other frenzied preachers, he was using every means, and, as it was said, moving heaven and earth, to prevail on the holy father to reject the prayer of the royal penitent, on whose behalf two dignitaries of the Church pleaded in vain for nearly three years.

During the time that the question of again welcoming the stray sheep, or refusing him entrance into the fold of the faithful, remained undecided, Spain and the League experienced many reverses, while Henri progressed slowly but surely towards attaining full possession of his kingdom.

Still Clement wavered, and probably would have continued to waver had not the final defeat of Mayenne in Burgundy roused him to put an end to his indecision, lest the next couriers from Paris should bring him news that the election of a patriarch of the Gallican Church, often threatened, had become an accomplished fact.

For the lieutenant-general the announcement of the pontifical absolution occurred at a most opportune moment. Without doing violence to his scruples of conscience, or suffering from feelings of wounded dignity, he could now swear allegiance to Henri IV., and without delay he did so, — with far more respectful humility, too, than from his former arrogant pretensions might have been expected. Henri, always a generous enemy, at once approved of Mayenne's choice of the president Jeannin (whose fidelity to his late chief in his adversity strongly recommended him to the king) as the negotiator of the terms of peace between them. He was unable then to communicate personally with his former enemy, from the necessity of proceeding post-haste from Lyons to Picardy, with the hope of arriving in time to prevent the surrender of Cambray to General Fuentés. But the Spaniards on his arrival were already in possession.\*

---

\* Cambray was so strongly and extensively fortified that without collusion from within it could have defied any efforts of the Spaniards to take it; and from hatred towards the newly created sovereign prince, Balagny, collusion occurred. But after the

The surrender of the strong fortress of Cambray, with the general failure of the campaign in Picardy, and the irreparable loss of several of his most esteemed and able generals, weighed heavily on Henri's spirits.* He frankly owned to Rosny (whom he left in Paris to observe the proceedings of the newly appointed, but very unsatisfactory, financial council he had established) that he fully recognised his error in entering into declared hostilities against Spain, as he feared it might replunge France into a war more disastrous even than that from which she was on the point of emerging. Yet he attributed much of the ill fortune that had befallen him to the want of energy and activity on the part of the Duc de Nevers, combined with his exceeding arrogance towards his officers.†

gates were opened to them the Spaniards forgot all the promises they had made respecting the privileges and franchises of the people. Balagny, it was reported, owed Henri's protection to Gabrielle, to whom he had promised to hold Cambray *en fief* for her and her son, César Monsieur.

\* Gabrielle did not escape the malignity of her enemy, the Princesse de Conti, even in this matter. That lady, who greatly envied the Marquise de Monceaux her position of mistress to the king, accuses her in " *Les Amours du grand Alcandre* " of having contrived the death of the Duc de Longueville, in order to ensure his concealment of certain tender missives that had passed between them. The duke was governor of Picardy, and was shot accidentally while inspecting the fortress of Doullens, one of the strong places of his province. It was a calumny without any foundation, like so many others invented by Madame la Princesse for the purpose of injuring her rival.

† *Mémoires de Sully.*

To reassure the people of the frontier towns, whom the sanguinary deeds of the Spaniards had filled with alarm and horror, the king determined on blockading La Fère, a small but very strongly fortified town which was occupied as the advance-post of the Spaniards in Picardy. At the same time he addressed very urgent appeals for reinforcements to Queen Elizabeth, James VI. of Scotland, and the German princes. The rebel French general, Baron de Rosne, who commanded a division of the Spanish troops, suggested to Fuentés to besiege Calais. He knew that stronghold, and that its strength lay less in its defences than in its reputation.

The council being assembled, Henri proposed to collect whatever troops were available, and with them to meet the enemy on his march. The Duc de Nevers was of opinion that the king ought not to expose himself to so much danger. "Such advice," rejoined Henri, contemptuously, "might be very suitable for you, who would not approach within seven leagues of danger." The duke made no reply, but took the implied reproach so much to heart that, being unwell at the time, grief so greatly increased his malady that he died a few days after. Henri endeavoured to console him by expressions of regret for the hasty and inconsiderate words he had spoken. The duke thanked him, but said "the balm came too late to soothe the rankling sting of those hasty words." Rosny, with his accustomed frankness, says : "The duke's death relieved the king of an adherent as troublesome as he was useless!" *

The king himself was also extremely unwell at this time, which occasioned considerable uneasiness to both Protestants and Catholics, for his death at so critical a moment in the affairs of France would have again filled the unfortunate country with political and religious strife, persecution and bloodshed; while the ravages of a

* The Duc de Nevers was not always so devoid of energy or so sensitive to reproach, having been one of the most urgent of the council assembled at the Louvre by Catherine de' Medici on the eve of the Saint-Bartholomew's Day, 1574, to goad the wretched Charles IX. into consenting to the proposed massacre on the following night. For a time he resisted the efforts of those demons, for the admiral's sake. But at last, in his usual frenzied manner, he raved out as he rushed from the room, "As you are determined to kill the admiral, kill them all, and let not one Huguenot be left to reproach me with his death." It was a sore trial to the Protestants when a man on whom was the blood of so many of their murdered coreligionists, friends and relatives, was welcomed and honoured in the camp of Henri of Navarre, and even deputed to intercede for him with the Roman pontiff. Nevers retired to his estates on the assassination of Henri III., horrified at the idea of a Huguenot king. But after the battle of Ivry, weary, probably, of his seclusion, he joined the "politique party," who supported Henri IV. on his promise to recant his errors and embrace Catholicism. The victory of Ivry appeared to Nevers to indicate, he said, that "God was on the side of the Béarnais." The pious duke hesitated no longer. He joined the heretic camp, and was the cause of endless dissensions, quarrels and misunderstandings. His departure was regretted by none, but rather gave general satisfaction.

faction scarcely yet suppressed, and which had brought the nation to the very verge of ruin, would have been renewed with more strenuous efforts and greater activity than before. Happily Henri's vigorous constitution speedily overcame the results of the extraordinary fatigue he had undergone in his last campaign. But a source of extreme anxiety to him yet remained in the utter inadequacy of that portion of the revenue which found its way into the treasury either to meet the requirements of the state or to enable him to reorganise his small army and to add to its numbers for the effectual carrying on the war with Spain.

The audacious project of confronting the Spanish army on its march with the insufficient force he then was able to assemble, was set aside by his indisposition. The siege of La Fère had made in three months but little progress, so strong was the situation of that fortress in the midst of the waters of the Oise and the Serre, its garrison being also numerous and amply provisioned. Charging the Connétable de Montmorency with the continuance of the siege, the king left Picardy to conclude with Mayenne the treaty which was destined to put an end to the League, if not immediately to place Henri IV. in full possession of his kingdom. It was signed in the course of the month of January, 1596, at the Château de Folembray, near Coucy, Jeannin representing the ex-lieutenant-general.

Considering Mayenne as a rebel chief, who for years, in arms against his king, had ravaged the country and oppressed the people, but being at last defeated and abandoned by his partisans, was entirely dependent on the royal clemency, even for sparing his life, the terms he demanded and obtained may well have caused such general surprise and general dissatisfaction. He could not have exacted more had he been dictating terms at the head of a victorious army. "Henri took upon himself, to the extent of 350,000 crowns, the debts contracted by Mayenne for the service of his party," besides the sums due — or pretended to be due — to the Swiss, the German cavalry, the lansquenets, Lorrainers, and other foreign troops, "which sums were to be added to the debts of the crown." His estates were to be freed from all claims or mortgages on them; and the king further recognised that the ex-lieutenant-general of the League and his party had taken up arms against him solely from religious motives.

"He also undertook strictly to enjoin that no search or inquiry should ever be made concerning any understandings, treaties, pacts, or conventions, entered into with foreigners by the League and its chief. All Mayenne's adherents who made with him their submission to the king were to be reinstated in their confiscated estates, and in the offices their chief had conferred on them. All his public acts of authority, as well as those of the magistrates of his party, together with their published financial accounts, were declared valid. Three cities — Soissons, Châlons, and Seurre, were allotted to Mayenne for six years, as security for the fulfilment of the stipulations of the treaty, and, in deference to his religious zeal and conscientious scruples, with the privilege of forbidding the Protestants to assemble in them. So comprehensively beneficent was this edict that, on claiming within a certain date to participate in its advantages, all persons banished for sedition were authorised to return and resume possession of their forfeited lands or other property."

The most embarrassing part of this treaty, as regarded the king, was Mayenne's demand that "he and the princesses and princes of his house should be declared innocent of any complicity in the assassination of Henri III." Absolute oblivion of the past Henri had promised to all, soon after his entry into Paris, private crimes alone excepted, and especially that crime of which the Guise family were not unjustly suspected of being the authors. But Mayenne also required that "the article referring to this crime should be so carefully drawn up that none could infer from the words or expressions employed in it that there had been favour shown or any need of royal pardon."

In the plenitude of his generosity (or, as some persons thought, weakness) towards the man who for seven years past had deluged France with the blood of her people and reduced his kingdom to a state of chaotic confusion, after having thoroughly drained it of its resources, Henri at once sent for Séguier, first president of the Sovereign Court, also for the procurator-general, who brought with them the documents relating to the inquiry into the circumstances of the assassination. After cursorily looking them over, it was determined to append these concluding remarks to the treaty: "It appears to the king, after inspecting the documents relating to the assassination of his predecessor, Henri III., that the princes and princesses who made war against him had no part whatever in that crime, of which they have further vindicated themselves by oath. His Majesty therefore prohibits his Courts of Parliament from instituting further proceedings against them respecting it."

Thus Henri IV. surmounted the great difficulty of this treaty, and, notwithstanding the promises he had made to Queen Louise, and the oaths he had taken to avenge the death of his predecessor, came to the conclusion that the memory of Henri III. was of little worth compared with the pacification of France. The widowed queen and her natural sister, the dowager Duchesse de Montmorenci, thought otherwise, and energetically opposed the king's decision before the assembled Parliament. Their complaints awakened some sympathy, and were so far entertained that the Parliament refused registration to Mayenne's treaty.

The Duchesse de Montpensier made no secret of her share in the late monarch's death, nor were proofs wanting of Jacques Clément's private interviews with Mayenne. Twice the royal letters commanding the registration of the treaty were set aside unnoticed; but a third, in a more startling tone — for Henri, when he pleased, could play the part of absolute sovereign as well as that of "*le roi bonhomme*" — convinced that dignified assembly that it would be wise to do as they were ordered without any further comment. Nevertheless, the Royalists who had looked for vengeance, at least in the humiliation of the arrogant family of Lorrainers and pretended descendants of Charlemagne, were indignant that Henri's should have been the hand to snatch this satisfaction from them.

The treaty being signed and registered, Mayenne lost no time in appearing at court in his new character of faithful partisan and loyal subject of the Béarnais. The first interview of these former enemies, but now fast friends, took place at Gabrielle's château of Monceaux-en-Brie. It was a favourite retreat of Henri's, and thither, to solace himself in the society of his amiable and *belle marquise*, he had gone for a brief visit after his many troubles, fatigues, and illness. Henri was walking with his confidant and counsellor, the

Baron de Rosny, in the gardens of the château when the Duc de Mayenne arrived. After the customary three embraces and mutual congratulations Henri resumed his walk, and with a quicker and more elastic step than the corpulent and gouty duke could conveniently keep pace with, pointing out to him as they went along the embellishments he had made and proposed to continue in the gardens and château.

The effort of dropping on one knee and embracing his majesty's thigh, according to the absurd etiquette of that period, Mayenne had accomplished with extreme difficulty, and much puffing, blowing, and perspiring. Yet, in spite of his bulky person, his gout, and sciatica, he made gallant attempts to step out with the king, though every movement in advance was agony to him. "*Pardieu!*" whispered the king to Rosny, "I shall kill this heavy Lorrainer if I drag him with me much further." Then suddenly stopping, "My cousin," he exclaimed, "I fear I am walking rather too fast, and have wearied you?" "By my faith, Sire," rejoined Mayenne, "you have indeed, and would have killed me outright had you gone on at that rapid rate much longer." Henri laughed, and, extending his hand, which the duke reverently kissed, said: "That is all the harm or annoyance, my cousin, you will ever receive from me."

To this the duke replied by expressing his gratitude to the king, whose generosity had freed him from the arrogance of the Spaniards and the intrigues of the Italians, and assuring him that henceforth he would serve him with all fidelity, should it even be against his own children. "I believe it, I believe it!" said Henri, slapping his "cousin of Mayenne" on the shoulder, as was his familiar habit with his officers in his camp; "and now go and seek refreshment and repose at the château, for you have need of both. Rosny, one of my oldest and most faithful friends, will accompany you, and bid them set out some of the fine wine of Arbois, to which I have heard you are partial." Henri was well aware of Mayenne's foible; he was not only partial to the fine wines of the Jura, but fond of them to excess, nor was he known to disdain those of other districts or countries.

Rosny then conducted the ex-lieutenant-general to an arbour to rest awhile after his exertions, and thence on horseback, escorted by several gentlemen, to the château. He was much gratified, Rosny observes, with the genial reception he met with from the king, and the attentions which Rosny was able to pay him, while the king on his part expressed himself equally well satisfied with their interview.*

Not many Catholics or Protestants shared the king's satisfaction. Both were much scandalised at his taking for his ministers and generals Leaguers who were scarcely yet able to reconcile

*Mémoires de Sully;* Mathieu.

themselves to acknowledging him as their king, and that he should have granted places of surety to the chief of the rebels, having refused them to the Huguenots, who had served long and well. Some of them were inclined to attribute the king's "impolitic and undignified concessions," as they were termed, in favour of his and the nation's chief enemy, to the influence of Gabrielle. Mayenne, it was asserted, in order to secure that influence, so powerful with the king, had promised her that should the question arise of her son César Monsieur filling the throne in succession to Henri, he would employ every means in his power to further the king's wishes, and support the claims of his legitimised son.

It seems very unlikely that such an arrangement should have been proposed by Mayenne, whose family had pretensions to the throne, as *soi-disant* descendants of Charlemagne; or, if proposed, that Gabrielle would be so eager to accept it, there being, for many reasons, not the slightest probability that the event it referred to would ever occur. Doubtless Henri would have married the woman to whom he was so devotedly attached had he been free to do so, however displeasing it might have been to M. de Rosny. But so long as the dissolute Marguerite de Valois opposed the divorce, lest her successor should not be, like her own degraded self, royally descended, it was impossible that the first step could be taken towards the realisation of Gabrielle's hopes — if she ever entertained them — of placing her legitimised son on the throne of France.

Henry's concession, say others, to the demands of the ex-lieutenant-general, so ably enforced and supported by Jeannin, was made with the same view as that which induced him to give the governorship of Provence to the young Duc de Guise — the conciliation of a still powerful and popular family, whom he was desirous of attaching to his interests and securing their aid in the pacification and much needed reorganisation of the kingdom. Certainly Henri had no more stanch supporter and faithful subject than the Duc de Mayenne, after he had sworn allegiance to him. That he had done so in good faith, an opportunity which occurred soon after enabled him to prove.

Meanwhile, the chief Leaguers included in Mayenne's treaty made their submission within the period allowed them. Amongst these was Duc Henri de Joyeuse, or Frère Ange, the Capuchin monk who, to oppose the heretic king, had cast aside his monkish cowl to put on his armour and draw the sword in the cause of religion. Henri gave him the marshal's baton, and — as he had ruled with discretion in Languedoc, and brought the people with him to acknowledge their king — he was rewarded with upwards of a million of *livres* and the lieutenant-generalship of the seneschal courts of that province.

*Catherine de' Medici.*
Photo-Etching. — From an old print.

Probably — as money was so scarce in the royal treasury that Gabrielle, from her own resources, lent the king 400,000 crowns — the million *livres* were but promised, and payment deferred until a more convenient season. Joyeuse was a duke and peer of the realm, of Mayenne's creation, afterwards confirmed in those dignities by Henri IV. His habits had been those of the dissolute court of Henri III. and Catherine de' Medici, until one evening, after having spent some days in more than usual profligacy, he fancied he heard angels singing. Evidently he considered that the burden of their song was a call to him to forsake his vicious courses, as he immediately entered a Capuchin monastery, and took the name of Brother Ange, in compliment to the angelic messengers. There he remained until Sixtus V. gave him leave to absent himself from his convent during the war.

But Joyeuse was in no hurry to return, and Rosny says he made himself full amends for the penances and restraints of convent life, becoming again the gallant cavalier and one of the most assiduous and brilliant of courtiers. Two or three years after he had made his submission, and accepted the terms of the general treaty with Mayenne, he was still lingering at court. But as he one day was standing on a balcony conversing with Henri IV., a number of people having assembled beneath it to gaze on them, the king laughingly remarked, "*Mon cousin*, these people seem to be extremely well pleased with the sight of a renegade and an apostate conversing together. This remark is said to have driven Brother Ange back to his Capuchins. He became very serious, and, after marrying his daughter and only child — who inherited the whole of the immense wealth of the Joyeuse family — to the Duc de Montpensier, in 1599, he bade a final adieu to both court and camp; and the gay world he had figured in so conspicuously saw Frère Ange no more.\*

Marseilles and Provence, included in the treaty, had not yet surrendered, and still had to be fought for. The haughty and brutally arrogant Duc d'Épernon was governor of Provence, ruling, or rather tyrannising, there in the name of the king, whom he detested — for "Épernon," as he said, "was neither Royalist nor Leaguer, but Épernon only." The Duc de Guise being appointed to supersede him, Épernon was summoned to evacuate Provence and appear at court. He curtly refused, regarding the province as his own, and declaring that "rather than give it up he would unite his arms with those of Savoy, of Spain, or even of the devil himself." He at once entered into a secret compact with Philip II. "against the Prince of Béarn, the heretics, and their abettors." Six thousand men were promised him, 12,000

---

\* L'Estoile, *Journal de Henri IV.; Mémoires de Sully;* Mathieu, *Histoire de France.*

crowns per month, and galleys in sufficient numbers to besiege and take Toulon.

But ere men, money, and galleys were ready the new governor had triumphantly entered Provence. The old popularity of the Guises was revived in an enthusiastic reception of the youthful head of that house. Town after town welcomed him, and heartily recognised the sovereign whose cause he now served; much, indeed, to the amazement, as well as mortification, of the ex-governor. For, notwithstanding the oppressive rigour with which he ruled the province, he very strangely expected that all would rise in his favour and expel the intruder who presumed to enter his domain for the purpose of ejecting him. Épernon was titular governor of several strong towns — Metz, Boulogne, etc.; but as they followed the example of Provence and took his expulsion quite calmly, he thought it well to tear up his treaty with Spain, and negotiate with the "Prince of Béarn" while yet there was time.

When Henri reproached him for his unfriendly feeling towards him, he replied very coldly, but with much gravity, "Sire, your majesty has no more faithful servant than myself in your kingdom. I would rather die than fail in my duty towards you in the smallest matter. But, Sire, as regards friendship, your majesty knows full well that it can be acquired only by friendship." This reply pleased the king, and converted his indignation into esteem.* But it is certain that if he thus gained the king's esteem, his own feeling towards him remained unchanged. "Épernon detested the king," says the Baron de Rosny, "because he detested everybody, and had often much difficulty in keeping on tolerable terms of friendliness with himself."

But the discomfiture of the Duc d'Épernon was not the only service the Duc de Guise rendered the king. He successfully rescued Marseilles when that important maritime city was on the point of being grasped by Spain. A fleet of galleys under Carlo Doria was in the port, having 2,000 troops on board ready to disembark. Another more numerous fleet was following, and Philip believed that, aided by two traitorous tyrants — members of the municipal body — to whom 150,000 crowns were promised, his and his father's dream of getting permanent possession of Marseilles was about to be fully realised. A counterplot, however, by means of which the gates were opened to Guise and his troops, entirely changed this promising state of things.

Some resistance was offered, but the people hailed with loud and enthusiastic vivas the entry of Guise and his army. After a conflict of an hour and a half's duration, the traitors, Casaulx and Louis d'Aix, fled from the city, and contrived to reach one of the galleys. No landing of troops

* *Vie du Duc d'Épernon.*

was attempted, and the galleys disappeared speedily, the rowers rowing their swiftest, while the victors were welcomed with hearty cries of "*Vive le roi! Vive Henri IV.! Vivent Guise et la France!*"

When these tidings reached the king, he is said to have raised his hands towards heaven and exclaimed that "God had had pity on France!" It was the most important victory achieved for his cause since the subjection of Paris.

## CHAPTER III.

Elizabeth, Requested to Send Her Fleet to the Coasts of France, Refuses. — Consents When too Late. — Spaniards Take Calais. — La Fère Surrenders. — Impoverished Treasury. — King Anxious to Place Rosny in the Financial Council. — Great Opposition Encountered. — A Perilous Journey. — King's Emotion. — Proposal to Revive Feudalism. — King's Indignation with Montpensier. — Explains to Him How He May Repair His Error. — Montpensier Penitent. — Rosny Refuses to Attempt to Conciliate Opposing Members of the Council. — Disappointed, He Determines to Leave the Court. — Death of His Brother a Pretext. — Bouillon Ambassador, Rosny Refuses to Accompany Him. — Gabrielle Approves Rosny's Conduct. — He Is Appointed Director of the Council.

WITH the exception of Brittany, which had yet to be conquered or ransomed, the League was now actually extinct throughout France. The Duc de Mercœur, who had maintained himself in that province for ten years, began to regard it as actually his own. A sort of desultory warfare, between skirmishing parties only, had been kept up on its confines since Queen Elizabeth, who required Brest to be ceded to her for her services, had withdrawn her troops from Brittany, having need of them in Ireland. But hostilities on a more extensive scale were looked for as soon as the king could sufficiently reinforce his army.*

Innumerable troubles and perplexities then surrounded Henri, chiefly arising from the ill-judged declaration of war against Spain, which he had neither money nor troops to effectively carry on. The council of finance robbed him in all directions. His dissatisfied Huguenots, who had just cause for complaint against him, declined to support his cause — "as he had abandoned them and their religion" — until such arrangements were made for their protection as in justice they had a right to demand; as sufficiently guaranteed also as were the concessions granted to rebels.

News arrived at this time that the irreconcilable Leaguer, the Baron Savigny de Rosne, who led the Spaniards with so much ability against his own country, was then before Calais, and had carried the bridge and the fort commanding the landing-places. The king, taking with him the *élite* of his small squadron of cavalry and the most active of his infantry, left the camp of La Fère in all haste on the 15th of April. But while on his march the disheartening intelligence reached him

* The duke, being one day asked by a friend if he was dreaming of making himself Duke of Brittany, replied: "I know not if I am dreaming; but if so, the dream that I am Duke of Brittany is one that has endured for upwards of ten years." The duchess had some fancied claim to the duchy derived from her grandmother, the heiress of the house of Penthièvre — whence Mercœur's pretensions.

of the failure of the Comte de Saint-Pôl to relieve Calais, as he had proposed, by landing a corps of troops in spite of the enemy. The weather rather than the Spaniards opposed his project. A terrific storm compelled him to beat a hasty retreat, and Calais, after the first assault, fell into the hands of the Spaniards, its governor being a man of little military capacity or experience.

Sancy was instantly despatched to London to entreat Elizabeth to give orders to the commanders of the armament prepared against Spain, and then ready in the port of Dover, to make a descent on the coast of France. The queen positively refused, unless Calais was to be the reward of her compliance.

Sancy replied: "The king would rather that it should remain in the hands of his enemy than pass into those of his friend"—a speech which appears to have displeased her.

"She was sure," she said, "that his master had not charged him with such a message."

Sancy acknowledged that he had not, such a request not having been anticipated. But he was aware that the king too highly prized her majesty's friendship to make her his enemy, which she would become if put in possession of Calais.

Sancy seems not to have played the courtier to Elizabeth's satisfaction. She, however, ultimately yielded, and the Earl of Essex was ordered to sail for Boulogne; but while the matter was under discussion Calais surrendered.

"We know," the queen wrote to Henri, "that the possession of Calais is earnestly desired by Spain as a suitable and convenient place for interfering with our power and domination in the channel, where we can suffer no associate."

The château was carried by assault on the 24th of April. The governor and all who were found there were either put to death or made prisoners. Consoling himself and his troops for their disappointment with the assurance that the retaking of Calais was but deferred for awhile, the king strengthened the garrisons of Boulogne, Ardres, and Montreuil, and returned to the siege of La Fère, where he was joined by Mayenne, who was very cordially received.

A Flemish engineer proposed to the king to submerge that fortress, but after two or three unsuccessful efforts the project was abandoned. The waters would not rise within six feet of the required height. Famine, however, did the work of the threatened deluge. The garrison had held out for six months; no provisions or ammunition could be obtained; death began to be busy among them, and further resistance being impossible, the governor surrendered. The château was much damaged by the siege. The king ordered it to be repaired, and gave the government of La Fère to his son, César Monsieur, — Philippe de Longueval, Gabrielle's cousin, acting in quality of lieutenant for the youthful governor.

The capitulation of La Fère was immediately followed by the loss of the strong town of Ardres, which, by the dastardly act of the Comte de Belin, Lieutenant-General of Picardy, was surrendered — in spite of the indignant remonstrances of the governor and garrison — to the new governor of the Netherlands, the Cardinal Archduke Albert of Austria. Here again the enemies of the Marquise de Monceaux step forward to assert that her protection saved the head of the cowardly Belin, who was merely deprived of the offices he held and banished to his estates.

Notwithstanding the smallness of his army, Henri would have risked a battle; but the Spaniards would not be drawn into accepting his challenge. They strengthened the defences of Calais and Ardres, then reëntered the Netherlands, and made desperate efforts to drive the Dutch from the positions they held in the North of Flanders. When besieging the town of Hulst they lost their French deserter, the Baron de Rosne, — a loss that was gain to the French, as it deprived the Spaniards of a commander of great military ability, who was thoroughly acquainted with the then deplorable state of France, and, further, was a determined enemy of Henri IV.

Elizabeth's fleet also took its departure to harass the coast of Spain, where it did considerable damage. The Spanish fleet was beaten, Cadiz burnt, and large quantities of merchandise destroyed. Henri and Elizabeth, towards the end of May, signed a treaty binding themselves never separately to make peace or enter into a truce with Philip II. Other states were invited through their ambassadors to join in this alliance with the Queen of England and the King of France. But the apostasy of Henri IV. had gradually disinclined the Protestant princes towards interfering in the affairs of France or aiding the king in his troubles. Very few troops were sent to him, and Elizabeth herself would not promise him more than two thousand, whom he must pay and provide for himself. She, too, had her troubles — Spain abroad, Ireland at home.

Henri was really in a very desperate condition. So entirely were his efforts for the pacification of France paralysed for want of money, that he would have been unable to complete the siege of La Fère but for another loan of 300,000 crowns from the Grand Duke of Tuscany, the Swiss and German mercenary troops having with difficulty been restrained from leaving his camp, requiring to be instantly paid. The financial council appointed on the death of the superintendent D'O supplied him with funds no less sparingly than when that officer ruled at the treasury. The king wished to undertake the siege of Arras, but on applying to his council for 800,000 crowns they replied that it was impossible to furnish him with so large a sum.*

Henri's thoughts had often turned towards the Baron de Rosny since the death of the Duc de Nevers, nominal president of the financial council. His methodical and successful management of his own affairs, his integrity, order, punctuality, application, and general aptitude for business — conspicuous in all matters, diplomatic, military, or civil, in which occasionally he had availed himself of his services — seemed to point him out as the most capable man to take charge of the coffers of the state, and to aid the king in the general reorganisation of France. Rosny's personal devotedness to Henri IV. also essentially fitted him to carry into effect the views and wishes of his sovereign.

In the preceding year — 1595 — Henri had introduced him into the Council of Finance, but without any official title. The councillors, who were well aware of the stern, unbending character of the king's Huguenot friend and zealous partisan, soon found means to disgust and get rid of him. He, however, had seen and acquainted himself with more than enough to warrant him in stigmatising the conduct of the financial affairs of France as "organised pillage." Hitherto Henri had forborne to give him a surer footing or more responsible position in the council. He seemed

* *Mémoires de Sully.*

to be fearful of offending his intimate and lively companion, Sancy, on whom the chief direction of that branch of the government had latterly devolved, but who, if not a participator in the frauds of his colleagues, seems to have been either unwilling or unable to assume the unpleasant office of suppressing them.

Rosny, with Madame la Baronne,—a helpmeet who was as active-minded and domesticated as himself,—was visiting his estates at Moret and Rosny, and superintending the building of a new residence, when urgent letters were brought from the king. His majesty informed him that he had an idea of convoking the States General in the course of the autumn; that he desired him as speedily as possible to join him at Amiens, whither he also charged him to escort the Marquise de Monceaux from Pontoise; his majesty adding that they were the only friends to whom, in his many perplexities, he could fully and freely unbosom himself.

Rosny would gladly have dispensed with the honour conferred on him; for, notwithstanding his many good and great qualities, he was a man of strong prejudices, which, at times, made him very unjust in his estimate of those persons who did not stand high in his favour. The *belle marquise* was one of those who were not permitted to bask in the sunshine of his good graces. Very readily he lent an ear to the slanderous reports of the envious, who ascribed to her influence, or her abuse of it, with the king, their failure to obtain the pensions, places, or governments they coveted, whether merited or not. Equally he believed that through the same influence favours were secured to those who promised to aid her in her asserted ambitious scheme of sharing the throne of France with Henri IV.

However, this journey to Picardy was very near having a tragical result and putting an end to all her schemes. Rosny met the marquise at Maubuisson, a faubourg of Pontoise. She travelled in a litter, followed at some distance by her women attendants, who occupied a large, heavy coach, having four horses and a driver. Before and behind the coach were several heavily laden baggage mules, while Rosny, with his faithful La Fond, rode six or seven hundred paces in advance of the marquise's litter.* At about a league distant from Clermont — where there is a steep declivity on one side of the road, which becomes narrowed, allowing scarcely space sufficient for two vehicles to pass each other — the coachman having left his seat to arrange some part of the harness, one of the mules, in passing the coach, set up a furious neighing. This, with the jingling of his bells, so frightened the horses, which

---

* La Fond on the death of Admiral Villars had again passed into the Baron de Rosny's service, as his principal *valet de chambre.*

were young and skittish, that dashing suddenly forward and dragging the coach with them, they threw down the foremost baggage mules and seemed inevitably destined to overthrow the litter. The women screamed, and Gabrielle, perceiving that something serious had happened, looked out to ascertain the cause of it. One glance revealed the fate that threatened her, and she uttered a piercing shriek. Rosny and La Fond, being in advance, could afford no aid, but rode wildly back, exclaiming, "Ah! should any harm happen to her, how terrible will be its effect on the king!"

By one of those fortunate occurrences which seem at times to have some connection with the miraculous, in the very height of danger, and at the moment of the expected catastrophe, the axle-tree broke, and the big, lumbering coach came with a crash to the ground. Kicking aside their traces, the horses rushed on. Rosny says "his heart leaped into his mouth." But as these skittish young animals approached the litter — as if aware of the preciousness of the burden it bore — they gave it as wide a berth as the narrowness of the road permitted, actually, as they passed, grazing the edge of the precipice, but not going over it. Rosny "breathed again."

He had now to devote himself to calming the fears of the marquise, who was half dead with fright. La Fond performed the same duty to the maids, who thought that the coachman was the cause of the mishap that had occurred, and ought to be punished. To oblige them, Rosny "gave him a volley of blows with his cane." When all had in some measure recovered from the effects of the great danger so providentially escaped, the big coach by some means was set on its wheels again, and the horses caught and harnessed, at least securely enough to carry them on a slow-marching pace some part of a league further—the king being expected to meet the marquise at Clermont. Her litter was, of course, uninjured; but she was naturally much flurried, and Rosny left not her side again until they reached their destination, where Henri arrived a quarter of an hour later.

The traces of recent agitation on Gabrielle's fair face did not escape the royal lover's anxious eyes, and Rosny observed, while giving him an account of their perilous adventure, that he turned ashy pale with emotion. Certain nervous movements, as of terror, which he had never remarked in him on going into battle or in the extremest personal danger, fully revealed the depth of his passionate love for la belle Gabrielle. Henri had sent for Rosny to consult and discuss financial and other matters with him. He, however, thought it necessary, after his mistress's narrow escape from death, first "to devote some moments to tenderness." *

A few weeks before the occurrence of the

\* *Memoires de Sully;* L'Estoile, *Journal de Henri IV.*

above mentioned incident, and immediately after the loss of Calais, an assured means—according to the Duc de Montpensier—of having always a fine army on foot, and avoiding in future his recent embarrassment of appearing before his enemies with insufficient forces, was suggested by that prince to the king. Henri was at Saint-Quentin when the duke proceeded to inform him, on the part of his nobility and general officers, of the manner in which this desirable state of things was to be accomplished. "He had but to decree that the governors of provinces then holding their governments by commission should henceforth hold them as their own, by right of inheritance and sovereignty, and bound by no obligations to the crown, except simply that of homage, as had been the practice formerly."

The duke then began to point out to the king the advantages that would result from this return to the feudal system, by each of those newly created petty princes undertaking to hold in readiness a certain number of troops expressly for his use whenever he needed them; "thus," he was continuing, when Henri, in an imperious tone, commanded this ill-advised young prince to be silent. "He had heard him thus far," he said, "without rebuke, only because amazement and indignation at such an affront being offered to the royal dignity by a Frenchman, a prince—a prince, too, of his own house—had so utterly overwhelmed him that he had found no words fully to express his feelings, or give an idea of the great compassion he felt for his cousin, who had undertaken to play a part so unworthy of him."

He perceived that advantage had been taken of an easy temper and yielding disposition to put forward a prince, much nearer the throne than he himself had formerly been, as the advocate of a scheme, of which, had he given it a moment's reflection, he could not have failed to see all the baseness. So far, however, was he from fearing to be ever reduced to lend himself to so preposterous a proposition, and so determined rather a thousand times to die than consent to cover his family and the royal dignity with so much infamy, that he would not condescend to give it one word of reply, or enter into any discussion respecting the grounds on which it was founded.

Montpensier at once acknowledged his fault. Henri's joviality in the camp probably led the prince to expect a jesting rather than a reproachful reply to a proposal he may scarcely have thought made to him in actual seriousness. But the air and tone assumed by the king convinced him of his mistake, and that he was considered to have offered him an insult. As far as words and protestations of loyalty and fidelity could avail, he made ample apology, and entreated the king to forget that he had been guilty of conduct so unworthy. After some further lecturing, Henri, in token of reconciliation, extended his hand to his erring cousin, who, dropping on one knee, kissed it.

He then explained to him how he might in some measure repair the fault he had committed, as regarded those who had urged it on him. "On the first occasion of the authors of the proposition touching on the subject, he should inform them that, having reflected on what they exacted of him, he must beg them to charge some other person with it, as he entirely disapproved their proposition, and should esteem it his duty, if ever it was brought under his majesty's notice, to oppose it as an indignity by every means in his power."

Montpensier appears to have very accurately followed the king's suggestion, and freed himself from any suspicion of complicity with those nobles who affected to desire the revival of the feudal times, and, necessarily, to replunge France into anarchy and bloodshed, instead of loyally coöperating with the king for her peaceful reorganisation after so many years of calamity. In reality, however, and as Henri well knew, it was but a renewed attempt of the Ducs de La Trémouille and de Bouillon, with other influential men of the Huguenot party, including D'Aubigné, to wrest from him certain concessions, and a recognition of their rights — long promised, but still withheld — by a seeming threat, indirectly conveyed to him by a "politique prince," of withdrawing their troops from his army.

Henri had intended on the arrival of the Baron de Rosny to notify to him his reappointment as a member of the Council of Finance, and by royal warrant, in order to give him a firmer footing there than before, and greater liberty of action. But the council strenuously opposed his entrance, professedly because of his want of financial experience, which, they said, required considerable time to attain. Without it, many errors and blunders would inevitably ensue. The real objection, however, was Rosny's inflexibility of character, and the determination he had once expressed to unravel the mystery of why and wherefore the people complained that they were bowed to the earth by their oppressively heavy burden of taxation, when so scanty was the sum — derived from the various sources of revenue — that found its way into the royal treasury, that it was insufficient for the most pressing needs of the king and the state.

The council generously admitted that the baron was a brave soldier, a good officer, well suited to take his place in a council of war; but in a council of finance, far more likely — from, as they hinted, his harshness of manner, and attachment to his own opinions — to create confusion and banish that harmony so desirable amongst its members. Though the king was persuaded that there was great need of a more economical administration of the revenues of the state, he did not believe the members of the council so thoroughly corrupt as Rosny declared them to be. The introduction of a man of such strict integrity, great intelligence, and untiring application to the duties of his office, would soon, he imagined, accomplish the needed reforms, when all would work together smoothly.

To conciliate "the gentlemen of the council," so disturbed in mind under the prospect of their peculations being revealed to the king, he assumed towards them the tone of appeal rather than command when referring to the projected appointment of a new colleague to aid them in their labours. They could not absolutely refuse to receive him, but did not actually consent. Henri was very fearful of offending the Catholics, or of appearing to have still a leaning towards the Protestants, and very dilatory in making those moderate concessions in favour of his heretic subjects which he had once, as well for himself as them, so urgently demanded of his predecessors on the throne.

It is rather amusing to find the stiff, unbending Huguenot baron secretly requested by Henri to play the amiable and deferential towards the "gentlemen of the council"—"seeking their society," as he said, and banishing from their minds by acts of complaisance the idea they entertained that Rosny was anxious to enter the financial council simply for the sake of doing them some ill turn and bringing them into disfavour. In a word, he would have him assume a conciliatory tone and a friendliness of manner that should convince them they were mistaken, and thus lead them to see so clearly the advantage of his coöperation as even to request that he might be appointed to join them.

Rosny confessed that "such docility was not in his character;" nor did he hesitate to tell the king that "he could imagine no more objectionable way of entering the council than that of owing the appointment to the favour of those who composed and governed it. Knowing, too, so well as he did the kind of spirit which animated that body, it would be impossible for him to serve it and at the same time serve the state." Henri disliked contradiction, and was piqued at his views being opposed. He resented, too, the haughtiness, as he conceived, of the reply, and Rosny's obstinate attachment to his own opinions. His frequent differences with the late Duc de Nevers crossing his mind at this moment, he referred to them, and exclaimed, in an irritated tone, "he had no mind to be on quarrelsome terms with all the world for his sake alone. He should think no more of introducing him into the Council of Finance, but would seek some other employment for the occupation of his time and thoughts." Henri, temporarily much displeased, then left his stern friend to his own reflections.

Rosny understood this as being henceforth destined by the king to make treaties with his rebellious nobility, and negotiate alliances with foreign powers. The post of ambassador he considered his means unequal to, — as one leading, indeed, to almost certain ruin, if he would support his rank with dignity and his reputation with honour. Already he had successfully combated the king's idea of sending him on an embassy to London. The Duc de Bouillon had told the king that one cause of the embarrassments he suffered from was having no regular representative at the court of Elizabeth and elsewhere.

The duke being one of the most intriguing of the Huguenot chiefs, Henri thought that his absence for a time might be advantageous to both of them; he therefore offered him the appointment. The duke accepted, and speedily made his arrangements for departure. But ere he left the shores of France the "gentlemen of the finances," as Rosny describes them, seriously advised the king to send with him "that able negotiator" the Baron de Rosny, whose tact and diplomatic ability would enable him to render the duke valuable assistance. The king liked the idea, the more so that it occurred to him that De Bouillon might avail himself of the opportunity of laying before the queen the many grievances of which the

Protestants complained, and soliciting her protection.

He imparted his views to Rosny, desired him to provide himself with money (from his own resources, of course), and to prevail on Madame la Baronne to accompany him to the English court. Rosny respectfully declined; nor was he more willing to accept, as secretary of embassy, the responsibility of the duke's errors, by the promise of recalling De Bouillon in the course of a few months in order that he (the baron) might succeed to the post with the same title and honour as the duke. "In a court," he says, "where everything was effected by underhand practices, he had no difficulty in comprehending the object of those gentlemen's commendations, and their feigned generosity on his behalf." The king was at first much annoyed by this refusal, but afterwards determined that Rosny might serve him more usefully in Paris than in London.

Rosny, however, by no means for the first time, proposed to withdraw from the court, and to devote himself to the management of his private affairs. A younger brother had recently died, and Rosny, becoming his heir, availed himself of it as a pretext for his decision, and for mentioning it to the king. He also desired to make some arrangement with him for the eventual repayment of several large sums of money he had advanced by way of loan for the king's service. But at his next interview the king prevented his entering again on the subject by at once informing him that he had decided on giving him the chief direction and control of the Council of Finance.

With much surprise Rosny heard that he was indebted for this change in the king's hitherto wavering intentions to the advice of the Marquise de Monceaux. She had inquired the cause of the vexation evinced by the king on entering her apartment after his recent conversation with Rosny, and had approved the baron's firmness when told of his obstinate resolve to pay no court to the gentlemen of the council. "You will never," she said, addressing the king, "be well served until you have met with such a man, who, purely from motives of public interest, fears not to draw upon himself the displeasure, and even the hatred, of the financiers."

In the afternoon, while the king was out hunting, the Baron de Rosny paid his respects to the Marquise de Monceaux. It was strictly *une visite de rigueur*. He had no more friendly feeling towards her than before, though he owed to her influence (well employed in this instance, it must be admitted) the post he had been anxious to obtain, in order to free both king and state from their embarrassments. This, he felt assured, might be readily effected, not by laying more burdens on the people, but simply by putting a stop to embezzlement and by practising a wise economy.

## CHAPTER IV.

Assembly of Notables Convoked at Rouen.— Rosny Enters on His Duties as Superintendent of Finance.— Great Opposition from Members of the Council. — Obtains 500,000 Crowns for the King's Use. — Arrival of Legate in Paris. — Little Prince Henri of Condé Sent to Meet Him.— Clement VIII. Anxious for the Cessation of War.— Henri Not Unwilling, yet Prepares for War.— Henri's Harangue to the Notables. — Gabrielle Surprised to Hear the King Speak of Putting Himself *en Tutelle*.— The Notables Dismissed. — Birth of a Daughter. — Her Royal Christening at Rouen. — The Edict of 1577 in Favour of Huguenots Registered.

INSTEAD of the long promised convocation of the States General, Henri resolved to substitute an assembly of notables — to give France at least the semblance for the reality. The general agitation of the public mind, resulting from years of religious warfare, was not yet sufficiently calmed down to tempt him to try the larger measure, which had been looked for on the termination of intestine strife. But the king had engaged in foreign war, and, however unwisely, it must now be carried on, and money to enable him to do so be obtained from some quarter, and by means other than an increase of taxation.

Until the assembling of the notables in October, Henri suggested to the Baron de Rosny that it might be advantageous to make a general survey of the principal financial divisions of the kingdom — a sort of voyage of discovery — with the view more particularly to inform himself of the real value of the various branches of revenue, and the ameliorations it might be desirable to introduce into the mode hitherto employed in collecting the amount and the disposal of it. He was also, if possible, to obtain a little money in advance of the ordinary receipts.

This project the king undertook to mention to the council as his own, in order to prevent any adverse criticism on the manner of the new superintendent's entry on his duties. It was approved by the council; of course, on the supposition that they and their subordinates would be required to undertake it. To their extreme confusion, the superintendent took four of those districts for his own inspection, and placed others in the hands of men whose probity was known both to him and to the king. These last, however (who were either less fortunate or less firm than Rosny, with the exception of the *maître des requêtes*, M. de Caumartin, who obtained for the king 200,000 crowns), found obstacles raised in the way of their research from the very outset, rendering all information, except that of the utter emptiness of the state's coffers, unobtainable.

The registrars, receivers-general, and clerks of various grades were desired by the council to refuse inspection of their registers "to all persons whomsoever." Some of these people produced their orders when asked for their registers, others closed their offices and absented themselves. But no obstacles or pleas of that nature sufficed to arrest the inquiries of the indefatigable Rosny. Using the unlimited powers confided to him, he very unceremoniously broke up the coalition of the subordinate officers of the financial department, who, supported by the members of the council, sought to conceal from him the mysteries of the system adopted in the administration of the public moneys.

Several of the employés were suspended from the exercise of their functional duties until the abuses detected could be more closely inquired into. The registers of the last four years Rosny himself cursorily examined and revised, and gleaned so successfully amongst the falsifications, overcharges, etc., of various kinds, that he carried home triumphantly to his impoverished royal master the acceptable sum of about 500,000 crowns.

An imperative command from the king to return without delay greatly surprised the baron, and brought his mission to an end sooner than he expected or had intended. It also left him no time to put his 500,000 crowns; the whole of which was in specie, into a more portable form.

He therefore packed up his money-bags in barrels, and then again in seventy small carts, for conveyance to Rouen, where the notables were about to assemble, because of the plague then making sad havoc in Paris. The silver-laden carts were accompanied by the receivers-general of the districts visited by the superintendent, and protected by a provost's guard of thirty mounted archers, with the baron and his own retinue in the rear. He had "taken possession of all the registers and falsified accounts, to serve him as a clue," he said, " to guide him further through that maze of injustice, knavery and robbery."

The baron's enemies, in their extreme vexation at having been "trapped," as they termed it, into approving a scheme which could only result in an exposure of their fraudulent tricks and corruption in office, resolved on making another attempt, either to force him to retire or the king to dismiss him. They complained that the Huguenot baron was "playing the tyrant with a very high hand;" that he was filling the prisons with the officers and subordinate clerks of the finance department, and that from mere vanity and bravado he was dragging after him, in chains, fifty of the principal employés. It seems surprising that Henri should have given any credence to charges so absurd; yet he is said to have suspected no falsehood in them because of the persistency with which they were pressed on him.

Believing, at least, that Rosny's zeal had outstripped his judgment, he thought it necessary speedily to recall this hitherto most prudent, moderate, and circumspect of his advisers; now playing such fantastic tricks before high heaven that, if perchance they made not the angels weep, at least fired the righteous souls of the gentlemen of the financial council with rage and indignation. They had warned the king, as they now reminded him, of the confusion and disastrous results that could not fail to follow the appointment of a soldier to so important a post as superintendent of the Council of Finance, with the duties of which he naturally was utterly unacquainted.

With so pretty a sum as 500,000 crowns for his pressing needs, and 200,000 more following, Rosny might well have expected a pleasant reception; but Henri received him very coldly. "Certainly," Rosny says, "he did him the honour to embrace him, but by no means in that friendly manner and with the cheerful salutation to which he was accustomed." In the same frigid tone, unusual with him, he inquired the reason for so uselessly encumbering himself with money which those for whom it was destined — the princes of the blood, pensioners of the state, etc. — were in the habit of applying for themselves to persons whom, as he well knew, he was desirous neither to vex nor to mortify.

The king was greatly surprised to hear in reply

that the sum amassed was entirely for his majesty's use in his preparations for war, there being no claims of princes or pensioners upon it; that it was, in fact, a sum that would have passed into the pockets of those who had no right to it, and have been utterly lost to him. Nothing had been anticipated on the current imposts, and he presented the 500,000 crowns to his majesty as an earnest of what he hoped to accomplish in the future. Henri found this statement so difficult to believe that he required Rosny to swear to its truth.

"*Pardieu!*" * he then exclaimed; "what a malicious set! and what an audacious imposture! Yet tell me," he continued, "why put so many people in prison, and drag hither in chains those receivers, treasurers, and other officers I hear are with you? What do you propose to do with them?"

Overpowering amazement at these questions prevented Rosny from replying. He knew that the king was fond of jesting, and the unexpected supply of cash had put him, it seems, into an excellent humour. The blank astonishment, however, on Rosny's countenance appears to have been a sufficient reply to the king's inquiries, as he burst into a fit of laughter, though the questions

---

* "*Ventre Saint-Gris*" had fallen into disuse, except occasionally, since Henri had become a Catholic,— Saint-Gris being looked on with suspicion as a Huguenot.

were not asked in jest. The idea of the Baron de Rosny accompanied by such a *cortège* amused him for the moment, but none the less he was exceedingly indignant at the malevolence displayed by the council towards a man of such honour and integrity. Its secret motive, too, stood fully revealed to him. He asked for no further explanation, but warmly embracing his long-tried, faithful friend, desired him to proceed fearlessly with his reforms, and to rely on his constant support.*

During the Baron de Rosny's absence the legate, Cardinal Alexandro de' Medici, Archbishop of Florence, arrived in Paris, deputed by Clement VIII. to receive the king's ratification of the engagements entered into for him by his agents at Rome on the occasion of his absolution. Henri rode out a considerable distance from Paris to meet the legate, and was accompanied by the Duc de Mayenne, that his reconciliation with the

---

\* Rosny's efforts to bring order out of disorder in the administration of the finances met with the most determined opposition at every step. Equally determined was he to carry his point; it amounted, he says, almost to a passion with him; and if this personified genius of order did not quite succeed in realising his own ideal of the conduct of his department, he, at all events, placed the finances of the country on a footing that eventually released the king from his pecuniary embarrassments, private and public, while tending also to diminish the burdensome taxation borne by the people. The difficulties he encountered, and his contentions with members of the council in the early period of his superintendence of the finances, are related at much length in the " *Œconomies Royales*."

*Prince Henri of Condé.*

Photo-Etching. — From Portrait in the Chantilly Collection.

League might thus be plainly made evident. On the following day the legate made his public entry into Paris, — the latest converted heretic, the little Prince Henri of Condé, being sent to receive him, — a mark of respect doubly gratifying, as evincing the sincerity of the king's conversion in snatching this brand from the fire, while at the same time it humiliated the Huguenots, who had thought this child their own.\*

The choice of Cardinal de' Medici as legate was intended as an assurance from the Vatican of the perfect confidence and good-will subsisting between Clement VIII. and the Most Christian King Henri IV. The cardinal was a man of singular discretion, excellent intentions, amiable temper and pleasing manner — in a word, "*vera persona grata.*" Unlike his predecessor, the Cardinal de

---

\* For eight years Charlotte de La Trémouïlle had remained in prison under an accusation, brought against her by the three princes of Condé, of having poisoned her late husband, their brother, Prince Henri of Condé. The civil wars had occasioned the suspension of the inquiry into the circumstances of the prince's death. It was now resumed by the Parliament of Paris. But the Prince de Conti and the Comte de Soissons (the third brother having died in the interval) appealed to the jurisdiction of the king and peers of France. The Parliament, however, disregarded the appeal and acquitted the princess — July, 1596 — who then claimed her son from the Huguenots and gave him up to the king. Almost immediately after, she abjured Protestantism in the hands of the amiable cardinal legate, who gave her absolution. The spiritual remission of sin following so closely on the parliamentary acquittal gave rise to much significant comment amongst Catholics as well as Protestants.

Plaisance, he remained two years in France without interfering with the Parliament or quarrelling with its decrees. Instead of encouraging the clergy, many of whom still nourished hostile feelings towards the king, he strove to subdue their violence and to pacify that restlessness of spirit yet pervading all ranks of the people.

Clement VIII. being very desirous that war should cease between France and Spain, the legate was authorised to offer Henri his mediation. The resumption of the sanguinary struggle between the two countries prevented Philip from giving effectual support to Austria against the Turks, which grieved his holiness exceedingly, as the Protestants of the Netherlands were favoured by the Turks in the consolidation of their heretic republic. This state of things also retained the Most Christian King in forcible alliance with powerful Protestant princes: an evil influence from which the holy father, in his anxiety for the spiritual welfare of his returned prodigal, was anxious to release him.

Henri was not indisposed for an honourable peace. He had keenly felt his error in rejecting Rosny's advice to defer vengeance until order was restored in France, and strength regained by a long period of repose and peace. However, the legate was informed that the king would consent to a negotiation for peace, but on the basis only of the treaty of Câteau-Cambrèsis, and a satisfactory indemnity for the losses of the state. In order to ascertain Philip's view of the subject, the Pope desired the legate to send the general of the Cordeliers, Calatagirone, to Spain, and for nearly two years these ecclesiastics carried on privately a correspondence on the subject with Philip II. and his confidential ministers.

Henri IV. meanwhile continued without relaxation to prepare for the retaking of Ardres, Doullens, and Calais. While waiting for the assembling of the notables — whose discussions he hoped would lead to some feasible proposal for raising a little more money without pressing too heavily on the people — he made an excursion to Normandy. Accompanied by the Marquise and the Baron de Rosny, he revisited the scenes of his former brilliant exploits, — Arques, Dieppe, Caudebec, etc., — returning to Rouen to address the notables on the opening of the session. This he did in one of those brief, lively speeches which, under an appearance of soldierly frankness and good humour, concealed so much shrewdness and gained so many hearts.

The assembly was held in the great hall of the Abbey of Saint-Ouen, and the king was accompanied by the legate, several cardinals, and bishops, the first presidents of the Sovereign Courts, magistrates, etc. Having taken his seat on the throne, placed under a canopy in the middle of the immense hall, he said :

"If I were ambitious of the reputation of an orator, I should have studied some elegant harangue and have spoken it before you with all due gravity. But, gentlemen, my ambition has a higher aim, it points to the two glorious titles of Liberator and Restorer of France. In order to acquire them I have assembled you here. You know to your cost, as I do to mine, that when called by God to the throne of this kingdom I found the country not only almost ruined, but very near being absolutely lost to Frenchmen. But, by the grace of God; by the prayers and good counsels of those of my subjects who are not of the profession of arms; by the sword of my brave and generous nobility (from whom I distinguish not the princes of the realm, "*Foi de Gentilhomme*," being our best and noblest title), and by my own efforts and exertions, I have saved France from being lost to us. Let us now save it from ruin. Share with me, my dear subjects, in this second glory, as you shared in the first. I have not summoned you hither, as some of my predecessors have done, to compel your blind approval of my 'good-will and pleasure;' but have called you together to receive your counsels, to trust in them, and to follow them, — in a word, to place myself in tutelage in your hands, which is what kings, graybeards, and conquerors have rarely shown an inclination to do. My extreme desire, however, to add those two grand titles, 'Liberator and Restorer,' to that of king, together with the great love I bear my subjects, renders everything easy and honourable to me."

His discourse ended, the king, the legate, and others who accompanied him rose to withdraw.

"My chancellor," he said, "will inform you further of my wishes. I will not by my presence put any restraint on your discussions."

The chancellor, in a long discourse on the necessities and perils of the state, then urged on the notables the sacrifices which the king — himself so prodigal of his exertions and even of his life — had a right to expect from his subjects; concluding his harangue by exhorting them to adopt the most speedy and efficacious measures for procuring the aid, which was absolutely necessary, to enable the king to support the heavy expenses of the war.

As usual, the Marquise de Monceaux was present to hear the king harangue the notables. Behind a screen or draped curtain, secluded from the general gaze, she was in the habit of listening to his public addresses. On the occasion above referred to she replied to Henri's question, how she liked his speech, that "she had rarely heard him speak better; but that she had felt much surprise when he told the assembly he was there to place himself in tutelage in their hands."

"*Ventre Saint-Gris!*" rejoined the king, "that's true; but, as I understand it, in tutelage with my sword by my side."

He was by no means desirous of being taken at his word. Rosny was obliged to remind him, when he expressed dissatisfaction with the opinions of the notables, that he had declared his readiness to accept their counsels and to adopt suggestions that were not exactly in accordance with his own views.

The notables did little or nothing for the relief of the king's embarrassments. They proposed a variety of impracticable plans: suggested withholding for a twelvemonth the pay of the officers and the salaries of the government employés; also proposed the tax of a *sou* per *livre* on all goods whatsoever entering the cities, towns, and bourgs of the kingdom. This tax the king accepted for a time. To remedy the gross mismanagement of the finances, the notables appointed another council, called the "Council of Reason," who succeeded only in introducing confusion worse confounded into the already entangled state of affairs existing in that department. These and other innovations were accepted only that the king might seem to keep his word of putting himself entirely into the hands of the legislators he had convened. Rosny had already doomed them.

The king was then enjoying his favourite pastime of hunting, and generally was amusing himself in Rouen. A daughter was born to him there, whose christening, notwithstanding the scarcity of funds, was celebrated with royal magnificence, to the great scandal of the public. Early in February Henri IV. once more appeared in the great hall of Saint-Ouen. The notables had completed their labours, if not to every one's satisfaction, at least, it would seem, very much to their own, and were now released by his majesty from their arduous duties. Temporarily, to gratify the Huguenots (the terms of the famous edict afterwards signed at Nantes being then supposed to be under consideration by three or four able statesmen), Henri obliged the Parliament of Rouen to register the edict of 1577, granted by Henri III. to the Protestants, but never registered, nor carried into effect. The Parliament at first remonstrated and resisted the command as strenuously as they had done twenty years before; but Henri, no longer in tutelage, ordered them to " cease cavilling and do his bidding " (another form of " *tel est notre bon plaisir*"), and forthwith he was obeyed.*

The epidemic prevailing in Paris in the autumn having nearly passed away, the king and the court returned to the capital. Rosny was busied in preparing for 1597 an official document concerning the revenue and the expenses of the state. This was to pave the way for reforms still more searching, and the utter abolition of the abuses then existing in the management of the finances, — forming a supplementary statement to the very able memorial drawn up by him in 1593 on the reëstablishment and reorganisation of the kingdom.

* The Protestants, believing that this edict was intended by the king to be the only permanent one he was prepared to grant them, were not disposed to accept it as a final measure. For while the Catholics regarded it as an exorbitant and impious compact with heretics, the Protestants considered it of no force whatever; in fact, a mere mockery — secret promises to the Catholics concerning its concessions having rendered void whatever the edict might, when first issued, have contained advantageous to them. Numerous assemblies were held by the Protestants at this period, when they inveighed greatly against the king's ungrateful treatment of his Huguenot subjects.

## CHAPTER V.

Unsatisfactory Result of the Discussions of the Notables. — Astrologers Prophesy Evil Things. — Court Festivities and Efforts to be Mirthful. — A Last Appeal to Madame Catherine. — Rosny Entreats to be Excused from Making It. — The King Will Accept No Excuses. — The Visit to Fontainebleau. — The Princess, Indignant That He Should Meddle in the Affairs of Persons above Him, Calls Him a Sycophant and Complains to the King, Who at First Receives Rosny Coldly. — Reconciliation. — A Grand Christening. — Amiens Taken by Surprise. — Great Consternation.

HENRI IV. left Rouen far from satisfied with the lukewarm efforts of the notables in his favour, the deliberations of that assembly having mainly resulted in a mere display of incompetence to deal with the questions referred to them. But the time for reforming abuses and reorganising the state had scarcely yet arrived. Had money and troops been sufficiently at his command, Henri doubtless would speedily have cleared his kingdom of Spaniards, and probably have done fuller justice to his Huguenots. Unfortunately they were not; but news of a victory by the Netherlanders over the Spanish forces revived his hopes, as of good augury for the success of his own arms.

While Rosny and other members of the council were laying up at Amiens provisions, cannon, ammunition, and other material of war for his next campaign, the king, as well from policy as from his own love of gaiety, thought that the interval might be advantageously employed by the court in a brief round of festivities. His idea was to revive the spirits of many of his officers and nobility, who, while faithfully attached to him, were influenced, as so many were in those days, by the prophecies of the astrologers.

They announced that Henri's star was declining, and would set in dark clouds at the close of the century; that the success which had so far attended him in conquering his kingdom was about to desert him — the prize when just within his grasp being destined to elude it. Not publicly, of course, were these dire events proclaimed. They were secretly disseminated by active foes in order to discourage his friends. Great troubles were said to be surely coming on France and her king; and the minds of many persons, not the poor and ignorant only, but also those of high station and reputed intelligence, were very seriously impressed by them.*

Henri IV. was not superior to such weakness. Being anxious about the future of his little son César, whom he would have gladly had to reign after him, he sent for an astrologer to "cast the

* L'Estoile, *Journal de Henri IV.*

child's nativity." The result, though doubtful, yet excluded not hope. Gabrielle was made quite unhappy by frequently consulting the soothsayers, who, in her case, appear to have always prophesied evil things. Rosny himself — strong-minded though he was — was not wholly free from such influences; while the loss of the fortified places in Picardy, and especially the loss of Calais — regarded as foretokens — seemed to the credulous to confirm what was predicted to follow. Efforts were, however, made to shake off these gloomy forebodings in a vortex of pleasures, and to treat them mirthfully, as tales wherewith to frighten old women and other weak-minded persons.

Several betrothals appear to have taken place during this sojourn of the court in Paris. Rosny's eldest daughter, a very young girl, was betrothed to the Protestant Duc de Rohan, and the king had been so sanguine as to believe that another effort to induce his sister to give her hand to the Duc de Montpensier might be crowned with success and joyously celebrated. That young prince had regained the king's confidence and favour by strictly observing the line of conduct required of him towards the would-be feudal nobles, and had again, within the last few months, expressed a great desire to marry Madame Catherine. Henri therefore determined that a final appeal should be made to her on the duke's behalf, as he had not the courage, it seems — knowing Soissons to be still in the ascendant — to make his appeal in person.

Madame Catherine then resided chiefly at Fontainebleau, where she had an hôtel of her own.* She had thus the advantage of the unrestricted society of several Protestant ladies and families of rank, some of whom had accompanied her from Béarn. The dissolute manners of the court had filled her with horror, while the Calvinist receptions she held three times in the week, when at the Louvre, were a great scandal in the eyes of rigid Catholics. It was discovered, too, that she had sinned beyond redemption by sending meat and other provisions, on a Friday fast-day, to some of the famished people suffering from sickness and poverty, then so prevalent in the capital, — filling up the measure of her iniquity by endeavouring to obtain Christian burial in consecrated ground for her heretic friends, with ordinary funeral rites. She wrote on the subject in a reproachful tone to Gondy, Bishop of Paris.

"Madame Catherine, the king's sister, considers it very strange indeed that the Reformers should be deprived of decent sepulture. It is a flagrant act of inhumanity."

---

* Henri also gave her a château at Saint-Germain and a house in Paris, — probably that the Catholic ceremonies he was compelled to observe might not come into open conflict with the Calvinist form of worship she so steadfastly adhered to, as they had done in the royal residences.

Furious preachers called her the "Navarraise Jezebel," others the "Serpent of the Mountains of Navarre," whilst many, with less envenomed feelings, yet knowing little of her, were inclined, from her unswerving attachment to the faith in which she was reared, to believe her a frigidly forbidding and harsh Calvinist.* But Madame Catherine in temper and disposition greatly resembled her brother. She possessed the same gaiety, and with far more refinement — naturally, as a woman — she rivalled him in sparkling repartee and lively badinage. That she was fond of pleasure we have had already the testimony of Rosny, who knew Madame Catherine when, as queen, she presided at the little court of Nérac, before Henri became King of France, and where the grave Rosny was commanded by the lively princess to take his part in the ballets.

Very arbitrarily Henri again imposed on the unwilling Baron de Rosny the ungrateful task of attempting to prevail on Madame Catherine to "gratify the wishes of her brother and her king" by transferring her affections from the man she loved to the man whom she had plainly declared to him she hated. Rosny naturally shrank from undertaking such a mission a second time, and earnestly implored the king not to insist on laying it upon him. His majesty's choice of an agent was, he contended, in every respect infelicitous,

* L'Estoile, *Journal de Henri IV.*

as both Madame and the Comte de Soissons regarded him with the most unfriendly feelings. This, he said, did not surprise him, as he had acted with great duplicity towards them and prevented their marriage, which Henri—not having then received the Pope's absolution—could not, as king, have legally forbidden.

Vain, however, were his remonstrances and entreaties that the princess might be spared this second affront from him. Henri only replied by quoting the old proverb, *À bon maître, hardi valet*. Finding all opposition useless, he requested the king to furnish him with a written statement of what was required of him, and with what object his mission, authorised by the king, was undertaken. Kings sometimes disavowed their agents; and, although Henri piqued himself on his word of honour being regarded by both friends and foes as sufficient guarantee of his good faith in whatever transaction he took part, the baron nevertheless considered that the delicate mission so persistently forced on him, and which was sure, he said, to make him eternally hated by both Madame and the count, demanded his requiring a *plein pouvoir* from the king to produce to them, if necessary.

Henri, hasty in temper, and considering his honour called in question, positively refused it. Rosny, calm and unmoved, then repeated his request to be allowed to decline so thankless a task.

Firmness at last triumphed, and Henri not only made in writing the required statement and handed it to Rosny, but also despatched a courier to Fontainebleau with a letter for the princess, informing her of the baron's arrival in that neighbourhood on important business,— the nature of which he did not tell her, — and his desire to pay his respects to her. On receipt of this letter Catherine's hopes rose high. "The king had at last resolved to make amends for the unhappiness he had caused her, and Rosny, whom he had employed to deceive both her and the count, was to bring the consent to their union."

This was the dream of poetic justice poor Catherine indulged in; now it vanished — now reappeared, hope and fear alternately, until the moment of Rosny's arrival, rudely to break the spell and dash her hopes to the ground. She received him rather coldly, which increased his embarrassment, and two visits were paid without advancing beyond compliments and civilities. On presenting himself the third time, Madame was surrounded by her ladies, and perceiving his confusion, she requested him to explain the nature of his business at Fontainebleau. Rather abruptly he entered upon it by informing her that the Comte de Soissons, by his many imprudences, to say no worse, had drawn upon himself the king's extreme displeasure. She must therefore divest herself of all expectation of obtaining his majesty's consent to their marriage. He had proposed, should she listen to this statement with any composure, to explain the views of her king and brother, and to conclude with a eulogium on M. de Montpensier.

But Madame's countenance warned him not to proceed. At first flushed with anger, it then became pallid as death, and assuming an air and tone of disdain, she assured him, after a most energetic defence of the count, that "he was exceedingly imprudent in presuming to meddle in the affairs of a person so very much above him." She treated him as "the most contemptible of men —as one who set himself up as a person of importance and an able politician, when he in fact, she said, was but a base flatterer who, to pay his court to the king, sought to draw from her the avowal of faults which neither she nor the count had committed." Many more reproaches to the same effect did she heap upon him; nor did she spare " her affectionate brother the king," upon whom she poured a torrent of invective and sarcasm.

In vain Rosny endeavoured to justify himself. She would neither listen to him nor allow him to read the statement by which the king authorised him to visit her and make known his decision respecting her marriage. She wished not to hear it, and " would hold him excused," she said, "from repeating anything he might have further had the intention of presuming to say to her." On leaving him she immediately sent off a courier with a letter to the king, to complain of the insults she had received from the sycophant Rosny, who boasted of being authorised and supported by his royal master. The baron, on his part, hastened also to despatch his confidential valet with an account of the upbraidings and accusations with which Madame Catherine had overwhelmed him, and the humiliating position it had placed him in. His messenger, he expected, would arrive before Madame's.

It, however, happened that on the road Rosny's messenger by some means sprained his ankle, which prevented his getting on so quickly as he would otherwise have done. The first account that reached the king of the interview at Fontainebleau was, therefore, his sister's. Very strangely, on reading it the king made no allowance for the excited feelings he must have known that the object of Rosny's visit would naturally occasion her. Equally strange, too, was his ready belief that his long-trusted, attached, and hitherto most discreet friend should have so far exceeded his instructions as to offer insult by word or manner to the princess, for whom he professed to entertain the greatest respect and esteem. Yet with an indignant gesture he took up a pen and wrote:

"His majesty cannot suffer one of his subjects to offer an offence to the princess, his sister, without immediately punishing it, unless the offence be effaced by expressions of regret and pardon sued for."

No sooner had the king despatched his letter than Rosny's messenger arrived with an account that gave an entirely different colour to the whole affair, and Henri then perceived that over-hastiness had led him into error, as well as an act of injustice towards his friend. However, with equal promptitude he penned a second letter, but of very dissimilar tone, concluding with:

"Return at once, and give me further particulars of what has passed at Fontainebleau; and be assured that you will be received by me as you have ever been, should I even be obliged to take the old Bourbon motto *Qui qu'en grogne. Au revoir, mon ami.*"

The first epistle the baron read with consternation. "Its effect," he says, "was as though a heavy blow had been struck at him and stunned him;" while, that his humiliation might be complete, it had been sent unsealed to Madame for perusal before passing into his hands. She, therefore, was triumphant. The second royal missive found Rosny meditating on the dangers which they who serve kings and princes are exposed to. He had faithfully served his king for a period of twenty-four years, and this disgrace was to be the reward of it. He would henceforth abandon the court, and devote himself wholly to his own private affairs.

This was not the first time he had made that resolve; but, happily for France and her king, he was not destined to carry it into effect. He read his sovereign's second letter with much satisfaction, and at once prepared to obey his summons. As had happened before, so it occurred after the slight misunderstanding in question, the Baron de Rosny rose in importance in the state and higher in the king's confidence and friendship. Not long after he was again received into the good graces of the Princesse Catherine. She was much attached to the Baroness de Rosny and her friend, Madame de Pangeac. Through these ladies explanations took place and reconciliation followed,—Madame, as Rosny says, either acknowledging herself in the wrong, or pardoning him for the wrong she imputed to him. He was not quite sure which; but, at any rate, "he accepted it as gracious and generous, as her words and her acts usually were."

Henri, however, though he gave up the idea of enlivening the court festivities of 1597 by a royal marriage, and allowed his sister a respite, as she was then suffering from chest disease, had still a husband in view for her. He was firmly resolved, too, that she should marry him; also that an effort should be made to induce or compel her to renounce her heretical opinions, and, following his melancholy example, enter with him the fold of the faithful.

Meanwhile, the king and his court commenced

a round of noisy dissipation, Henri varying the monotony of balls, ballets, masquerades, pantalonnades (Italian farces), and other similar diversions by little domestic episodes of the "good father of the family" kind. Then, with his belle Gabrielle and their little son César, of whom Henri was devotedly fond, he would amuse himself at the fair of Saint-Germain in bargaining for fairings, offering about a fourth of the price asked. Now and then he would buy trifles which the child took a fancy to, showing much pleasure in gratifying his every request and listening to his infantile prattle.

"On the other hand, the nobles," writes L'Estoile, "vied with each other in the splendour of the *fêtes* offered to the king. But while, in the abodes of the rich and noble, mirth and feasting, dancing and gambling prevailed," with an extravagance in dress that seems to have thrown into the shade even the prodigality of preceding reigns, the courtiers and ladies being literally almost covered with jewels — the king one of the rare exceptions — the sorrowful people were parading the streets in procession to implore God for mercy, for relief in their great trouble, and especially for deliverance from among them of the hated Huguenots.

Urged by their priests, several of whom were still violently opposed to the king, in spite of the legate's endeavour to restrain them, at least, from openly expressing their ill-feeling towards him, the women ran excitedly through the city, loudly comqlaining of the assembling of the heretics at Madame's hôtel in Paris. Catherine was staying there for a short time for the advice of the king's physician respecting her increasing complaint of weakness of the chest; but she took no part in the revelries of the court. Yet all the woes of France — pestilence, sickness, war, etc. — were attributed to her, and the vengeance of God would be further visited, they were led to believe by the priests, on the already afflicted city if she did not immediately leave it.

Side by side with this misery and fanaticism, pleasure and prodigality gaily continued their course. Lent was at hand, and the last and most splendid of the series of court festivities was announced. It was given by Henri, Duc de Montmorency, Marshal and Constable of France, at his recently erected spacious and elegant hôtel, on the occasion of his son's christening. The christening was, in fact, rather the pretext for this entertainment than its actual motive. It was really given in honour of a very young, recently married, and lovely lady, who was the object of the duke's assiduous gallantries. There was no offence in this against the morals of the court, where extreme laxity had so long prevailed; and as the lady's husband was rather elderly, it was thought a subject more for jest and ridicule than otherwise.

The king was present as the child's sponsor,

the legate, Cardinal de' Medici, officiating at the baptism as the chief ecclesiastical dignitary.* Gabrielle also appeared at this *fête*, magnificently dressed in green satin woven with gold, and wearing a profusion of pearls and diamonds. The king noticed that she had fewer diamonds in her hair than she should have had. There were but twelve, it appears; three more were required, he said, to make her coiffure perfect.

L'Estoile informs us that "all the cooks in Paris were engaged eight days before the *fête* took place to prepare the banquet." "The fish was served in the disguise of joints of meat. Two sturgeons cost 350 crowns, the dessert 150. The *bon-chrétien* pears, as many as could be obtained, cost a crown each. After this ample dinner of three courses — in which were many more dishes costing from 45 to 100 crowns each — followed a dessert of preserves, *massepains* (biscuits of almonds and sugar), and various kinds of fruits and bonbons, all in such profusion that the ladies left the greater part of these delicacies, so liberally supplied to them, to be eaten by the pages and lackeys." To the banquet succeeded the ball, and dancing was kept up until a very late hour with great spirit and vigour; so much so, observes L'Estoile, that "it seemed as if all our troubles, all presages of the anger of

* This child was the famous Henri de Montmorency who thirty-five years later was beheaded by order of Cardinal Richelieu.

God, were entirely lost sight of in the enjoyment of that amusement.

The Baron de Rosny, though no ardent votary of pleasure, was present at this *fête*, being one of the twelve courtiers whom Montmorency selected for special invitation, as the most likely to add brilliancy to his *fête* by the number and splendour of their retinues of gentlemen. He would have preferred to pore over his financial schemes, and the means of providing the munitions of war for the defeat of the Spaniards and recovery of Brittany in the next campaign; but his royal master commanded him to attend. On such occasions Maximilien de Béthune, Baron de Rosny, considered it incumbent on him to uphold in suitable manner the high dignity of his ancient house — connected with royalty by the marriage of its daughters.

Soon after two in the morning, Rosny and Madame la Baronne left the Hôtel Montmorency — the former very characteristically expatiating on the excellence of the general arrangements and the orderly way in which they were carried out. But scarcely had he retired to rest when a messenger from the king arrived requiring his immediate presence at the Louvre. "What had happened to his majesty?" he inquired, much alarmed, for rumours of intended attempts on his life were constantly afloat. "Nothing to his person," was the reply, "but news of great importance had just been brought by a courier."

His first fears relieved, Rosny in all haste repaired to the palace. The king, but partly dressed, was pacing his apartment with hurried step, his hands joined and passed behind him, his head bowed, and his countenance showing marks of profound grief. Several courtiers were with him, looking very serious, but uttering not a word. When Rosny entered, the king advanced, and taking him by the hand, exclaimed: "Ah! my friend, what a misfortune! The Spaniards have taken Amiens!" It was now Rosny's turn to be overwhelmed by this unexpected blow. So strong a place as Amiens; so well provided in every respect; but thirty leagues from Paris, and the only key to the kingdom on the side of Picardy. Yet taken in an instant and without the remotest idea that it was menaced.

"Henri, who was not easily daunted," says another chronicler of the events of this period, "appeared astonished at this blow. Looking, however, to God, as he usually does in adversity more than prosperity, he said aloud: 'This blow is from heaven. Those poor people, from having refused a small garrison which I desired to give them, have brought this trouble on themselves and me.'\* After a moment's reflection, he exclaimed, 'I have

---

\* The exemption from governor, garrison, and citadel — an ancient privilege confirmed by Henri IV. on the voluntary surrender of Amiens — had, in other instances, led to the same unfortunate results as had occurred in that frontier city.

played the King of France long enough ; it is time to resume the part of King of Navarre ; ' then turning towards his marquise, who stood weeping beside him, he said very tenderly: 'My mistress, we must now give up our pleasures, put on our armour, and mount our horses to make war once more.' "

Had troops been ready in sufficient number he would have taken the command of them, he declared, that same day, to show that fear lodged not in his breast and could take no root therein. This greatly reassured the people, for confidence in him began to be shaken, and it served as a stimulus to the nobility to fight gallantly and be firm under the conduct of a king so brave and generous. Yet it must be confessed that the taking of Amiens might have been avoided could Henri have left the fair of Saint-Germain and the balls and ballets of Paris to listen to the counsels of the Duc de Mayenne, who had recently advised him to revisit that city. But God, who wished to humiliate and reawaken him, and from time to time to chastise the people, who well deserved it, did not permit those good counsels to be followed.*

Amiens was taken by surprise on the 11th of March by the Spanish Governor of Doullens, Fernando Teillo de Porto-Carrero, a man of high courage, but a dwarf in stature. Having been informed by an exiled Leaguer that the citizens

* L'Estoile, *Journal de Henri IV.*

of Amiens, though carefully guarding their city at night, were extremely negligent of precautions during the day, he quietly assembled three or four thousand of his best troops and placed them in ambush, concealed by trees and hedges, not far from the walls of the city. In the morning, when the gates were opened, twenty or thirty soldiers and two officers, disguised as peasants — men and women — presented themselves, carrying sacks and baskets of fruits and vegetables, as supposed, for the market. One of them as he entered pretended to stumble, and his sack of nuts falling to the ground, its contents were scattered in all directions. Amidst much laughter the sentinels of the watch, thrown off their guard, began to scramble for them. A cart in the meantime was driven up and so placed under the portcullis that the gate could not be closed.

The sham peasants then drew their swords and pistols, which their long frocks had concealed, and attacked the guard, who, except one or two who fled, were all killed. At a signal given, Porto-Carrero and his troops appeared, and Amiens, with scarce any attempt at resistance, was taken in half an hour. A few of the city militia assembled on the Grande Place, but Porto-Carrero disarmed them. He exacted ransom from the wealthy, otherwise the lives of the citizens generally were spared. The city, however, was thoroughly pillaged, the booty proving immense. All Rosny's artillery, with other material of war stored at Amiens, with the intention of making that city the *place d'armes* of the next campaign, fell into the hands of the Spaniards.

This event for a time put an end to the negotiation for peace, Henri declaring that until Amiens was retaken the word " peace " must not be spoken in his presence. To carry out this determination money and troops were needed — in abundance, too, and without delay. Yet, when his bold resolve was announced, he knew that his coffers were empty, and that he had not at hand a single regiment in a condition for service.

## CHAPTER VI.

Raising Money to Carry on the Siege of Amiens. — Parliament, Refractory, Refuses to Register the King's Edicts. — Rosny's Successful Efforts to Equip the Army after Some Delay. — Elizabeth Refuses to Take Calais. — Huguenots Again Rally Round Henri. — " Charmante Gabrielle." — Successful Siege. —Henri's Imprudence. — Amiens Capitulates, 19th of September. — *Te Deum* Chanted. — Tomb of Porto-Carrero. — Death of Saint-Luc. — Entry into Paris. — The Grand-mastership of the Artillery. — D'Estrées Reappointed. — Rosny's Ill-feeling towards Gabrielle.

AFTER leaving the Louvre Rosny passed the night in racking his brains to devise a means of keeping his promise to submit a project to the king that would enable him to regain possession of his "good city of Amiens." Some project, indeed, the baron had always on hand for putting money into the state's coffers; but in whatever direction he, with that view, now turned his thoughts, blank despair alone met him. The notables had done nothing that could avail to assist the king in his present dilemma, and he was averse to imposing new taxes on the people while the country was in so piteous a state and poverty so general.

Yet on an emergency like the present one, involving the safety of the kingdom, some sacrifices, he thought, might surely be demanded of all classes. Nothing better, however, suggested itself than to require of the clergy a free gift (its amount to be mutually agreed on), paid a year in advance for two years, and from the wealthy — as well of the court as of the principal cities of the kingdom — a forced loan of 120,000 crowns. The late managers of the state's finances, who had realised in that capacity fortunes so immense, should be compelled to contribute, he considered, by way of a tax towards the state's needs, under pain of judicial proceedings for fraudulent practices while in office. A limited number of new offices also might be created, for sale to the highest bidder; and the northern provinces be required to raise three regiments of infantry, and to furnish the means for their pay and equipment. His most objectionable proposal was that of adding fifteen *sous* per *minot* to the price of salt — an infamous tax, which fell entirely on the poor, already compelled to purchase daily or weekly a certain specified quantity far in excess of what they needed, and with a prohibition to dispose of it to other families.

When morning dawned Henri of Navarre was himself again, prepared gallantly to confront this fresh rebuff of adverse fortune. He knew and keenly felt the difficulties of the enterprise he was about to engage in. But though some of the courtiers spoke of it despairingly, and several of the Huguenot chiefs forsook him, or threatened to do so in this hour of peril, he gave not way to despondency, but gaily prophesied that he and his troops would return triumphant from the battlefield. Victory he knew would turn the tide, and complainings give place to acclamations.

The king and his minister duly discussed the measures proposed by the latter as the most likely to secure with promptitude the necessary sinews of war. Neither would have willingly chosen them, nor would they then have been accepted, but in a case of such urgency as the necessity of saving the state at all hazards. Henri, therefore, determined to lay them before the council of war as measures of his own. He read them himself, and explained that it was not intended to employ all at the same time, but successively and according to the probable duration of the war. He then waited for the opinion of the council; but as all remained silent, as if hesitating to offer an opinion, Henri adroitly accepted their silence as a unanimous acceptance of his measures. At all events, they seem to have had nothing more feasible to suggest, as the king's proposals were at once agreed to and Rosny deputed to give immediate effect to them.*

A difficulty, however, arose with the Parliament concerning the registration of these measures as

* *Mémoires de Sully;* Mathieu; Pérefixe.

edicts issued by the king. The creation of a number of useless offices was vehemently opposed by the Parliament of Paris, and very severe remonstrances were addressed to Henri respecting it. The verification of those extraordinary, or "bursal" edicts was refused both to the constable and the chancellor; and the king was compelled, in order to obtain it, to attend the Parliament in person, when a very animated scene took place between him and Achille de Harlay, first president of the Sovereign Court.

While Henri was forcing the hand of the Parliament of Paris, Sancy, sent by the king, was contending with that of Rouen, whose members long held out stoutly against all the edicts presented to them. But especially they resisted with courageous firmness the imposition of an increased charge on salt, and endeavoured, though for a time unsuccessfully, to free Normandy entirely from the detestable system of its enforced purchase.

A month had glided away in the endeavour to obtain the resources without which the assault on Amiens could not be undertaken with the necessary vigour. Paris was greatly agitated by the unseemly discord between the king and the Parliaments. "Would he but gamble less," * it was said, "there would be no need of these forced loans, these new sinecures, and the burying of

* L'Estoile, *Journal de Henri IV*.

the people under avalanches of salt." Meanwhile, Elizabeth was appealed to for aid, and Calais was offered her to retain as a pledge, if she would besiege and take it while Henri assaulted Amiens. Fortunately she refused, preferring to employ her ships in harassing the Spaniards on their own coasts. She, however, sent the king 3,000 troops, which by treaty she was bound to do, though for this small service she thought the cession of Boulogne would be but a suitable acknowledgment. Henri, however, differed from her.

The Protestant princes, more or less engaged in war themselves, assisted the king but feebly; but as soon as money began to flow into Rosny's hands, there was a speedy change in the general aspect of things. Yet ere the royal mandate to the Sovereign Court was obeyed, Rosny, by his activity, intelligence, and a liberal use of his private resources for the king's service, had assembled, equipped, and provisioned an army of several thousand men, ready to march with the king. With the exception of two regiments sent by the Prince of Orange, they were drawn from the various garrisons in the provinces where peace then prevailed, and with them were four or five thousand Swiss, to whom Rosny guaranteed the punctual payment they were ever clamouring for, but were little accustomed to obtain. Sancy, who had left off meddling with financial matters, prevailed on the Swiss to remain in France, and took the command of them himself.

The clergy and nobility began also to respond liberally to the appeal to their patriotism; even the treasurers and financiers, moved either by fear or perhaps the prickings of conscience, contributed a considerable sum, in lieu of the tax, towards the expenses of the war. In that respect, therefore, the success of the campaign may be said to have been already assured. Several hundred noble cavaliers, amongst whom were the Duc de Mayenne and sons, the Duc de Guise and younger brothers, prepared to escort the king, and as volunteers to take part in the siege. The chief men of the Huguenot military commanders — the Duc de Bouillon and one or two others excepted — also joined him; some secret promises that their just demand for a permanent edict in their favour should be conceded to them without delay, the siege being ended, having once more rallied them around him.

Not until the 21st of May was Henri able to leave Paris, though Biron, with a corps of 3,000 men, had been despatched some weeks before. The king's army was then increased to 12,000 men, and other levies were expected to add to its numbers shortly. The Protestant Baron de Saint-Luc was grand master of the artillery, and seconded by Rosny, who had a special liking and talent also for this branch of warfare, a few cannon had been got together, and more were in course of construction. Power to act with authority in his absence was conferred by the king on Rosny, with the full control of the finances. His ability to guide the ship of the state in troubled waters was soon apparent, and Rosny assured the king that, "should the war terminate in a *solid peace*—a peace that would last, say, ten or twelve years— he would venture to promise that the prosperity and generally flourishing state of the kingdom should attain to a height it had never yet reached in any preceding reign."

La belle Gabrielle was anxious to accompany the king. She had hoped that the wars were ended, and the thought of new perils filled her with fear. But Henri, though inclined to take her with him, on reflection judged it better that she should retire with her children to her château of Monceaux. There, at the moment of setting out, he sent her the well-known *chant de départ*, which is attributed to him, though perhaps written by one of the court poets:

> "Charmante Gabrielle,
> Precé de mille dards,
> Quand la gloire m'appelle,
> À la suite de Mars,
>     Cruelle départie,
> Malheureux jour,
> Ah! que ne suis-je sans vie,
> Ou sans amour.

> "L'amour sans nulle peine,
> M'a par vos doux regards
> Comme un grand capitaine
> Mis sous ses étendards.
>     Cruelle départie,
> Malheureux jour,
> Ah! que ne suis-je sans vie,
> Ou sans amour."

The siege of Amiens occupied several months, and was carried on with great vigour and valour by both besieged and besiegers, Porto-Carrero displaying as much ability in his defence of Amiens as he had shown adroitness in surprising it. The garrison consisted of 3,000 infantry and 1,000 of the *élite* of the Spanish cavalry, "their dwarfish commander, in whom dwelt the soul of a hero," inspiring his troops with redoubled energy by his own exceeding bravery. He greatly disturbed the French approaches, blew up their mines, and ruined their works by murderous sorties. Nevertheless, the besiegers advanced — if slowly, yet surely. They had taken up their position on the border of the moats, and were able to batter the ramparts with forty-five pieces of cannon.

But so anxious were the Spaniards to retain possession of this key to the kingdom of France on the side of Picardy, that the cardinal-archduke declared, in a letter to Porto-Carrero, that "should Brussels and Antwerp and even the whole of the Netherlands be lost to Spain during his absence, he yet would certainly leave them to compel Henri of Navarre to abandon the seige of Amiens." Provisions were beginning to fail, ammunition was becoming short, and the middle of August had brought with it neither the promised revictualling of the city nor the cardinal and his army. He was, in fact, waiting the arrival of Philip's treasure-laden Indian galleons, for not until then could supplies be obtained of the value of a single *pistole*. A year had not elapsed since Europe had resounded with the news that the King of Spain was a second time a bankrupt; that he had repudiated his debts, both interest and principal, and as the bankers would advance him nothing more, he had withdrawn the domains which had been assigned to them to hold as security.

The besiegers availed themselves of the cardinal-archduke's forced inaction to push forward their own operations, and to complete and fortify their positions. Henri's army was then more than 25,000 strong, and foundries were established in the very midst of the camp, where efforts were successfully and continuously made to reconstruct artillery to take the place of the cannon captured at Amiens. Rosny had more than fulfilled the assurance given to the king that "his army should be liberally and punctually paid, well nourished, and well cared for when sick or wounded." The dangers and fatigues of warfare were therefore cheerfully borne.

Anything in the way of hospital arrangements

for the army had hitherto scarcely been dreamed of. Great credit was therefore due to the Baron de Rosny for providing that aid for the soldier of which he had himself so greatly experienced the need when lying helpless, wounded, and uncared-for on the battle-fields of Arques and Ivry; D'Aubigné, Mathieu, and other contemporary writers bear witness to the excellence of his arrangements. "He may be said," remarks D'Aubigné, "to have brought Paris to Amiens, few of the conveniences and supplies of the capital being wanting at the camp; while the sick and wounded, from the unwonted care bestowed on them, gave the siege of Amiens the name of 'the velvet siege.'"

It was the baron's custom to visit the camp once a month, provided with the necessary funds for paying both officers and men, — a system of ready cash very novel to them, but which they greatly appreciated, and which gained for the harsh, inflexible Rosny golden opinions on the one hand, envy and calumny on the other. It may be inferred from the king's purchase of the duchy of Beaufort in the month of August that he also was liberally supplied with cash, though Rosny would doubtless have preferred that he should have otherwise employed it. For the duchy was a present the king then made to his "charmante Gabrielle," whom he had sent for to join him at Pequigny, and there conferred on her, with the estate, the title of Duchesse de Beaufort, with remainder to her second son, very recently born, but not yet christened, the ceremony of his christening being deferred until the end of the siege, — an event that appeared to be near at hand.

Reports were brought to the French camp at this time that the cardinal-archduke had begun to assemble his forces at Douay, and would shortly advance on Amiens. On the 3d of September the Spaniards made a desperate sortie, in which the valiant Porto-Carrero was killed by a ball from an arquebuse. He exhorted his men not to lose courage, but to hold out bravely until succour reached them. A few days after, the cardinal arrived at Doullens at the head of 20,000 troops. The French army exceeded it in numbers by several thousands, with a finer corps of cavalry than Henri had hitherto commanded, — better equipped, better mounted.

Though slow in his movements, the cardinal daily drew nearer and nearer to Amiens; but Henri firmly believed that he would not dare to attack him in his lines. He knew that his enemy was encamped half-way between Amiens and Doullens, yet by way of bravado, on the morning of the 15th of September, he set out for the chase, accompanied by a large party. Towards the middle of the day the Spanish army appeared within sight of the French camp, drawn up in the order of battle introduced into Spain by that famous military tactician, the Duke of Parma.

The king's imprudence would probably have resulted in the loss of Amiens, if not of France, had not the Duc de Mayenne, seeing the threatened danger, promptly made the necessary disposition of the troops and taken the command of them himself. The cardinal may have intended a surprise in the king's absence; but whether or not, it is certain that Mayenne then rendered an immense service both to king and country, and fully justified the confidence Henri reposed in him since the day he laid down his arms, made his submission to his sovereign, and swore obedience to him.

Not until four in the afternoon did Henri return from hunting. He then found Mayenne actively engaged in putting the village of Longpré into a state of defence, to prevent the Spaniards from taking possession of the bridge, which the intriguing Maréchal de Biron (following his father's traitorous tactics of protracting war by opposing some obstacle to complete success, while avoiding absolute failure) had left undefended, to enable the Spaniards to take advantage of his "error," and revictual the city.* Henri immediately headed

---

* Biron himself confessed this and other similar traitorous acts to the king two or three years later, and asked his pardon, which the king readily granted. Yet Biron, notwithstanding the king's pardon and many subsequent favours bestowed on him, continued his career of intrigue and treachery, which was to prove fatal to him. — MATHIEU.

a corps of cavalry and harassed the Spaniards, while Mayenne completed his arrangements.

The cardinal retreated with his army to Arras. On the 16th Henri followed, but could not draw him into hazarding a battle. A persistent deluge of rain, lasting for several days, and reducing the country around to the condition of a swamp, compelled him also to refrain from besieging Doullens. But patience was rewarded on the morning of the 19th, when, after a vigorous onslaught of the French on Amiens, the garrison, seeing no chance of their much-needed supplies reaching them, compelled the governor, General Montenegro, to capitulate.

By the first article of the capitulation, Henri engaged, both for himself and his army, to respect the monument the Spaniards had placed in the Cathedral of Amiens to the memory of the valiant Porto-Carrero. He respected valour in his foes as well as in his friends, and willingly submitted to this condition.* On the 25th of September the garrison marched out with arms and baggage, drums beating, colours flying, and on the same day Henri reëntered his "good city," and was received with immense enthusiasm. But the exemption of Amiens from receiving a garrison was

* The cuirass, helmet, and arms of this valorous Spanish officer were examined by the French with much surprise and curiosity, being so small that they seemed intended for a boy of twelve years or less. — MATHIEU.

no longer reckoned amongst its privileges. It had turned out so disastrously that the inhabitants readily concurred in Henri's determination to abolish it.

Every city in France chanted a *Te Deum* and sent congratulations to the king on his successful siege of Amiens. All the denunciations of fanatical preachers, all the evils foretold by the astrologers, were at once dismissed from the minds of the people as vain imaginings of frenzied priests and soothsayers, and higher than ever rose the military reputation of the soldier-king. From Amiens he hastened to Paris, and made his triumphal entry into his capital with great éclat, and amidst the enthusiastic acclamations of the Parisians of all classes.

His entry took place by torchlight at between seven and eight in the evening. He rode a dapple-gray horse; his dress was a doublet of gray velvet bordered with gold, with trunk-hose to match. Also he wore a gray felt hat with a waving white plume. The garrisons of Mantes and Saint-Denis went out to meet him, with the municipality of Paris, the sheriffs (*eschevins*), and a numerous cavalcade of the city archers. The gentlemen of the Sovereign Court in their red robes waited his arrival at Notre-Dame, where a *Te Deum* was chanted. It was eight o'clock when he crossed the bridge of Notre-Dame, accompanied by a numerous escort and surrounded by a magnificent *cortège* of the noblesse. He was evidently in his gayest humour, well pleased to hear the people crying so joyously, "Long live the king!" His hat was continually in his hand, as he saluted the ladies, old and young, who filled the windows and balconies. He especially distinguished three beautiful women who wore mourning, and were at the upper windows of a house opposite Notre-Dame.

The Marquise de Monceaux, now Duchesse de Beaufort, was a little in advance of the king, in a splendid litter, entirely open. Her dress was of black satin, spotted with white, and so covered with pearls, diamonds and other glittering gems, that when the light fell on them, they dazzled the eyes of all beholders — their brilliancy completely throwing into the shade the red glare of the torches. Splendid *fêtes* and illuminations, with hunting-parties, in the vicinity of Paris — Gabrielle and other ladies accompanying on horseback — succeeded for some days the king's return to his capital. On these occasions the duchess was dressed entirely in green. After the hunt, she reëntered Paris, riding beside the king, he holding her hand.*

Henri's devotion to his belle Gabrielle was now so marked, and the respect and attention paid her by the court so general, that many believed that — the divorce obtained — Marguerite was to

* L'Estoile, *Journal de Henri IV.*; Mathieu; Sully.

give place to Gabrielle as Queen of France. She was greatly in favour with Madame Catherine; and several other ladies, Protestant and Catholic, were no less pleased by her amiability, beauty, and fascinating manners. But, unfortunately, she had a persistent enemy in the Baron de Rosny, who, though an able financier and a man of unswerving integrity — so rare in those days — yet was arrogant, harsh, and repelling; full of prejudices, and generally, from a jealous feeling, opposed to all whom the king was inclined to favour. True, his counsels and warnings were more frequently for the king's advantage than otherwise, yet he was sometimes inflexibly unjust, and was more than ever inveterate against Gabrielle when he found that he owed the control of the finances to her influence, which really overcame the king's inclination to listen to the cabal of the council against him.

He was also very desirous of obtaining the post of grand master of the artillery. He had been offered that of lieutenant-general; but pride would not allow him to accept the subordinate command. On one of his monthly visits to Amiens, during the siege, the grand master, the Baron de Saint-Luc, while examining the gabions, was shot dead by a ball from the ramparts of Amiens. Rosny lost no time in seeking the king, and applying for the vacant *grande-maîtrise*. But already Villeroy had asked the post for his son, and the Marquis de

Châteauneuf had sought it for himself. The king was not disposed to gratify either of these applicants, and the idea that it was an office incompatible with that of the control of the finances made him hesitate to bestow it on the Baron de Rosny.

Of course the baron thought otherwise. The king, however, without any definite promise, decided on leaving the post vacant until after the siege. During that time, he said, he could render him more service in Paris than at Amiens. "I did not see the king the next day," Rosny relates; "but, unfortunately for me, he saw Madame de Beaufort (as she now calls herself), who left no means untried to make him change his resolution, and give the *grande-maîtrise* to old D'Estrées, her father. *La dame* wept," he says, "and declared she would retire to a convent if he refused — a pretended threat that at once subdued the king. He told me this," he continues, "on the following day, with much confusion of face for his weakness."*

The *grande-maîtrise de l'artillerie* belonged to Gabrielle's father, Jean Antoine d'Estrées. It was

---

* This is probably one of those exaggerations to which Sully's secretaries were prone, and which impart to the memoirs, or "*Œconomies Royales*," as they are called, an air of boastfulness little intended by the aged minister. Sully's memory was then failing him — one of the causes, doubtless, of the confusion of dates and events in the otherwise most valuable record of the career of a great man and of the times of Henri IV.

one of those great offices of France made hereditary in certain families — as that of Constable of France in the Montmorency family. That now in question was conferred on Antoine d'Estrées, Jean Antoine's father, by Henri II., for the great ability with which he had personally directed the siege of Calais, and his previous distinguished services under François I. and Henri II. His son succeeded to his post; but after Henri's death, the confusion, terror, and bloodshed that prevailed for many years in France, together with the subsequent wars of the League, caused many high offices to change hands, as Catholics or Protestants were temporarily in the ascendant. Sometimes they were nominally held by both at once, or, as in the case of the grand-mastership of the artillery, left vacant altogether, there being generally no need of a grand master and his staff of officials to take charge of two or three guns.

Henri, however, gave the appointment to the Baron de Saint-Luc, an able officer, who was known in the army by the epithet of "*le brave*," and under whom the department became of greater importance. On hearing of his death, Gabrielle reminded the king of her father's claim, and he, being a lover of justice, could not refuse to acknowledge it, even at the risk of disappointing M. de Rosny. Brantôme refers to it as "an act of tardy justice to Antoine d'Estrées, and the conquest of right and truth which he well deserved." Rosny was consoled for the time with the governorship of Mantes, vacant by the death of his younger brother — the second of his family who had held that post and died at Mantes.

## CHAPTER VII.

Renewal of Peace Negotiations. — Elizabeth and the United Provinces Withdraw. — Henri Marches on Brittany. — Huguenots Press Their Claims. — A Bribe to Gabrielle from Mercœur, Who Offers His Only Child and Heiress in Marriage to César Monsieur. — The Offer Accepted. — César Made Duke and Peer, and Presented with the Duchy of Vendôme. — Magnificent Betrothal. — Rosny Greatly Mortified. — Movement to Nantes. — Famous Edict Signed There. — Visit to Rennes. — Chenonceaux Exchanged with the Queen for Moulins. — Peace Signed by the King and the Archduke. — Death of Philip II.

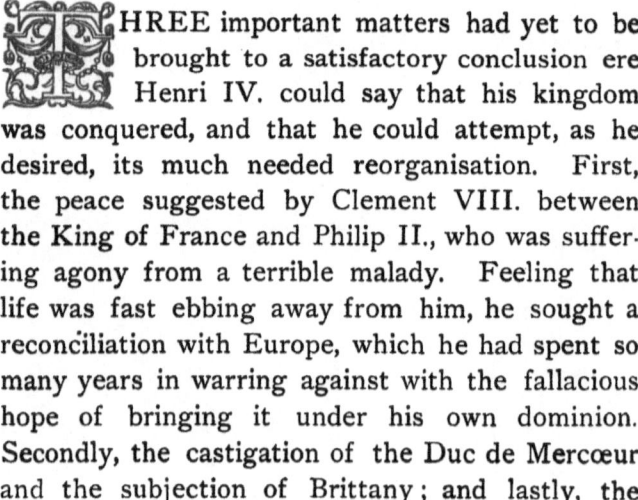HREE important matters had yet to be brought to a satisfactory conclusion ere Henri IV. could say that his kingdom was conquered, and that he could attempt, as he desired, its much needed reorganisation. First, the peace suggested by Clement VIII. between the King of France and Philip II., who was suffering agony from a terrible malady. Feeling that life was fast ebbing away from him, he sought a reconciliation with Europe, which he had spent so many years in warring against with the fallacious hope of bringing it under his own dominion. Secondly, the castigation of the Duc de Mercœur and the subjection of Brittany; and lastly, the

speedy satisfaction of the just demands of Henri's Huguenot subjects.

Early in January the plenipotentiaries named by the king — Pompone de Bellièvre and Brulart de Sillery, the legate, Cardinal de' Medici, and the Cordelier Calatagirone, with Richardot, Tassis, and Verreiken, Philip's envoys — assembled at Vervins to reopen the suspended negotiation. Henri's intended march into Brittany was delayed by the non-arrival, owing to stress of weather, of the ambassadors from Elizabeth and the united provinces. They were to have joined in the treaty, but now sought the king at Angers to urge on him the continuance of the war with Spain, promising substantially to aid him both with money and men. But Henri was firm in his determination to make peace, which, as he explained to the envoys, was, for the well-being of France, an absolute necessity.

"Long years of civil warfare had destroyed," he said, "all subordination. His own power was not yet firmly established, and royal authority was no more respected than were the most sacred laws of the state. Peace alone offered a remedy for these and many other evils; to delay it would be but to send France with hastening steps towards her ruin." He pressed them to join in the treaty, a general peace being for the welfare of Europe. The ambassadors departed, vexed and grieved by his determination. But Henri did not abandon his allies, as the Pope would have had him do, and join the Spaniards in making war against them, according to the maxim of there being "no obligation in an oath made to a heretic."

The Huguenots had become aware of the holy father's views; hence much of their restlessness, their anxiety, their unwillingness to aid the king in achieving success that was to result in peace between him and Spain and renewed persecution of the Protestants. But in this they did him an injustice. He had often declared rather vauntingly that "so much reliance was placed simply on his word of honour that even his enemies never required an oath from him." In this respect, at least, his acceptance of Catholicism had made no change in his sentiments.

The subjection of Brittany was expected to give much trouble, but was accomplished speedily and effectually without unsheathing the sword. For when France and Spain began seriously to discuss terms of peace, and a detachment of troops, with the king at their head, began to march westward to castigate the usurper, the Duc de Mercœur — who so long had assumed almost sovereign rights in that duchy — then felt that the hour of his downfall had arrived. He, however, resolved to fall easily, and being aware of Henri's weaknesses, sent his wife and her mother to Angers to make his submission to the king, and to solicit favourable terms from him (which he hardly dared otherwise hope for) through the influence of the king's mistress, who, with little "César Monsieur," accompanied Henri.

The Duchesse de Mercœur (Marie de Luxembourg, Princesse de Martigues) came prepared to offer a bribe for the services she sought, which at once secured Gabrielle's warmest pleadings on the duke's behalf. His daughter, sole heiress of his immense wealth, was offered in marriage to Henri's and Gabrielle's son. An interview with the king was arranged for the duchess and her mother, and Henri, of course, could refuse nothing to two ladies in tears and on their knees before him, in whom also his own *belle duchesse* took so deep an interest. A treaty was signed at Angers on the 20th of March between Henri IV. and the Duchesse de Mercœur, deputed by the duke to sign in his name. Religious zeal was the motive assigned in the treaty for his tardiness in swearing allegiance to the king. His forced resignation of the governorship of the province was assumed to be voluntary, in favour of his future son-in-law, who was created by the king duke and peer of France, and endowed with the duchy of Vendôme.

"Secret articles to the treaty granted pensions and indemnities to Mercœur and his chief partisans. But the States of Brittany, who had been prepared to deliver the duke into the king's hands, as they had informed him, should he show any intention of resisting the royal authority, objected to register the treaty, but afterwards yielded to the king's command, and also voted him a loan of 800,000 crowns, that the pacification and reorganisation of the duchy might be thoroughly completed."

The betrothal of the youthful Duc de Vendôme, who was four years of age, and Françoise de Lorraine, his *fiancée*, who was in her sixth year, was celebrated at Angers with no less magnificence than if "César Monsieur" had been the legitimate heir to the throne; so that, instead of the expected fighting and bloodshed, dancing and rejoicing became the order of the day, and Henri entirely banished all thoughts of castigating the Duc de Mercœur.

But what mortification awaited M. de Rosny! He had remained for awhile in Paris to make such arrangements in his official department as would enable him to leave the capital for awhile to join the king, whom he expected to find far advanced on his march into Brittany. Great was his surprise, therefore, on approaching Angers, to learn that the king was still there. Immediately on his arrival he sought his royal master, "his countenance betraying all that was passing in his mind." Henri embraced him cordially. "Welcome, my friend!" he said, gaily. "I am glad to see you here." To which Rosny, "incapable," as he tells us, "of those base condescensions which flattery inspires," replied: "And I, Sire, am very sorry to find you here, and —"

Interrupting him, Henri rejoined: "To understand each other's sentiments, half a word suffices between such old acquaintances. I, therefore, am quite aware of all you were about to say to me; but you would change your opinion if you knew how I have advanced matters since I came here."

Rosny answered that whatever were the advantages he had secured, he might have obtained a thousand more considerable ones if, instead of stopping at Angers, he had presented himself before Nantes at the head of his army. The king excused himself on the ground of the inadequacy of his artillery for such a siege. "Nantes was prepared for voluntary surrender," rejoined the baron, "and would have delivered the duke into your majesty's hands." Henri agreed that it probably would have so happened — an avowal which drew from Rosny the remark that "in what had taken place he did not recognise his valorous king;" but as he clearly perceived who had restrained his hand, he would say no more about it. He did not fear, he remarks, with Henri, the results of a perhaps too great sincerity. "He at once, with some confusion, acknowledged all; mentioning, as an excuse, the pity he naturally felt towards those who humbled themselves, also confessing his unwillingness to disoblige Madame de Beaufort," which must have greatly exasperated his monitor. Their conversation then turned on other subjects.

Henri on the following day advanced as far as Nantes, intending to wait there the result of the long and numerous conferences, which, without making much progress, had been carried on almost continuously during the past three years, between the accredited agents of the king and those of the ministers and chief men of the Protestant party. Peace was near at hand, and there was an evident desire on both sides that the famous edict, also, by which the rights of the two religions were about to be defined and solidly established, should no longer be unnecessarily delayed, but that the respective parties to it should endeavour seriously to come to an amicable agreement on the one or two disputed points which might then be under discussion.

Many sleepless nights and anxious days had this edict cost the king. It was, in fact, wrung from his fear of a Protestant rising against him; while, on the other hand, he dreaded a renewal of the violence the Catholics had always exhibited when any concessions were made for the safety or advantage of the Protestants. But what he had claimed for himself before his separation from the Huguenots he could not now well refuse when, from the suppliant for grace and favour, he had become their dispenser.

The famous Edict of Nantes was the three years' work of four generally considered able and conscientious men, — Maréchal de Schomberg, the minister Jeannin, the historian De Thou, and the Protestant councillor Suffroi-Colignon. It was signed by Henri IV. on the 15th of April, 1598.

Correctly speaking, it was but a renewed confirmation of the several treaties concluded between the Catholics and Protestants in the course of the last half of the sixteenth century — treaties constantly infringed by the party for the time being victorious. The edict began with an act of oblivion of all past wrongs. The sentences pronounced against the Huguenots on the subject of religion were annulled and effaced from the registers of the recorders of the Sovereign Courts. Families established in foreign countries were invited to return to France, and the children born in exile declared French.

Protestant prisoners, not excepting those sent to the galleys for their religious belief, were to be liberated, and full liberty of conscience conceded to all. The public exercise of the Protestant form of worship was formally prohibited in Paris, and limited to those cities where it had remained publicly established until the promulgation of the edict. All colleges, schools, and hospitals were to be open equally to Protestants as to Catholics, and permission was given them to publish in their own cities books concerning their religion. Also, they were henceforth to be eligible for all government offices and employments, notwithstanding treaties to the contrary, and were not to be required to make any form of oath or take part in other ceremony against their consciences.

In every city, town or village a place of sepulture was to be allowed them; their children were not to be taken from them and brought up in another faith; and all lawsuits in which Protestants were interested were to be judged in the new "Chamber of the Edict," and by an equal number of Protestants and Catholics. Other articles there were relating to their fortified places, garrisons, and cities of surety, into which, as well as in the above, many modifications were afterward introduced.

This solemn edict was sealed with the great seal of green wax, to denote that it was perpetual and irrevocable. It was registered with all the required forms by all the Parliaments, and particularly that of Paris; sworn by all the Sovereign Courts, the governors of provinces, magistrates, and even by the principal inhabitants of all the cities of France.*

That due effect might be given to the edict, Henri despatched two commissioners to each province of the kingdom, though its publication was

* Weiss, *Histoire des Réfugiés Protestants*.

deferred until after the signing of the Peace of Vervins and the departure of the cardinal legate, to whom it would have given umbrage, which Henri was anxious to avoid. The cardinal had promised to support an intended application to the Pope for a divorce from Marguerite, and he had just hinted that there was an unmarried princess of Tuscany, a relative of his own, who might perhaps be a suitable successor. Henri's thoughts were, however, then turned in another direction.

While awaiting the conclusion of the conference at Vervins, Henri with Gabrielle visited the capital of Brittany, where he was received with much enthusiasm and magnificently fêted. His affability and complaisance in attending the numerous balls, ballets, and other entertainments given by the ladies of Brittany in his honour, excited their unbounded admiration. These amusements were varied by matches at tennis, jousts, and running at the ring; but it was remarked that the king allowed none of these sports to interfere with his assiduous attentions to la belle Gabrielle, whose beauty and grace gained her many admirers.

The Bretons, it appears, were fond of making complimentary speeches and long harangues, which greatly tried Henri's patience. To one of these unconscionable speechifiers, who began his discourse with "Agesilaus, King of Lacedæmonia, Sire," the king, foreseeing what was in store for him, interrupting, said: "I have often heard of that Agesilaus, but, as I understand, before he was harangued he always dined, which I have not, so pray excuse me." To another, who addressed him by very long titles of honour, and continual repetition of "O great king! king most benign! king most clement!" "And why not add," exclaimed Henri, "king most weary?"

But Henri was anxious to visit Chenonceaux, where Queen Louise, the sister of the Duc de Mercœur, of the younger branch of the House of Lorraine, then resided. Madame de Beaufort and little César accompanied him.* The Duchesse de Mercœur was there to meet them and Jean Forget, Councillor of State, commissioned by the king to accept, in the name of the Duc de Vendôme, the estate of Chenonceaux, which Queen Louise gave to her niece, receiving at the same time, as a gift from the king, the splendid château and domain of Moulins, which had belonged to the unfortunate Charles de Bourbon, Constable of France in the reign of François I.† Some formalities were also

* L'Estoile, *Journal de Henri IV*.

† The morbidly pious Queen Louise had almost transformed Chenonceaux into a nunnery and dedicatory chapel of prayer for the worship of the memory of the most worthless of the kings of France. When the pleasant domain of Chenonceaux, whose embellishment had afforded Diane de Poitiers so much agreeable occupation, was ceded by her to Catherine de' Medici, it became the scene of the disgraceful revels with which the infamous Catherine was accustomed to amuse and ensnare the victims of her wily policy. Henri IV. was fond of Chenonceaux. He had

completed with reference to the age at which it was contemplated that the marriage of the betrothed young couple should take place.

Henri left Chenonceaux for Amiens to await the conclusion of the peace with Spain, which was signed at Vervins by the plenipotentiaries on the 2d of May. All the towns they possessed in France, including Calais, which the Spaniards would have preferred to retain, and which, it was suspected, Elizabeth would have been willing to purchase from them, were given up to the French, and Cambray and La Franche-Comté restored to Spain. On Sunday, the 21st of June, Henri, in the presence of the Duc d'Arscot, Prince de Chimay, and Don Francisco de Mendoz, — the legate, Cardinal de' Medici, officiating for the Pope, — signed the treaty in Paris, and solemnly swore faithfully to fulfil its conditions. The cardinal-archduke at the same time took a similar oath at Brussels, in the presence of M. de Bellièvre, M. de Sillery, and Maréchal de Biron, to whom the king then gave the rank of duke and peer, to qualify him to take part in the ceremony, a dignity which, the Baron de Rosny declares, completely

passed some time there in his early youth — to which the exchange of gifts with the queen was probably due. Then all had been life and gaiety there, and this change to solemn silence, black draperies, and the apotheosis of Henri III. impressed him uncomfortably — knowing too well the character of the monarch so honoured. Chenonceaux as a bridal gift was to undergo yet another change.

turned the head of that arrogant and intriguing officer.

The peace was greatly fêted in Paris and the principal cities of France. It was regarded as "a glorious peace," the most advantageous that France had made with her enemies since the time of Philippe Auguste, a conquest chiefly due to able negotiation.* All concerned in it were right royally rewarded. But fearing this might alienate the States of Holland, who had refused to listen to or to take any notice whatever of the archduke's conciliatory proposals of peace, as he did not recognise them as an independent sovereign state (which, having definitively thrown off the yoke of Spain, they claimed to be), the king immediately sent them an ambassador, M. de Buzenval, charged to keep on excellent terms with the States General, and to pay the stipulated portion of the sum due to them. The only unsatisfactory point in the settlement of peace was that the decision concerning the marquisate of Saluzzo was left to the arbitration of the Pope. The Duke of Savoy persisted in retaining it, the king in refusing to forego his claim to it,— the dispute being eventually settled by again having recourse to arms.

Like many other high dignitaries of the Roman

---

* After signing the treaty the king wrote to his ministers that "he had just achieved by a stroke of his pen more exploits than would have been possible in a long war with the best swords in his kingdom."

faith, the cardinal-archduke was not a priest; yet, from some sort of vow, it was needful that the Pope should absolve him before his marriage could take place. This being accomplished, he left Brussels for Madrid to receive the hand of the Infanta Isabel Clara Eugenia, to whom — the archduke representing her — the States General of the Catholic Netherlands made oath of allegiance. This marriage, by which Philip still hoped firmly to establish his house after him, he did not live to see concluded. His sombre despotism came to an end on the 13th of September.

The tortures he had endured in the last nine or ten months of his life made death a welcome visitor. His strange and agonising malady was generally regarded as the effect of Divine vengeance, a providential expiation of the many atrocious cruelties he had inflicted on thousands and tens of thousands of unfortunate people. "He looked on men as born to serve his ambition, and could he have waded through the sea of blood and have climbed over the million piled-up bodies of the men who were sacrificed by him, to the throne he so coveted of Europe and the new world, it would not have cost the barbarian a single sigh." *

For many days before his death blood is said to have flowed from every pore, his body was covered with ulcers, and devoured by vermin.

* *Esprit de la Ligue.*

One recoils from describing so frightful a condition, and, monster though he was, still must pity him. He displayed a sort of dogged resignation, a gloomy, silent patience under his terrible infliction, which impressed those about him with the belief that his blind religious fanaticism yet sustained him. But whether he really felt any remorse for the past, or cherished any hope in the future, none knew. The testament addressed to his son, and attributed to Philip, is generally considered unauthentic. "He died as he had lived — impenetrable," passing away amidst the execrations of Europe, and designated by the people, who rejoiced at his death, "The Demon of the South."

## CHAPTER VIII.

Rosny Remarks That the King, Notwithstanding the *Fêtes* Given in His Honour, is Frequently Silent and Meditative. — He is Troubled about the Succession to the Crown. — He is Recommended to Marry Again, but None of the Princesses of Europe Possess the Qualities Personal or Mental Which Form His Ideal of a Wife. — Only in His Mistress Does He Find Perfection. — Rosny, Astounded, Remonstrates with the King. — A Council Discusses the Marriage Question. — Opinions Vary, and Marguerite is Consulted. — Grand Christening of Gabrielle's Second Son. — Rosny Indignant. — A Terrible Scene. — Gabrielle Faints, and Becomes Ill and Unhappy. — Marriage of Madame Catherine. — A Worthy Archbishop. — Festivities. — Departure for Lorraine.

DURING the festivities which took place while the king was in Brittany, Rosny remarked that his majesty frequently fell into a silent, meditative mood, very different from his usual frame of mind. Twice he desired the baron to accompany him to the chase, observing that he had something to communicate to him; but on both occasions he returned without in any way referring to this secret trouble. One day, however, as Rosny was entering the courtyard of the royal residence, the king made a sign to him to follow him into the private garden leading from his apartment.

After speaking of the progress of the negotiation at Vervins and other public matters,* he said that it was in vain that he had sought and procured the blessings of peace for France, as at his death the kingdom would be inevitably replunged into the horrors of civil war by the disputes between the Prince de Condé and the other princes of the blood concerning the succession to the throne. He must marry again, Rosny suggested. The king's agents at Rome, the Archbishop of Urbino and Cardinals du Perron and d'Ossat, had assured him there would be little trouble in obtaining from the holy father the dissolution of his marriage with Marguerite de Valois, when the application should be made to him by both parties.

Marguerite had not yet been consulted on the subject. Henri III., several years before his death, had imprisoned her in the Château d'Usson in Auvergne, and there, after his assassination, she continued to reside from choice, leading a life of great depravity. This would not secure a divorce in the Roman Catholic Church; but the pretext of spiritual affinity, for which no dispensation had been granted, was generally, as in this case, discoverable — Henri II. having been the

---

* There had been a vehement contention amongst the plenipotentiaries on the question of precedence, which at last was conceded to the French, with some **extenuations to save the** *amour-propre* of the Spaniards.

godfather of Henri of Navarre. Marguerite had also unvaryingly declared, from the time the *noces vermeilles* took place, that her consent to marry the heretic prince had been obtained solely by undue coercion. This was true, too, for she was then very much in love with the Duc de Guise, and very desirous of marrying him.*

Until peace was signed, it was not proposed to send any formal embassy to Rome connected with the application for divorce. Meanwhile, Rosny undertook to ascertain Marguerite's sentiments on the subject. The king, however, did not let it drop here; but, supposing his marriage with Marguerite dissolved, "in what royal house," he said, "was he to find her successor?" That he might not have to repent of so hazardous a bargain as marriage, or fall into that greatest of all misfortunes, the having a wife destitute of pleasing qualities of mind and body, he required that his second wife should be young, beautiful, prudent, gentle in disposition, gracious in manners, lively and spirituelle, — a woman who could fix his

* Charles IX., with his usual violence, conceived so furious a hatred to Henri of Guise for his presumption in asking of him his sister Marguerite in marriage, that immediately after refusing he sent for the *grandprieur*, natural son of Henri II., and, placing before him two swords, said: "With one of these swords I intend to kill you, if, to-morrow when I go to the chase, you do not kill Henri of Guise with the other." This was secretly reported to the duke, who abstained from joining the royal hunt that day, and prudently withdrawing his attentions from Marguerite, shortly after sought and won another bride. — L'ESTOILE.

roving affections, and with whom he could live happily.

Having passed in review the marriageable princesses of Europe, and decided that all were wanting in one or more of the necessary qualifications, he added that, without going to foreign courts, he believed he could name a woman who entirely fulfilled his ideal of the wife who would ensure him domestic happiness, and as, in the ordinary course of nature, he must die before her, could also bring up his children satisfactorily, and conduct the state with prudence during a minority. "Now reflect a little," he continued; "you may then bring to mind some one in whom all these qualities are centred. If you can name no one, and cannot even venture to guess, I will name her."

"Name her, then," replied the baron. "I have not wit enough to do so."

"Ah, cunning fox!" exclaimed the king, "you could name her if you pleased; but as you choose to affect ignorance, confess that the qualities I have named are possessed by the Duchesse de Beaufort, my mistress."

Confused, as Rosny imagined, by such a confession of his weakness, he resumed: "Not that I mean you to infer from this that I have any intention to marry her, but simply that I desire to know what you would say should I take the fancy to do so."

"It was only too evident to him," Rosny says,

"that the king had already more than a fancy to contract this unworthy marriage." It surprised him greatly; but he thought it prudent to conceal his surprise, and to affect to treat the king's last words as a mere jest on his part. This, he thought, would make him feel ashamed of having expressed so absurd an idea. But Rosny's *ruse* was not successful. The king, he presumed, had not brought himself to make this painful avowal without considerable effort, and his words and tone appeared to ask pardon for it. Yet he bade the baron speak freely and seriously to him. By his long and faithful services he had acquired the right, he said, to tell him the truth, and, "if done in private, he would never feel offended by his frankness."

Rosny availed himself of this to lecture the king at some length, wisely pointing out to him, should he marry his mistress, the evils likely to ensue from the illegitimacy of his children, and the strife that would probably follow between them and others that might be born after his marriage. The king listened attentively for some time, then, interrupting, thanked him, and said he had told him enough for once.

But a few days after leaving Brittany, he assembled a sort of council at Saint-Germain, consisting of Rosny, Villeroy, and Sillery, and desired them to advise him on the subject of marriage with the Duchesse de Beaufort. Rosny repeated his former objections, — " the king would cover himself with shame in the eyes of the universe." Villeroy was of opinion that "he would do well not to marry at all, and to leave the succession to the Prince de Condé, to whom, by right of birth, it belonged." Sillery, more courtier-like than the others, gave the king the advice he seemed to wish for, namely, to marry his mistress and legitimise her children. "He could not do better than that," he said. The king replied to his advisers: "I thought to be confirmed by your united advice in the course it would be best for me to take in this matter. But as you have all advised me differently, and have supported your several opinions by very convincing arguments, I am more irresolute than ever. I must, therefore, give deeper thought to the subject myself, and abide by my own decision." *

Rosny perceived that the bands of love and habit, stronger than marriage vows, which united Henri to Gabrielle, could not be easily severed, and that ere he succeeded in tearing them asunder

---

* It was intended by the king, it appears, that this assembling of his friends in council should be kept a profound secret — not a word of it breathed to any one. He would see that Madame de Beaufort was not informed of it. Yet it was no secret to L'Estoile, or to any of the courtiers, and, notwithstanding the Baron de Rosny's disapproval, it was afterwards generally believed that if death had not taken from the king this tenderly loved mistress, he would either have married her or have forborne to marry any other.

a terrible conflict awaited him. He "regarded him as one who had received a deadly wound, and as such he was prepared to treat him." He lost no time in writing to Marguerite, and, as usual, piquing himself on his straightforwardness, he mentioned that the king desired to satisfy the nation's wishes by giving them a legitimate heir to his throne. He gave her a hint, too, which would interest her far more, of a probable increase of pension, regularly paid, should she "patriotically" fall in with the king's views.

Marguerite took five months to decide on her answer. During that time the peace of Vervins was signed, and Henri had despatched the Duc de Luxembourg to Rome to solicit from the Pope the dissolution of his marriage. The duke was, however, shortly after recalled, and Comte Brulart de Sillery, who favoured the idea of Gabrielle's elevation to the throne, named to succeed him, with the title of ambassador, and to flatter the Pope, a numerous retinue of nobles and gentlemen, splendid new carriages, and a long train of valets and lackeys. Rosny remonstrated, but in vain. "That woman," as the baron invariably speaks of poor Gabrielle, "had persuaded the king," he said, "that all this *éclat* and grandeur were necessary to secure the success of the mission." The ambassador was also well provided with money, probably by Gabrielle herself, who is said, by some chroniclers of the time, to have been wealthy, — able to lend money to the king, who so rarely had any for his own necessities. Sillery, too, had told her that there was no agent more powerful at Rome than money.

Rosny had his revenge soon after. The christening of the king's and Gabrielle's second son, which had been delayed by the settlement of peace, and discussions on the Edict of Nantes, took place at Saint-Germain on Henri's return from Brittany. It was celebrated with great magnificence, the sponsors being Madame Catherine, the king's sister, and the Comte de Soissons, the Cardinal-Duc de Joyeuse officiating. The ladies and gentlemen of the court attended, as at the baptism of the royal children, and none of the ceremonies usual on such an occasion were omitted. The child was named Alexander, in compliment to the king's heroic deeds, as the elder child had been named César Monsieur.*

All this was of course, and rightly so, highly displeasing to M. de Rosny, to whom the order for payment of the fees of the "heralds, trumpeters, and other subaltern officers" who assisted at the ceremony, was, in the usual course, sent for signature. Putting aside this document, which, on looking it over, he regarded "as handing down to posterity a monument of shame to the king,"

---

* Henri IV. was frequently represented in the prints of the day under the allegorical figures of Hercules, Alexander, Cæsar, etc.

he drew up another, "simple and modest as it should be," — that is, he suppressed the titles of "Monsieur" and "*fils de France*," and every word that conveyed the idea that a royal child was referred to.

This made a very considerable reduction in the amount due to the heralds, etc., who by no means took M. de Rosny's view of the matter. They urged that "the order for payment was given by the Councillor of State, M. Forget de Fresne, and that their rights were regulated by law." Rosny, in a passion, bade them begone, and to understand from him that there were no royal children of France. Fancying that this might lead to an unpleasant scene, he immediately sought the king, who was walking in the gallery of Saint-Germain with Épernon and several other gentlemen. Quite unceremoniously, it would seem, he placed De Fresne's order before him, and said: "It now only remains for you to declare yourself married to the Duchesse de Beaufort."

The king, having read the document, desired Rosny to tear it up; then, turning to his courtiers, said: "What malice there is in the world! and what vexations those who serve me well are doomed to encounter! An order has been sent to M. de Rosny, apparently to offend me should he comply with it, or to offend my mistress should he refuse." To Rosny he continued: "Madame de Beaufort is no doubt very angry; but go to her and give her a satisfactory explanation. If that does not suffice, I will speak to her *en maître*."

The duchess received her enemy haughtily, and, after listening to a part of his explanation, interrupted him, and with many reproaches accused him of always "endeavouring to make the king believe that black was white."

"Ho! ho! madame," he replied, "if that is the tone you adopt, I wish you good-morning; but none the less shall I do my duty."

As far as bad feeling would allow him, he gave, no doubt, a correct version of this interview to the king. It put the latter into a very bad temper with his belle Gabrielle, the result being that the king accompanied Rosny to the duchess's apartments in the cloister of Saint-Germain. There — instead of acknowledging that he alone was to blame for any undue splendour in the christening arrangements, having, of course, sanctioned all that was done by his presence at the ceremony — he reproached her with listening to the unwise counsels of her ambitious aunt, the Marquise de Sourdis, declaring — after some tears on the part of the duchess, and unkind remarks on the other side — that "he would rather part with ten mistresses such as she than with one faithful servant like Rosny."

The latter was scarcely satisfied with this cruel, almost brutal speech (if, which is doubtful, it ever was made). Some writers slightly qualify it thus: "Know, madame, that a friend like Rosny must be dearer to me than even such a mistress as you!" Gabrielle sank senseless on her couch. "The king had insulted her," she exclaimed, "in the presence of one of his valets." This stung Rosny to the quick. Nothing she could have said in the way of reproach would have touched him so deeply, for he greatly piqued himself on his ancient lineage, and on some of the daughters of the house of Béthune having married into that of Bourbon.

This was the second affront of that kind he had brought on himself from the excited feeling of an angry woman. Madame Catherine had contemptuously termed him " *un petit gentilhomme,*" a base sycophant, who meddled in the affairs of those above him in order to curry favour with the king. Much, however, might be excused by him in a king's sister, which he would find impossible to tolerate in a king's mistress; though she, too, was of noble birth, and even connected with royalty by the intermarriages of the D'Estrées with the house of Courtenay.

Worse than all, the king, who certainly was much afraid of offending Rosny, was not so firm as the latter thought desirable when he saw his mistress fall in a swoon. He mentions in his "*Œconomies Royales*" that he kept an observant eye on the king, and remarked that he trembled;

that he was ready, of course, to fall on his knees beside her, and implore her to revive and forgive him. But it was necessary to summon her women, for Henri had become anxious, and the baron himself says he was a little alarmed also. The rigid monitor, therefore, took his departure, and the king, it is presumable, lost no time in placing himself on the stool of repentance, confessing his sins and imploring absolution.

But however impetuously the king may have spoken to Gabrielle while fretting, probably as was often the case, under the inflexible Rosny's iron hand, it seems to have occasioned no change in their ordinary relations toward each other. His attentions to her were even more marked than usual, while she perhaps took his incautious words more deeply to heart than he imagined. The letters he then wrote almost daily to her — when, owing to the various and important affairs of state then occupying the attention of the king and his ministers, he was compelled to absent himself for a few days from her — are full of expressions of tenderness and passionate love for her and her children. On one of those occasions he wrote consoling her, for Gabrielle was now often oppressed with sad forebodings :

"You are depicted in my eyes, as in my heart and soul, as all perfection. My love for you is greater now than when I first knew you; my desire to return to you when absent more intense."

In another, announcing his return, he says:

"*Mes belles amours*, two hours after the arrival of the bearer of this missive you will see a cavalier who loves you most fondly, and who is called King of France and Navarre, — a very honourable title certainly, but a very troublesome one. That of your subject is far more delightful. All three are good in their way, and I am resolved to cede none of them. But as we are to meet so soon, I will chat no more with you for the present, so *bonjour*, or rather *au revoir*, my beloved."

Another letter, less pleasant than the king's, which Rosny had received from Marguerite, would, he believed, effectually put an end to "that woman's" presumptuous hopes of marriage with the king, could he but make its contents known to her. It was Marguerite's second letter. Her first he describes as "what might be expected from that princess, — being modest, prudent, and submissive, and expressive of her readiness to concur in the king's views on the subject." To this Rosny responded more emphatically that the king desired to gratify the nation's wish for an heir to the throne. In reply, Marguerite wrote "she had learned that the king intended to put the indignity upon her of elevating that disreputable Gabrielle to his throne. She would never consent to such an affront being offered her."

Even the grim baron must have smiled at the idea of Marguerite de Valois venturing to apply the term of "disreputable" to any one, — a woman so thoroughly abandoned, whose dissolute life was beyond the tolerance of even the grossly depraved court of Henri III., from which she was expelled. Yet, in spite of her resolve of no surrender, she appointed an agent to negotiate terms for her; named a large sum for the payment of her debts and a considerable pension. M. de Rosny, whom she adroitly flattered for his management of this delicate mission, thought her demands very moderate. Eventually they were fully complied with, and Marguerite duly applied to the Pope to annul her marriage.

Her determination not to yield to that Gabrielle was made known to the latter by the Marquise de Sourdis. "Everything," as the baron has informed us, "was accomplished at court by underhand means." He therefore adopted the usual course, and, taking his wife into his confidence, informed her of the preposterous views of the king's mistress and Marguerite's intention to thwart them. She in her turn, but by Rosny's orders, confided the tale to one of the most gossiping ladies of the court, who lost no time in whispering it into every one's ears, until at last it reached the one for which it was especially intended. Gabrielle did not, it seems, give much heed to this rumour. The king was ill, but more devoted than ever, to atone, perhaps, for the unpleasant episode of the christening bill. Therefore, for awhile little was said about the divorce; Clement VIII. also habitually taking an unconscionably long time to make up his mind.*

The Edict of Nantes had not yet been presented to the Paris Parliament for registration, and a regular opposition to it was organising in all parts of the country; even processions, as in the time of the League, of priests and people, to pray that God would avert the evils which astrologers and fanatical priests declared were coming on the country, and of which the "heretic edict" was believed to be the cause. But Henri turned a deaf ear to all such remonstrances, intending to have the edict registered and its stipulations carried into effect as soon as the legate, on the point of quitting Paris, had finally taken his departure.

Meanwhile a domestic event, likely to embroil him a little with the Church, but which he had resolved on completing, occupied much of his time and thoughts. This was the marriage of Madame Catherine with the Duc de Bar, eldest son of Charles III., the reigning Duc de Lorraine. It had been in contemplation for nearly a year; Henri also proposing to bring his sister into "the true fold," that she might enter on her married life as good a Catholic, at least, as her brother. A vain struggle ensued against both marriage and

---

* Henri had fallen ill of fever at Monceaux, and for a day or two it was severe enough to occasion some alarm; but his excellent constitution triumphed over the exhausting remedies then in such indiscriminate use.

conversion on her part, and a determination to dominate on both questions on his. The duke was a fervent Catholic, the princess a zealous Protestant, clinging more than ever to her religion when an attempt was made to turn her from it. Unlike Henri, Catherine had never wavered in her love or her religion, and "her heart could still acknowledge no other *fiancé* than Soissons, as she told her brother when expressing her repugnance to the proposed alliance. She had all the steadfastness of character that distinguished her mother, Jeanne d'Albret, while Henri, with the bravery of Antoine of Navarre, had inherited also some of his weaknesses.

Still the negotiations went on, — the old Duc de Lorraine, for political objects, being as anxious as Henri to conclude the arrangement. But no sooner was it publicly announced that this marriage was on the *tapis* than Catholic priests and Protestant ministers vied with each other, though from contrary motives, in their efforts to prevent it.* Less hopeful than at first of his sister's conversion, the king sent to Rome to ask the Pope for a dispensation. Cardinal d'Ossat — Henri's treacherous agent at the Papal Court — was commissioned to present his request, and to urge

---

* The Catholics looked with horror on the union of a pious son of the Church with the inveterate "heretic princess, while the Protestants were in terror lest so true a daughter of 'the religion' should be led by priestly crafts to forsake God for the worship of idols."

Clement to comply with it. The king's missive was duly laid before his holiness, but the cardinal strongly recommended refusal.

Clement adopted the cardinal's advice, and Henri was informed that the sovereign pontiff could not grant his request. "One of the parties had not only refrained from joining in the application, but had neither recognised him as the Pastor of the Catholic and Apostolic Church nor believed in his power to pronounce a dispensation. Further, she did not regard marriage as a sacrament, or believe it unlawful if contracted between cousins-german." The cardinal professed to have employed all such arguments as the case permitted to overcome the Pope's decision, though, he added, it was against his own convictions, and that he was forced to agree with his holiness, who in a matter of conscience such as this could only reply as he had done. It was supposed that the courts of France and Lorraine would at once either unite to compel Madame Catherine to change her religion, or that the marriage would be given up altogether.

However, it was determined to meet the Pope's refusal by dispensing with his dispensation. Towards the end of December the marriage-contract — drawn up by the Baron de Rosny — was read in Catherine's presence. The king, having affixed his signature, handed the pen to his sister, he protesting that she was not constrained to this marriage in any way, or urged to be a Catholic.

Rosny, Villeroy, Jeannin, and other ministers of state being present, also attested it. Catherine, suffering from chest disease, and apparently worn out by her brother's harshness and importunity, had at last resigned herself to her fate — saddened, sorrowful, and deeply melancholy. She and the Comte de Soissons seem to have bidden farewell to each other when they stood together at the font as the sponsors of Henri's son, — the cause of great searchings of heart to M. de Rosny.

A few days after the signing of the contract, the Duc de Bar, with a younger brother and a retinue of three hundred gentlemen, arrived at the Louvre. "Madame received them with as much graciousness as agitated feelings allowed her to assume, assisted by the king, and supported by the pious couusels of Du Plessis-Mornay." Catherine was then in her thirty-ninth year, the duke several years younger, and described as very handsome, elegant, and brave; and, from his generosity and piety, surnamed "the good." She, too, was not unpleasing. Her figure was slight and graceful; her countenance animated, which, with the natural liveliness of her disposition — when not saddened by Henri's unkindness — gave her still a youthful air.

A final effort was yet to be made to bring this Huguenot princess to a sense of the perilous condition of her soul. A conference of bishops and doctors was named to instruct her in Catholicism, at which Du Plessis-Mornay and one or two Protestant ministers were to be present at her desire—as some points on which both faiths could agree were to be discovered if possible. Rosny and the duke also attended. But the prelates and doctors of the Sorbonne overwhelmed her with theological subtleties, and shocked and distressed her with reference to the punishment which—in order to alarm her into seeking in the bosom of the Church a refuge from a similar fate—they contended that the soul of her heretic mother was then undergoing.

Henri had spared himself the infliction of listening to the prelates' arguments, but entered the apartment when the conference was closing; in time, however, to hear his sister declare that "she neither understood nor believed anything they had told her." Being of a very hasty temper, he reproached her angrily with thwarting all his efforts for her advantage; to which she replied, "These Catholic prelates would have me believe in the damnation of our dear mother." The king was silenced. His eyes became suffused with tears in spite of his efforts to suppress his emotion. For he cherished a profound regard for the memory of his noble mother, whose mysterious death at the court of the infamous Catherine de' Medici was so soon followed by the slaughter of so many of his then Huguenot friends and allies.

Henri was not moved, however, to release his

sister and the duke from their unwelcome engagement. The latter had not sought Catherine in marriage; like herself, he was the victim of circumstances, a sacrifice to the political views of his elders. There was that sort of sympathy between them; and Catherine really pitied the duke, though she gave him no love, and expected none from him. But it would seem as if fate had determined to aid in setting them free, for yet another obstacle to their marriage presented itself: none of the bishops would venture to marry them, the Pope having refused the dispensation, and the conference having failed in its object.

What must be done in such a dilemma? The king at last bethought him of sending for the Archbishop of Rouen, — a prelate of an unscrupulous and dissipated character, on whom he had lately bestowed, at the instance of the Duc de Roquelaure, that very important see, though wholly incompetent to fulfil its duties.* M. de Rouen positively refusing to comply with the king's request, his majesty flew into a violent passion, called the archbishop ungrateful, and sent for Roquelaure, the companion of his orgies, to bring him to his senses. Threatened with the loss of his archbishopric, he at length gave an unwilling consent.

\* He was Henri's natural brother, — the son of Antoine of Navarre and Mademoiselle de la Baraudière la Roüet, one of Catherine de' Medici's frail bevy of beauties.

On Sunday morning, the 29th of January, the king, taking his sister by the hand, led her to his private apartment, where the duke, evidently anxious and troubled by this unusual celebration of a royal marriage, was waiting with his brother to receive them. On the arrival of the archbishop, the king commanded him to proceed with the ceremony. He observed that the customary solemnities which took place in a chapel ought not to be omitted, when the king replied, very learnedly (as the *Chronologie septénaire* remarks), that "his presence was above all other solemnities, and his apartment a no less sacred place than a chapel."

The ceremony was as little prolonged as possible; the new-married pair afterwards kneeling and remaining some time in prayer, but speaking not a word to each other. Catherine wore only a plain white morning dress without any ornaments, and looked more pale and fragile than ever. In the afternoon the king gave a banquet, at which Catherine was present in splendid bridal dress, with royal mantle, and wearing magnificent pearls and diamonds.

Three days were devoted to balls and festivities, and a medal was struck in commemoration of the event. A few days after, the melancholy pair took their departure for Lorraine. Catherine expressed great regret at leaving France, and fainted with emotion on bidding adieu to her brother. Rosny speaks of the magnificent presents he received both from the king and the Duc de Lorraine, in acknowledgment of the trouble he had taken to bring this affair to a conclusion, if not to a very happy one. Amongst other presents of great value from Lorraine was a beautiful Barbary horse most richly caparisoned. This, and the rest of the bridal gifts, he sent, as was his custom, to the king, who always returned them with the request that he would keep them.*

* Soon after the marriage of Madame Catherine the Comte de Soissons consoled himself for the loss of his princess by marrying Mademoiselle Anne de Montaffié; but his resentment towards the Baron de Rosny continued unabated. The Duc de Montpensier also married, a few months later, the daughter of the Duc de Joyeuse.

## CHAPTER IX.

Henri Now Determines to Delay No Longer the Verification of the Edict of Nantes. — Henri's Address to the Remonstrances of the Deputies. — Edict Registered 15th February, 1599. — Parliament of Rouen's Resistance. — King's Divorce Applied for. — Secret Negotiation of Rosny, Villeroy, and Others with Tuscany. — Henri Shrinks from a Medici, but Rosny Is Enamoured of Marie's Dowry of 600,000 Crowns. Signs and Wonders. — Gabrielle Depressed. — King Seeks to Reassure and Console Her. — Their Parting. — Gabrielle Seized with Strange Pains at Zameti's. — Her Death; Magnificent Funeral. — King's Grief. — Court Mourning. — Duke of Tuscany Suspected. — The Divorce Granted.

THE marriage of Madame Catherine being accomplished, and Cardinal de' Medici on his way back to Rome, the king determined to defer no longer the verification of the Edict of Nantes. It was therefore sent to the Parliament of Paris with the royal mandate to register it. The king's command was met by violent opposition, no less by the clergy of the University and doctors of the Sorbonne than by the magistrates of the Sovereign Court. A deputation was therefore named to remonstrate with the king.

Henri received the deputies in his private apartment, "not," as he said, "like a monarch in royal robes or armed *cap-à-pie* to listen to ambassadors, but simply in his gray cloth doublet, as the father of a family to converse with his children. You have exhorted me," he continued, "to do my duty. I now exhort you to do yours, and request you to verify the edict which I have granted to the people of 'the religion' in the interests of peace. Having secured peace without, I would now have peace within my kingdom. There must be no more such distinctive terms as Catholics and Huguenots; all henceforth must be Frenchmen and good citizens.

"I will have my edict observed, and that such is my will ought to be sufficient reason for your immediate acceptance of it. Never in an obedient state is a prince asked for his reasons. I hear, too, that at Tours and elsewhere there have been street processions of priests and people for the purpose of intimidating the judges, and inciting them to reject my edict. This is the sort of thing that has led to barricades and civil war. But I, who have leaped over the walls of so many cities, shall easily jump over barricades." This address of mingled seriousness and banter he concluded with: "I am your king; I now speak to you as king; I will be obeyed!"

The Edict of Nantes was registered by the Parliament of Paris on the 15th of February, after much difficulty. For, in spite of the tone adopted by the king, so many modifications were secretly conceded, so many verbal promises given not to do what the edict promised to do, that before it obtained a general, but most unwilling, acceptance, it had become a very different document from that which left the hands of the four statesmen employed in drawing it up. The Parliament of Rouen frequently implored the king to revoke his edict, and on various pretences resisted his order to verify it until 1609.

The king's divorce and probable remarriage were but seldom alluded to just then. A mysterious silence was observed on the subject, though it was well known to many persons of the court that, without even the king's consent, and before Marguerite's demand to be released from her marriage vows had reached the Pope, some sort of negotiation was being carried on with the Duke of Tuscany, the uncle of Maria de' Medici. Henri himself shrank instinctively from a Medici, and from placing another "banker's daughter" on the throne of France. Her dowry of 600,000 crowns had an attraction, however, for M. de Rosny, on whom the king early in this year conferred the title of superintendent of the finances of the state, — a post whose duties he had already for some time fulfilled without being distinctively nominated chief of the financial department.

Peace being concluded, the much needed reorganisation of the kingdom was to begin. Reforms innumerable were floating in the king's mind; and who so fit to enable him to realise them, to bring order out of disorder, as M. de Rosny?— the man whom Providence had given him, and especially, it would seem, designed for that task. A man of harsh temper, proud and obstinate, whose rough manners rather alienated than attracted friends; yet a man of great ability, industry, perseverance, and irreproachable integrity, though by no means disinterested, but expecting that the king should make his fortune while he made that of the state.

The salary of the superintendent was fixed by the king at 20,000 *livres*, to which was added the vacant post of inspector of the roads of France (*grand-voyer*), salary 10,000 *livres*, with another small appointment, surveyor of buildings and fortifications (*intendant des batiments du roi*), which the capricious M. de Sancy had resigned, together with his place in the Council of Finance, not caring to serve under M. de Rosny, who had treated him with some discourtesy. The king, who was rather too liberal a master, — considering the smallness of his revenue, the enormous debt he owed, and the misery of the people, from whom the means of its payment had to be wrung, — added to the baron's salaries a "yearly gratification of 60,000 *livres*, making an annual stipend of 90,000 *livres*, the *livre* being then of the value of three *francs*.

He was not unworthy, certainly, of these marks of royal favour. France owed much to the Baron, afterwards Marquis, de Rosny, but generally better known as Duc de Sully, — a title which, with that of peer of France, was not conferred on him until 1606. The king had offered it some years back, but Rosny declined to accept it, for although very wealthy, and his wife also rich, he thought himself not rich enough to incur the expense of adding a hundred or more gentlemen to his retinue, a train of ladies of honour for the duchess, and generally of keeping up the state and magnificence which the custom of the day expected of the *haute noblesse*.\*

The season of Lent this year was passed by Henri and Gabrielle at Fontainebleau, where many rumours were afloat of strange sights seen, strange sounds heard, and remarkable occurrences in various parts of the world, all announcing woe to the nation and dire events about to happen; these wretched superstitions being encouraged by the discontented priesthood. The black huntsman was said to have been seen in the dusk of the evening in the forest of Fontainebleau, the echoes of his winding-horn and the baying of his hounds being distinctly heard on stormy nights above the moaning of the forest trees as they bowed before

\* The grand cordon of the order of Saint-Esprit should have accompanied the creation of duke and peer of France; but *his religion* forbade his acceptance of it. He therefore composed a decoration for himself, consisting of a chain of linked SS, set with diamonds, which meant probably, if it meant anything, Sully, or Sully of Sully, the estate from which, in preference to Rosny, it being a recently acquired possession, he took his title.

the force of the gale, striking terror into the hearts of the timid, and filling them with anxious fears.

If not only the ignorant people, but the court generally, were looking forward to new disasters instead of the promised blessings of peace, with much more reason might the beautiful young Duchesse de Beaufort give way to sorrowful forebodings, and find, in spite of hunting parties and other permissible Lenten amusements, the season of piety and penance more lugubrious than usual. Her spirits drooped; she was alarmed and anxious, and wept bitterly. The king strove to reassure her, and redoubled his attentions, often taking long rides with her in the forest with few attendants.

As the holy week was approaching, the king's confessor recommended that the duchess should pass that time in Paris, the king remaining at Fontainebleau for his Easter devotions. This was inflicting a penance on him, for which the confessor may have had his motives. But the historian Mathieu says that the object of the duchess's journey was to conclude the contract for the purchase of Châteauneuf, in Le Perche, and that the confessor then suggested that she should wait in Paris for the king's return a few days after, instead of going back to Fontainebleau. The king yielded to this suggestion, which seems to have grieved the duchess. To console her, he immediately wrote to Zameti, whose pleasant château, with Italian gardens reaching to the Seine, he thought would be less gloomy for her while so depressed than the Marquise de Sourdis's residence, or her own apartments in the Louvre.

Though their separation was to be but for a few days, the king, while consoling her, had become no less distressed himself. He accompanied her to Melun, whence she was to proceed in the royal barge to Paris. At the moment of parting some secret apprehension of evil about to happen, and that they were taking a final leave of each other, seemed to possess them both. She implored him to watch carefully over her children, and recommended her domestics at Monceaux to his favour. The king listened without attempting to comfort her, being overcome with sympathising grief. He seemed unable to leave her, and again and again renewed his parting endearments.

But at length the Duc de Roquelaure, Maréchal d'Ornano, and the Baron de Frontignac, who had accompanied the king from Fontainebleau, strove to prevail on him not to prolong a parting so painful to both. Yet a little gentle force was necessary ere they could induce him to reënter the carriage that had brought him and Gabrielle to Melun. He then especially charged La Varenne, his *maître d'hôtel*, to conduct her with the utmost care to Zameti's.

Desirous of pleasing the king, Zameti received

the Duchesse de Beaufort with the greatest courtesy. On Maunday Thursday, the 10th of April, after partaking of one of those exquisitely prepared Italian dinners to which Zameti, a rich financier, frequently invited his friends,— the king often sitting down unceremoniously to dinner with them,— the duchess wished to attend the musical evening service at the Petit Saint-Antoine, Mademoiselle de Guise and the Duchesse de Retz proposing to accompany her. Suddenly, while crossing the garden, she was seized with violent pains in the chest, and so burning a heat in the throat that she at once concluded she was poisoned, and attributed it to the salad she had eaten; others say to a poisoned orange.

She was immediately conveyed, at her request, to her aunt's, in the cloister of Saint-Germain l'Auxerrois. Fearful convulsions then attacked her, and the beautiful features became frightfully distorted. The king's physician — La Rivière — was summoned in all haste; but on beholding the terrible change in her countenance he turned from her with horror, exclaiming, "It is the hand of God!" Apparently, he made no attempt to assist or relieve her.* La Varenne then wrote to the

* D'Aubigné says that "La Rivière was accompanied by other physicians of the king's household, of whom he was the chief, and that on arriving at Saint-Germain he advanced but three paces into Gabrielle's room, and looked at her from a distance only, as she lay on her bed. Perceiving the sad distortion of her countenance, he turned towards his companions who stood nearer

king that the duchess was seized with fits, and at her desire had been removed to her aunt's. Instantly, he mounted his horse, and, accompanied by the above named cavaliers, set off at full speed for Paris.

But ere he had proceeded far a second messenger from La Varenne met him. His agitation became extreme. Tearing open the letter, he dismounted to read it. It contained but a few words; but at a glance he learned from it the fatal truth — his belle Gabrielle was dead. In the madness of his grief he threw himself on the ground and gave way to violent emotions of agony and despair. Suddenly rising, he said he "would at least have the consolation of looking on her loved face once more," and was about to remount.

The friends who were with him, having been told by the messenger of the fearful results of the strong convulsions in which the duchess died, were anxious to spare him the further agony of beholding the beauty of the woman he so loved turned to hideousness. They therefore thought it well to hint to him that the duchess's sufferings had occasioned a fearful and painful change in her. For a moment he seemed not to comprehend them, but when the truth flashed on his mind,

---

the door, and said: '*Hic est manus Domini.*' All then left the apartment." La Rivière afterwards attributed her death to apoplexy.

emotion so much overcame the dauntless soldier-king that he swooned and fell senseless on the ground. A carriage was procured at a neighbouring château, in which he was taken back to Fontainebleau.

When the Duchesse de Beaufort landed at the arsenal from the king's barge, the Baron de Rosny was there to receive her. Both he and the baroness thought it a part of their duty, notwithstanding the scene which some two or three months before had taken place at Saint-Germain, to visit and take leave of her before quitting Paris, as they were about to do with the Prince and Princess of Orange, to celebrate the Lord's Supper at Rosny, and to show the prince the new château the baron was building there. The duchess appears to have received them cordially, which Rosny attributed to a desire to "win him over to a relaxation of severity, and to obtain his support to her design of marrying the king. He returned her courtesy," he says, "by general protestations of respect, attachment, and devotedness, which signify anything you please or nothing at all."

Two days, or rather nights, after, while all in the château were sleeping, the baron was awakened by a violent ringing and knocking at the outer gates, a powerful voice at the same time calling, "*De la part du roi!*" M. de Rosny left his bed, and roused his drowsy lackeys, while he, wondering what could have happened, slipped on his dressing-gown to receive the nocturnal visitor. The gates being opened, a courier entered, who said he had been riding all night, sent by the Duc de Roquelaure and other courtiers staying with the king, to request M. de Rosny to repair with all speed to Fontainebleau.

"But the king — is he ill?"

"He is not ill, but overwhelmed with grief. Madame la Duchesse is dead!"

"Dead!" exclaimed the baron. "He could not," he says, "believe the man; it seemed to him so unlikely." But when he produced a letter from La Varenne, "which at first he feared he had lost," Rosny could doubt no longer, and his feelings for the moment were divided between regret for the affliction which he was sure this event would cause the king, and joy for the blessing it would prove to France. The latter sentiment predominated; for he reflected that for a brief, if acute, spasm of sorrow the king would purchase exemption from anguish of heart a thousand times more cruel than that which now weighed upon it. Heaven, he said, had come to his aid, by a blow certainly of a painful kind, but the only one which could effectually open the way to a marriage on which the repose of France depended, the well-being of her people, the destiny of Europe, and his majesty's own personal happiness; for he would have always regarded the advantages of a legitimate union as too dearly bought by the abandonment of a woman otherwise worthy of his attachment by a thousand good qualities.\*

After jestingly informing Madame de Rosny that she would not have to attend either the *coucher* or *lever* of the Duchesse de Beaufort, as she had suddenly died of apoplexy, the baron, with but two or three of his attendants, set out with the courier to Fontainebleau. They arrived in the evening of the following day. The king was alone, pacing to and fro in the gallery. He could not endure the presence of his courtiers, whose proffered consolation did but render his grief more acute. He scarcely desired the presence even of Rosny; for, as he told him on arrival,

---

\* This was a great concession on the part of M. De Rosny. Very recently he had denied her any good qualities, and declared her "universally hated," which was the reverse of truth. For she was generally liked by the court, except, of course, by such personages as the Princesse de Conti, who would have been very glad to step into her place, or by others whose political intrigues made her abandonment by the king, or other mode of "quiet removal," convenient to them. The historian Mathieu speaks very favourably of her. He says "her judgment, too, was good, and she often gave excellent advice to the king." Another contemporary writer, who was far from being a flatterer, after speaking approvingly of her, mentions her extreme beauty, which he says was of a refined style, without the slightest trace of sensuality. "It is, indeed, remarkable," he adds, "that such a woman, who for nearly nine years had lived as a queen, and was treated as one rather than as a mistress, should have made so few enemies. Her influence was great with the king; but she used it very modestly. *The necessities of the state were her enemies; which I leave, as a doubtful thing, to every one's own explanation.*" — D'AUBIGNÉ.

he had feared that the sight of him would but add bitterness to his poignant sorrow, and that such indeed was the sensation he experienced when he entered.

Rosny, however, offered consolation by reminding him of passages of Scripture inculcating perfect trust in God, as well as thankfulness to Him under the most terrible and painful events as of the most pleasurable ones, — the former being frequently mercies in disguise. His aim, he states, was to place the king in that distressing, but to him inevitable, conjuncture, had his mistress lived, in which, combated on the one side by the powerful charm of deepest tenderness, and on the other by the voice of honour and duty, he would have been compelled to decide on a *liaison* he could neither break without lacerating his heart, nor continue without covering himself with shame. The baron then varied his theme, and launched out into praises of the late duchess, ascribing to her qualities he would have been far from crediting her with had she lived.

This had a much greater effect on Henri than anything he had said before, and he listened with pleasure to the praises of Gabrielle. He was gratified, as Rosny saw, that he now believed his attachment to Madame de Beaufort to have been founded on the real sympathy of their minds, and sincerest mutual esteem, — that it was by no means a mere libertine love. The king required the whole of his court to wear mourning for Gabrielle. Black was ordered for the first week, he wearing it for the first month; afterwards, with the rest of the court, violet for three months.

Her funeral could scarcely have been more splendid had she really shared his throne. For three days she lay in state under a royal canopy at Saint-Germain l'Auxerrois, and by her side was placed her prematurely born dead infant. The king and his children, with the whole of the court, knelt around her coffin, which was afterwards conducted with great funereal pomp to the Abbey of Maubuisson, where the bodies were buried. The ambassadors, in deep mourning, paid their visits of condolence to the king. The Parliament also sent a solemn deputation to express their sympathy with him. His sister — herself unhappy — wrote a very touching letter, assuring him that she fully shared in his sorrow, and lamented with him the great loss he had sustained. In his reply, he told her that "his heart was now dead to love; its root was withered, and would bloom no more. Sorrow and mourning must be his lot until the grave closed over him. Henceforth he should live for his kingdom alone."

Unhappily, the result proved otherwise. Yet the place which "la belle Gabrielle" had held in his heart was doubtless never wholly possessed by another. He never, indeed, entirely forgot her; and though time had its customary soothing effect, and the ardour of his love was too speedily quenched, there yet remained with him the cherished souvenir of a loved and valued friend. Latterly, influenced by Rosny — harsh and dictatorial — Henri had seemed to waver between love and political expediency; but had not the beautiful Duchesse de Beaufort, then in her twenty-seventh year, thus suddenly and mysteriously died, it can hardly be doubted that the marriage of Henri IV. and Maria de' Medici would never have taken place.

The king continued to reside at Fontainebleau, secluding himself during the period of mourning, and apparently finding consolation in the society of his children for a longer time than the Baron de Rosny had expected. Vainly, at first, he told him that, for dispelling grief and freeing the mind from the torture of useless regrets, there was no remedy like occupation, and that many important matters of state were now urgently requiring attention. Henri was not of a temperament long to hug sorrow or enjoy grief. Gradually he recovered his wonted cheerfulness, which Rosny was not slow to take advantage of. As long as Madame de Beaufort lived, few persons, he says, thought of pressing the king to be more urgent with his agents at Rome on the subject of his divorce, being unwilling to expose themselves to the anger of "that woman so universally hated," and wnose displeasure was always to be greatly feared, even had she failed in her designs on the king. Nothing, it seems, could mitigate the intensity of Rosny's hatred for Gabrielle. He must have known that it was the general feeling that she was the victim of a crime, attributed — *sotto voce*, of course — to the Grand Duke of Tuscany, the uncle of Maria de' Medici, and that pity was far more the universal feeling than hate.

But no sooner was it known that she was really dead than the Parliament of Paris, with the provost and municipal body, and a great number of the people, seemed to have conspired together to address the king, earnestly to request him to obtain his divorce speedily and to remarry. Henri was not very well pleased with this attempt to impel him to take a step on which, as regarded the choice of a queen, he had come to no determination whatever. He yet gave a sort of promise to the procurator-general that the wishes of his subjects should be gratified. Rosny at the same time wrote to Marguerite, who, to hasten the proceedings at Rome, sent a private letter to the Pope in terms intended to convince him that no violence was done to her feelings with regard to the dissolution of her marriage, but that, on the contrary, she was no less eager than the rest of France for its speedy accomplishment.

The final proceedings in this divorce could take place only in France, it seems. The Pope, therefore, appointed two French prelates, the Archbishop of Arles and the Cardinal-Duc de Joyeuse (Brother Ange), with the Bishop of Modena — the nephew and nuncio of Clement VIII. — to repair to Paris, there to declare Henri and Marguerite liberated from all mutual engagements, because of the nullity of their marriage, which had never been regarded as a binding one by Catholics or Protestants, neither the customary ceremonies of the Catholic Church nor those of the reformed religion having been observed. Several months, however, passed away ere the declaration was made in due form. Meanwhile the king recovered his wonted gaiety, and was prepared to wear the chains of any eligible new mistress.

## CHAPTER X.

**Parties of Pleasure, Banquets, and the Chase Again Occupy the King. — The Withered Heart is Revivified. — An *Intrigante* of the Court Sells Him Her Smiles for 300,000 Crowns and a Promise of Marriage. — Heaven Comes to Henri's Rescue. — A Scene with Rosny. — Secret Negotiations of His Ministers to Marry Him. — His Excitement on Learning That the Contract is Signed by Them. — Divorce Obtained. — Clement Also Annuls Catherine's Marriage. — Charles Emanuel of Savoy Visits France. — Rosny Buys D'Estrées's Post of Grand Master. — The New Cannon, etc., Shown to Duke of Savoy. — Plots, Intrigues, and Attempts to Assassinate. — War against Savoy Declared.**

WHILE the prelates were leisurely making up their minds to declare what was already so clear to every one, the king returned to Fontainebleau, where, surrounded by his courtiers, he now passed the greater part of his time in parties of pleasure, banquets, and the chase. It was at the dinner-table after one of his hunting parties that he first heard of Mademoiselle d'Entragues. The description which one of the party gave of her beauty, liveliness, and wit inspired the king with a desire to see her, and having gratified this desire, he fell violently in love with her. The image of his "charmante

*Catherine-Henriette d' Entragues.*
Photo-Etching. — From an old Portrait.

HENRIETTE, DE BALSAC, D'ENTRAGVES, EVT DE HENRY IV.
HENRY, EVESQVE DE METS, PVIS DVC DE VERNEVIL, ET GABRIELLE
ANGELIQVE, DVCHESSE, DE LA VALLETTE

Gabrielle," so recently and so vividly "depicted on his heart, his soul, in all her perfect loveliness," faded away into dimmest shadow before the attractions of this new and artful beauty, — a consummate and dangerous *intrigante*, whose smiles were to revivify the withered root of that desolate heart which he had believed was doomed never to bloom into love again. "Ah! why," we may exclaim with the Baron de Rosny, "could he not foresee all the misery this new passion would eventually bring upon him?" But, alas! it was the destiny of Henri IV. that the foible which tarnished his glory should also embitter his domestic life.

Catherine Henriette was the daughter of François de Balzac, Comte d'Entragues, and his second wife, Marie Touchet, the mistress of Charles IX. She was about three years younger than Gabrielle, but less beautiful; of a lively temper, but bold and ambitious. Though both amused and gratified to find herself the object of the king's ardent pursuit, her ambition was more particularly flattered by the thought that in the existing conjuncture of events it was not impossible, if she played her cards skilfully, that she might compel her lover to convert that title into husband. Like her father she was an adept in intrigue, and but recently he and her mother, with her half-brother, the Comte d'Auvergne, and herself, had received an order from the Baron de Rosny, by the king's command, to quit Paris, information having been obtained of their connection with seditious persons who were intriguing against the state.

When reminded of this, Henri, absorbed by the ardour of his new passion, gave no heed to it. The young lady meanwhile frequently met his assiduities with proud disdain; at other times her modesty took alarm while listening to his protestations of ardent and undying love. But at length she consented to become his mistress for the sum, immediately paid, of 300,000 crowns, and a written promise to marry her within a year. The latter, she said, was to satisfy her father and brother, whose anger she pretended to fear, as they would separate her from the king forever without that pledge of his true attachment to her.

"For herself," she said, "she was wholly devoid of ambition, and had no desire to make any use of such a promise. Let her have it, however, but to show her parents, and she would then place her destiny in the hands of the king, who alone had a right to dispose of it." This was her second request; for as the king at first had hesitated to give this promise, she did not urge it until the 300,000 crowns were obtained. That sum was wrung from the baron after a violent scene between him and the king. Rosny had introduced some additional stringent reforms in the financial department, which enabled him to put into the treasury for the needs of the state much that had hitherto continued to pass into the pockets of receivers-general, treasurers, etc.

Such a demand on his first savings as 300,000 crowns to purchase the smiles of a courtesan, when the greatest difficulty was experienced in providing for the payment of salaries and the gradual reduction, on a plan he had arranged, of the enormous debts of the state, greatly irritated him. It was indeed most disheartening, and so roused his anger that the king was told by M. de Rosny some very plain home truths on that occasion. It would not have suited the king to dismiss from his office of superintendent the only man able and willing to cope with the embezzlers of the revenue. He said then, as he had occasion to say many times after, that "the baron was naturally of a bad temper, but if not unduly provoked, it soon passed off."

Having obtained the 300,000 crowns, Henri hastened to lay them at the feet of the lady who had ensnared his heart.* The indignant father and brother then appeared on the scene, when, after much expostulation, the Comte d'Entragues, pitying, doubtless, the amatory monarch's loveless, widowed condition, consented to give his daughter to him "as a companion," if, besides the 300,000 crowns she had received, he gave him a written

* Some memoirs say 100,000, others 300,000 crowns. Perhaps the former is correct. Rosny had not very long had the entire direction of the finances.

promise, in his own hand, to marry her within a year, should she during that time give birth to a son. The king had the weakness to consent! He, however, had made it a habit rarely to conceal his plans and private arrangements, wise or unwise, from M. de Rosny, who, as he well knew, would strive to turn him from what, in his view, was hurtful to himself or the state.

Accordingly, the promise the king had consented to entrust to Entragues being written, he one morning, when ready to set out for the chase, called Rosny into the gallery at Fontainebleau, and placed in his hands this disgraceful document. As he read, he says, every word seemed to stab him as with a blow from a poniard. Perceiving its effect on Rosny, the blood mounted to Henri's face. He turned aside to conceal it. But while the terms of the promise were too ridiculous to be of any legal validity, they were calculated to bring shame and contempt on the king, and sooner or later to give occasion for a terrible scandal. Silently and coldly he returned the paper.

"Well?" said the king, expecting some remark. "Why affect so much discretion? Speak freely."

But Rosny had some unpleasant thoughts of his own. His efforts to displace poor Gabrielle, and her "removal," afterwards effected by others, had neither brought about, nor seemed likely to produce, the happy results expected. But, as he continued silent, the king became more desirous of having his opinion. He assured him that he would neither feel angry nor offended, whatever he might say or do. "It is just," he said, laughingly, "that I should make you some amends for the 300,000 crowns I extorted from you." Two or three times he repeated this, and each time more seriously, as a sort of oath; for he was especially anxious to know what Rosny, so rarely backward in speaking his mind, really thought of this promise.

Thus assured, Rosny took the paper he had returned to the king and tore it in pieces, but spoke not a word.

"*Comment, morbleu!*" exclaimed the king, surprised at the boldness of this act. "What do you mean by this? It seems to me you are mad!"

"True, Sire," he replied, "I am mad; and would to heaven I were the only madman in France!"

While the king was gathering up the fragments of the marriage promise, Rosny took the opportunity of reading him a lecture, which, notwithstanding his extreme irritation, he listened to unto the end. But so entirely was he enslaved by this new passion that no arguments could make him change his resolution respecting the promise. He was exceedingly displeased, also, with his too sincere confidant, and his first impulse was to banish him. He, however, fortunately for himself, succeeded in controlling his feelings in that respect. He then left the gallery, and rewrote his promise in his own private room; then, passing out, — affecting not even to see his friend and counsellor, — he mounted his horse and rode off in the direction of Malesherbes, where Entragues and his family had resided since the order to leave Paris. Madame d'Entragues, herself formerly a king's mistress, and who had no objection to her daughter following her example, received his majesty with eager pleasure, and Rosny saw no more of him for the next few days.

Mademoiselle d'Entragues soon afterwards appeared at court as Marquise de Verneuil, a title conferred on her by the king until she could legitimately assume that of queen. This was in October, six months only after the death of Gabrielle and Henri's overwhelming grief for "his irreparable loss." On that occasion it was said by Rosny and others that heaven had come to Henri's aid, and carried off an obstacle to the welfare of France and her king. So under the circumstances now in question Divine aid was said to have been once more vouchsafed to him and France to defeat the presumptuous hopes of a second unworthy queen-consort-expectant.

The aid was not in this instance sent in a poisoned *pâté* or Italian salad-bowl, but came direct from heaven in the form of a heavy storm with thunder and vivid lightning, which struck the house where the marquise was temporarily residing at Saint-André de La Coste. This event, together with the violence of the war of the elements, so terribly alarmed her that the child on whose sex and life depended her hopes of sharing the throne of France came prematurely into the world and dispelled them. The *liaison*, however, continued, and the promise of marriage was retained by the marquise; for though of no real value whatever, it yet might serve as a weapon for creating annoyance and trouble.

The French envoys had not been recalled from Florence or Rome, Henri having scarcely considered their mission as specially relating to the negotiation of a marriage, but rather as mainly connected with the Pope's mediation in reference to the marquisate of Saluzzo and the explanations required of the grand duke concerning the taking of the isles of If, in the roadstead of Marseilles, by the duke's brother, who had fortified them to prevent their occupation by the Spaniards. It was proposed, on peace being signed, to leave the decision respecting the possession of Saluzzo to Clement VIII., and that the three islets should be restored to France on payment of the cost of the fortifications.

Rosny, being very desirous of remarrying the king to keep him free from further entanglements, pressed him to authorise some overtures being made at the same time to the Grand Duke Ferdinand for the hand of his niece. Henri had no inclination for that match. The description he had received of the princess was not at all to his taste, and the house of Medici he regarded rather as a banking firm than a royal house. Still, greatly urged by the baron, he gave a sort of unwilling permission to touch on the subject, binding him, as he conceived, to nothing at all; therefore he gave no further thought to it.

His attention had, indeed, been fully occupied by his new mistress, and to the important work of establishing her in a manner suited to her new dignity of the king's first favourite. This compelled him, in order to avoid contentions with Rosny, to borrow money sometimes from Zameti or Gondy, under whose names Duke Ferdinand carried on his banking business, and farmed a part of the revenues of France. Clement VIII. greatly approved of the marriage of his niece with the Most Christian king, and Ferdinand was no less pleased with the prospect of placing her on the throne of France. With much surprise, therefore, Henri received the information that the grand duke had named his confidential adviser, Comte Joanino, to proceed to Paris to meet those representatives the king might appoint to discuss with him the terms of the contract.

The king at first treated it as a jest, though he ought to have known that Rosny was no jester. Finally, and, as the baron affirms, from importunity alone, — in order to be free from further trouble about it, supposing that obstacles would arise to prevent agreement, — he named as his agents the Connétable de Montmorency, the Chancelier de Chiverny, the minister of state Villeroy, and the Baron de Rosny.

Soon after the Italian count arrived, and Rosny determined that his mission should not fail from needless delay. All were anxious for the marriage of the king, desiring to liberate him from the hands of the artful *intrigante* into whose toils he had fallen, and — now that he had passed the meridian of life and had encountered and overcome so many troubles and hardships — to see him safely into the haven of matrimony and domestic bliss, where, as he had already proposed, he might devote himself to restoring peace and prosperity to his country.*

The contract was speedily drawn up, and but little disagreement occurred respecting its stipulations, — the king's agents securing all possible advantages for his majesty, the Italian complacently accepting all their propositions as far as possible. For the duke had desired him, within certain limits, to be yielding, as he had for some years past — from the time, indeed, of Henri's abjuration — been scheming to bring about this alliance, which procured him some desired political advantages. Maria de' Medici's dowry was larger

* Henri IV. was then forty-six; but the hardships of the rough life he had led made him in constitution and appearance at least ten years older.

than that of any of the princesses of Europe — 600,000 gold crowns, which atoned for the fact of the House of Medici being but, as it were, a parvenu amongst royal houses, and hardly yet accepted as royal.

The duke had lent the king 300,000 crowns, which sum was to be deducted from Maria's fortune, leaving Rosny still the 300,000 to replace the sum at which Mademoiselle d'Entragues had appraised herself. Not a *livre* of this windfall did he propose to offer the king. The several articles of the contract being agreed to, and the agents on both sides having affixed their signatures, the Baron de Rosny, as most capable of bearing the brunt of the king's displeasure, was deputed to be the bearer of the document to his majesty. He had expected the affair to be a long time on hand, and eventually to end in nothing; so that when Rosny, with his parchments and papers, entered his apartment, the king inquired with surprise where he came from.

"I come, Sire," he replied, in an unusual festive mood, "from having assisted in marrying you."

As the king listened to these words their effect on him, as described by the baron, was as though a thunderbolt had fallen on him. For a quarter of an hour, at least, he remained silent and absorbed in thought. He then began to walk rapidly up and down the apartment, biting his nails, scratching his head, and giving way so violently to the feelings which agitated him that for a considerable time he was unable intelligibly to utter a word. At last, recovering a little mental calm and firmness, like a man who has taken a final resolution, he exclaimed, striking one hand with force on the other :

"Well, if it cannot be avoided, if there is no remedy for it, *par dieu!* let it be as you wish! You say it is for the good of my kingdom that I should marry : marry, then, I suppose I must!" He then rushed excitedly from the room.

His aversion to this marriage must have been very great. He had a terror, a strong presentiment of the kind of life he was destined to with Maria de' Medici. The fascinations of the new mistress, who had not yet fully revealed her true character, may have also contributed to intensify the revulsion of feeling he so strongly displayed. He was far less excited on the discovery of two intended attempts to assassinate him towards the close of this year.*

* The first was by an Italian, who had visited Paris for the purpose of stabbing the king when opportunity offered. He had taken a Capuchin monk into his confidence, who at once sent the information to the king, and the would-be assassin was arrested on his arrival. The second aspirant for the honour of killing the king was a woman, Nicole Mignon, whose husband was a cook, who, as assistant in the king's kitchen, was to prepare the poisoned dish for his majesty. The Comte de Soissons, being grand master of the king's household, she fancied would ascend the throne on the king's death; she therefore ventured

The news from Lorraine and Rome, however, moved him greatly, for Clement VIII., while annulling the marriage of Henri and Marguerite, also annulled, by a pontifical brief, that of Madame Catherine with the Duc de Bar. Nor was this misery and mischief-making enough for him; he must also excommunicate the duke, and forbid all political and religious relations between the holy see and the duchy. The Easter devotions were also forbidden, and all hope of obtaining absolution denied him. Catherine was much affected by this persecution of her husband, who bore his troubles without complaint or reproach. But the people, in their superstitious terror of the vengeance of Heaven about to fall on them, implored the grand duke to banish the heretic princess in order to save their country.

The Duc de Bar made at that time a journey to Rome, ostensibly for the purpose of endeavouring, through the influence of certain cardinals favourably disposed towards him, to obtain a dispensation legitimising his marriage; but the real motive was said to be to protest against the pontiff's order to repudiate his wife and marry another. Catherine declared that she was quite willing to return to Béarn if her religion was in any way prejudicial to

to disclose her plans to him, believing that he would readily join in carrying them out. To her consternation he heard her with horror and immediately denounced her. She was arrested and, having confessed her guilt, was burnt alive at the Place de Grêve.

the states of Lorraine. Yet she continued to reside at the ducal court, and, so far as priestly interference would permit, calmly and pleasantly enough, as from mutual sorrow there had sprung up between her and the duke mutual esteem and sympathy.

The marriage contract with Maria de' Medici, which so greatly disturbed Henri's tranquillity of mind, was not signed at Florence by the duke and princess until the following April. Events political and military of some importance intervened and still further prolonged the king's respite by yet several months, while they also afforded M. de Rosny an opportunity for securing the long-coveted appointment of grand master of the artillery.

The marquisate of Saluzzo, a possession in itself of little value, but which Duke Charles Emmanuel of Savoy refused to relinquish to France, while Henri declined to forego his claim to it, was left at the peace of Vervins to the arbitration of the Pope. The duke's subsequent conduct respecting it determined Clement VIII. to decline interference in the matter. Having requested and obtained a safe-conduct from the king, in order, as he said, for the advantage of personally discussing the affair with him, Charles Emmanuel arrived at Fontainebleau a few days before the close of the year 1599, and was received by Henri IV. with his accustomed cordiality. The duke was a prince of great ambition, restless humour, and, to serve his own ends, profuse liberality.

He came to France laden with gifts for the new year, and, as he indiscreetly remarked in the presence of some of the courtiers, "he came not to reap, but to sow,"— sedition being understood by such as were willing to join him. The Duchess of Savoy was one of the daughters of Philip II., and the duke loudly complained that that monarch, while giving one of the infantas the Netherlands and La Franche-Comté for her dowry, which were worth more, he declared, than the two Castiles and Portugal, had bestowed only a crucifix and an image of the Virgin on the daughter he had married. This and similar indiscretions offended Philip III., who declined to reopen the war with France in support of the duke's pretensions.

Many banquets and balls were given by the king in the duke's honour, both at Fontainebleau and Paris; but from the first there was little expectation of a satisfactory settlement between them of the disputed possession of the marquisate. A commission was therefore appointed to investigate the matter. Meanwhile, the new year afforded the duke a pretext for making valuable presents to those courtiers whose defection from their allegiance to the king he was anxious to purchase, and in some instances succeeded. The ladies were enchanted by his munificent gallantry, and the taste and elegance displayed in his gifts. The marquise was especially favoured with several ornaments composed of fine diamonds. He and the king also exchanged presents of value, and no member of the king's household who, on New Year's morn, saluted the duke with the customary *Bonjour* and wished him *La bonne année*, but received some proof of his royal bounty, and, as he said, "his affection for the king."

To Rosny the duke sent his ambassador to present him with his portrait in a frame of diamonds, which the baron felt compelled, he said, to refuse, unless he might be permitted to separate the portrait from its surrounding brilliants. But the ambassador, M. des Alymes, replied that he was not authorised to make any changes in the duke's presents. Rosny therefore begged permission to decline it.

Nothing satisfactory resulting from the conference concerning the restitution of Saluzzo, the king proposed, as an alternative, the cession of Bresse, and the banks of the Rhône from Geneva to Lyons. To this a decisive answer might be given, he said, at once. Decision did not accord with the subtle Savoyard duke's schemes. He must have time for reflection, and proposed eighteen months as a reasonable time for making up his mind. The king considered it preposterous. At last he consented to three months, on remembering that within, or soon after the time specified, some astrologers, in whose predictions he had faith, had prophesied that there would be no king in France, therefore no necessity for making up his mind at all, as he had no wish to do.*

After more banquets, ballets, and balls, the Duke of Savoy, early in March, took leave of the king at Fontainebleau, apparently on terms of the greatest friendship.† He was attended by a brilliant and numerous retinue of nobles and gentlemen, all as anxious as the duke to reach Chambéry in order that it and other cities of the duchy might be strengthened in their fortifications to resist the new grand master's artillery, which had taken the duke by surprise, as well as the fact, which he had been at some pains to ascertain, that money was not wanting.

Rosny had long anxiously hoped to succeed to the post of *grand-maître de l'artillerie*, then held

---

* The prophecy, however, was verified, but not exactly as he desired to interpret it, for soon after the expiration of the three months there was no king in France; he was in Savoy, and the duke of that country at his mercy.

† D'Aubigné relates that while the king and the duke were one day playing at cards — the stakes being 4,000 *pistoles* — the king, fancying he had won, threw up his hand. The duke, who really held the winning cards, said not a word; but, leaning slightly towards the Duc de Guise and D'Aubigné, who sat on either side of him, allowed them to see his hand, then shuffled the cards into the pack. Whether this was politeness, generosity, or policy, D'Aubigné leaves to others to determine. Certainly, the king was greatly elated when he did win, it was an event that so rarely occurred; and had he at the moment been strongly pressed, he might, perhaps, have relinquished his claim on Saluzzo.

by the Baron Antoine d'Estrées, the duties of the office being mainly performed by the second officer in command, the Lieutenant-General Jean Durefort de Born, who, at the period in question, was desirous of resigning his office. The king a second time proposed its acceptance to the Baron de Rosny. He would have, he said, almost uncontrolled authority, D'Estrées having latterly, from grief for his daughter's sad death, been in a measure incapacitated from exercising the necessary surveillance as *grand-maître*. He, however, did not wish to displace him, "as he was the grandfather of his children." The appointments, already considerable, were to be increased, and additional advantages given to the post of lieutenant-general of the arsenal of Paris, — thus placing the holder of that post in authority over the lieutenants-general of the provinces.

Nothing that the king could say, with the view of increasing the importance of the subordinate post, tempted M. de Rosny to accept it. He could not bring himself to serve under another after having failed a year or two since to obtain the principal place. He excused himself from accepting it by pleading the duties of the charge he already-held. Many times the king — making light of this excuse — renewed his entreaties that he would accept the proffered office; but Rosny was not to be moved from what he had determined on. "*Aut Cæsar, aut nihil*" was his motto, or should have been. The king — a very weak person compared with his minister — went off into a terrible passion; declared that never again would he speak to him on the subject, and that, as he would follow only the suggestions of his own caprices, he, for his part, would also act only as his own will dictated.

In spite of this menace, Henri sent a confidential messenger to D'Estrées to ask if he would be willing to give up the grand-mastership. He did not seem anxious to do so; but Rosny having heard — probably from the confidential messenger — of the step the king had taken, immediately sent 3,000 crowns to a Madame Néry, a housekeeper or relative of D'Estrées, begging her to press upon the old man the advisableness of giving up a charge he found too wearying at his time of life to attend to. It was one of those hereditary offices which the holder, having no heir to succeed him, might either restore to the king, or dispose of to a person competent to fulfil its duties.

Female influence, however, prevailed with D'Estrées, who wrote to the king that he was willing to resign for a consideration. Informed of this by his lady agent, Rosny at once arranged the terms with D'Estrées, and stepped into the grand-mastership for 80,000 crowns, which was the large yearly salary attached to it. Some incidental expenses made the purchase-money 100,000 crowns. The king was well pleased, and said that all he would exact from the new grand master for having put him into a passion, was that the artillery, with as little delay as possible, should be placed on a footing of efficiency that would enable him to take Saluzzo.*

This change occurred but a few weeks before the expected arrival in France of the Duke of Savoy, who, as both the king and Rosny well knew, had no real intention of entering into amicable arrangements respecting the marquisate. He was rather prompted to visit France to see the nakedness of the land, hoping to find the king — who desired to give the devastated country and the impoverished people a long period of peace — utterly unprepared for the renewal of hostilities, his kingdom depopulated, his treasury empty.

As grand master of the artillery, the Baron de Rosny proved as able, active, and efficient an officer as in the other charges held by him. He at once removed to the handsome and spacious residence attached to the arsenal, that he might be at hand to prevent any dilatoriness in the founding of new cannon, and for the greater facility of introducing and enforcing a better-ordered system into the establishment generally. With unflagging dili-

---

* The king further confirmed the arrangement between D'Estrées and Rosny as satisfactory, and by royal warrant made the office hereditary in the family of the Baron de Rosny, as one of the great offices of state.

gence he pursued his work, with the hope of surprising the Savoyard visitor. The king was equally anxious; and with so much steady application had the work been carried on that three days after the duke's arrival in Paris the grand master was informed by a message from the king that "he and M. de Savoie, with the principal ladies and gentlemen of the court, proposed to take supper with him at the arsenal, intending afterwards to visit his magazines."

The grand master would have liked a longer notice, and have preferred to dispense with the supper and the company of the ladies and gentlemen. But while he was giving orders for the necessary arrangements to receive the royal party, the Duke of Savoy, attended by only two of the gentlemen of his suite, entered the arsenal. He, it seems, thought the morning a better time for inspecting the work going on there than an after-supper visit. Mutual civilities and compliments having been exchanged, the duke requested Rosny to show him his magazines.

As left by his predecessors, the old magazines did him no credit, he considered, and the new arrangements had not yet been carried out in that department; so, without replying, he led the way to his new foundries. There he pointed out, with some pride, twenty newly founded cannon, twenty more in process of founding, forty gun-carriages complete, and a prodigious quantity of arms of all sorts on which the workmen were diligently employed.

So amazed was the duke at all he saw that he inquired what it was proposed to do in a time of peace with all this warlike apparatus.

Rosny replied, intending to be rather jocose: "To take Montemélian" (the strongest fortress in Savoy).

"I presume that you have never seen Montemélian," responded the duke. The grand master acknowledged that he had not. "Know, then," he said, "that Montemélian is impregnable."

"I fancy that it would lose that character should the king ever be forced to attack it," rejoined Rosny.

The duke smiled; but though all this passed in a tone of pleasantry, it may be supposed that he did not find M. de Rosny's joke a very pleasant one, combined with what he had seen of his great guns and had heard of his well-filled and carefully hoarded money-bags.

As soon as the duke left France, the courtiers whom the tempter had not beguiled mocked at his discomfiture, and said "he had carried away from France nothing but mud and mire." Being informed of this, he replied that "the mud he had carried away was already dry, and had left no stains on his clothing, but that the footprints he had left in France would need the sword to efface them." Truly he had taken advantage of the discontent and disloyalty of the former Royalist chiefs, and had encouraged the revival of their idea of feudal independence. Perhaps among them none was more arrogant in his pretensions then Maréchal de Biron. He declared that it was he who had put the crown on the king's head, and that for this service the ungrateful monarch had rewarded him with merely a marshal's bâton, the rank of duke and peer of France, the government of the extensive and fertile province of Burgundy, with two or three pensions and some slender gifts of money.

He desired to hold Burgundy as its hereditary and sovereign prince, and Charles Emmanuel gave him hope that Spain would support his views on that province, while he promised him one of his daughters and a considerable dowry. Biron's military reputation stood very high, and the duke thought to avail himself, in the war he was seeking to prepare for, both of the marshal's skilful generalship and his treacherous design of thwarting the plans confided to him by the king to carry out. He is said by De Thou to have promised the Governor of Fort Sainte-Catherine that when joined there by the king he would lead him under the arquebuse of an assassin posted in ambush; but that when about to do this cowardly deed some better feeling arose in his mind, and impelled him to recoil from so base an assassination.

The duke had hopes of gaining over to his

schemes the Connétable de Montmorency and the princes of the blood, Montpensier and Soissons; but they were not found anxious to incur great risk for no compensating advantage in view. The Comte d'Auvergne, however, joined the ranks of the disaffected, though he had rendered no services whatever to found any claims upon. He pretended, therefore, to feel highly indignant, and to be wounded in his honour at the king's failure to place his mistress, Auvergne's half-sister, on the throne of France.

The king and his first minister (for such was the Baron de Rosny, though without the title) were not duped by these manœuvres. The three months had elapsed, and the king demanded the duke's immediate decision. He promised to cede the marquisate, but did not. War was in consequence declared against him on the 12th of August, 1600.

## CHAPTER XI.

The Dispute between Du Perron and Du Plessis-Mornay Occurs While Awaiting the Duke's Decision. — Biron's Treachery. — Rosny's Marvellous Exertions in This War. — The King Inactive. — Under the Spell of His New Mistress. — Clement VIII. Offers His Mediation. — The Grand Master's Reception of the Legate. — Marriage Negotiation Concluded. — Bellegarde Desires to Represent the King. — The Ceremony at Florence. — The State Galleys. — Arrival at Lyons. — Success of the Campaign Attributed to Rosny and Lesdiguières. — A Wet and Cold Journey. — Legate and Rosny Settle the Peace. — Biron's Treason. — Appointing the Queen's Household. — A Warning to the King. — Dinner at the Arsenal. — The Two Medals.

IN the course of the three months accorded to the Duke of Savoy to make up his mind concerning Saluzzo, there occurred the famous, or rather infamous, attack of the unprincipled Du Perron, "Rosny's Bishop of Evreux," on M. du Plessis-Mornay.* Mornay had written a work on the Eucharist, supporting the Calvinists' views by quotations from the

---

* Du Perron was thus called because the bishopric of Evreux was conferred on that worthy son of the Church, a renegade Huguenot, through the influence at the Court of Rome of that "zealous Protestant," the Baron de Rosny; Du Perron was a very learned man and could prove, as occasion required, that there was a God, or no God — a devil, or no devil, and so on.

Fathers. A copy of it was sent by M. de Rosny to Du Perron, who pronounced the quotations falsified. Mornay proposed to defend himself from this imputation, but in writing. The king decided otherwise; he would have the disputants argue the matter in public, that the Huguenot might be overwhelmed by the surprising fluency and astonishing memory of Rosny's bishop.

It was from memory he strove to confute his opponent, whom he at least amazed, if he did not confute, by the astonishing facility with which he rolled off from the tip of his tongue page after page of the Fathers, whose writings from time to time had passed through the hands of various doctors at Rome, and lately had been corrected by the Jesuits at the request of Clement VIII. Mornay retired, thoroughly disgusted. The king, much elated, wrote, strangely enough, to the Duc d'Épernon, who abhorred him, informing him that "the diocese of Evreux had vanquished that of Saumur," of which town Mornay was governor. Of Rosny he inquired what he thought of his pope, — Mornay's influence with the Huguenots having sometimes procured him in jest this title. The baron did not often perpetrate puns or *bons-mots*, but on the present occasion he replied: "I think, Sire, that M. de Mornay is more a pope than you imagine, as at this moment he is giving the red hat to M. d'Evreux." And this was true enough: the red hat very soon followed M.

d'Evreux's able defence of the Vatican edition of the Fathers.

But leaving disquisitions on the Fathers to prelates and doctors of the Sorbonne, Henri must once more unsheathe the sword. It had become evident that by force alone could anything be obtained from the Duke of Savoy. Yet Henri's courtiers would still have had him wait awhile, as the duke had again sent word that he would cede Saluzzo. When, however, the king's agents arrived to take possession, he refused to allow them to do so. His liberal gifts seemed to have purchased the voices of the Royalist chiefs in his favour, though, with the exception of Biron, few or none were disposed actively to aid him.

At all events, Rosny had improved the interval by the great diligence and ability he had displayed in the new and effective organisation he had given to the corps of artillery, the engineers, and army generally. The infantry he had speedily raised from ten to twenty-five thousand men, better equipped than any that had hitherto fought under the banner of Henri IV., and, to their great contentment, sure of their pay. They were divided into two corps. One, under the invincible Lesdiguières, to attack Savoy, the other, commanded by Biron, to lay siege to Bresse, left Lyons on the 11th of August. On the 13th, in spite of himself and his various contrary orders and secret information to the governor, Biron and his detachment, more loyal than their commander, took Bourg-en-Bresse, and Lesdiguières the town of Chambéry. To remedy a *contretemps* so disastrous to his treacherous plans, Biron asked for the governorship of Bourg, which was refused, and his conquest confided to safer hands than his.

The *grand-maître*, also on the 11th, forwarded his cannon and other material of war for the siege of Charbonnières and Montemélian to Lyons. Henri alone did not display his usual alacrity, but lingered in his lady's bower, unable to separate himself from her. By much importunity and urgent representation of the peril to which by delay he was exposing the kingdom and his own life too, Rosny prevailed on him to set out for Lyons. He thought of taking Madame de Verneuil with him, and some of the court flatterers encouraged him to do so. But again Rosny interfered, and it was determined at last that she should follow him. Some few days after she did so; but when the lovers met again — whether that the arrangements of war had not allowed of satisfactory preparations being made for her reception, or that there were other reasons for her displeasure — a very lively quarrel ensued, followed by an estrangement of one or two days' duration.

Then Henri was again at her feet imploring a reconciliation, to which she appears to have consented, as he then took her to Grenoble and afterwards to Chambéry. Several officers' wives were assembled at the latter place, and amongst them Madame de Rosny, who gave a ball to both besieged and besiegers, who were all as gay as possible, though Chambéry had changed masters.

Clement VIII. was not pleased with the renewal of hostilities, and fearing that Italy would again become the theatre of war between France and Spain, he despatched his legate and nephew, Cardinal Aldobrandino, to Henri's camp to intercede for M. de Savoie, and to offer his mediation. The cardinal was also deputed by the Pope to inform the king that the negotiation of his marriage with Maria de' Medici was concluded and the contract signed by Clement VIII., the grand duke, and the princess. It therefore only remained for him to appoint a proxy to represent him at the marriage ceremony at Florence, and to conduct the bride to France. Henri was not disposed to sheath the sword until he had obtained full satisfaction for the treachery and artifice with which Duke Charles Emmanuel had sought to foment dissension in France, and to incite his officers and nobility to rebel.

But as soon as it was announced that the legate was on his journey, Rosny was desired by the king to receive his eminence with every mark of respect and customary honours. The baron was really proud of his title of *grand-maître de l'artillerie*, and prouder still of the office, whose important duties he so well fulfilled. He determined, he says, that the legate, on approaching Montemélian, should at once be aware that he was received by a *grand-maître de l'artillerie.* The *château-fort* of Montemélian was not yet taken; the town had surrendered, and a truce of some days had been agreed on, which gave him the power of making use of the artillery of the place as well as his own. To do more honour to his eminence, he availed himself of it and employed both.

With a *corps d'élite* of 3,000 infantry and 500 cavalry the Huguenot *grand-maître* rode out half a league to meet this prince of the Church. A volley of musketry announced their approach to Montemélian, and the battery on the rock, above which waved the white ensign, then poured forth its thunderous welcome. This was taken up by the cannon of the château, and again responded to by the battery on the rock, and so on in perfect order, each quickly recharging and keeping up an incessant firing from one hundred and seventy cannon, echoed and reëchoed from the gorges of the mountains with the finest effect in the world — to the mind of the grand master. Probably it was less so to the mind of the cardinal, who is described as appearing more alarmed than gratified, often making the sign of the cross as the reports from the batteries rumbled and echoed through the mountains. Rosny afterwards entertained him at dinner, then despatched him with a strong escort to the king's camp at Chambéry.

Several of the younger nobility were anxious to obtain the honour of representing the king at Florence; the Duc de Bellegarde especially solicited it. But Henri allowed him to be the bearer only of his letter appointing the grand duke his *locum tenens*. The contrast between the bridegroom and his substitute might have appeared too striking, — Monsieur le Grand, as the duke was called from the office he held of *grand-écuyer*, being considered the handsomest man of the French court, while Henri had acquired the reputation of being "the ugliest gentleman in France."

The duke arrived in Florence, attended by a numerous and brilliant escort and forty cavaliers. Besides the letter to the grand duke, he was also the bearer of a missive from the king to his bride, a miniature portrait set in diamonds accompanying it. The marriage ceremony took place a few days after, when, those present having signed the contract, a *Te Deum* was sung, and the bridal party then repaired to the Pitti Palace to partake of a sumptuous banquet in the great hall. A daïs under a canopy was prepared for the queen, her uncle being placed far below her. The golden basin of scented water to dip the tips of her fingers in was presented by the Duc de Bacciano; the perfumed gold-embroidered napkin to dry them was handed to her on a gold salver by the Comte de Sillery, who accompanied the Duc de Bellegarde.

Maria de' Medici left Florence on the 13th of October for Livourna, where an escort of seventeen galleys awaited her. For magnificence, such a flotilla had never before been seen on the sea, nor such a vessel as the grand duke's galley, destined to convey his niece to the shores of France. Both within and without it sparkled with gold and precious stones. The arms of France and Tuscany were placed in front of the queen's seat. They were beautifully emblazoned, and adorned with gems, and cost, it was said, 210,000 *livres*. That the fortune of the grand duke — who was not a man to spend imprudently what he could not afford — was large enough to enable him to construct and equip such a vessel, excited great and general astonishment, and scarcely less so the magnificent jewels he and the grand duchess presented to the bride.*

The queen landed at Toulon on the 3d of November, where she was received with a salute almost as alarming as that with which the *grand-maître* welcomed the legate. The Grand Duchess of Tuscany accompanied her niece, also the Duchess of Mantua; her cousin, Virginio Orsini; her uncle, Don Joăn, the bastard of the House of Medici; and an Italian named Concini. Report said they were her lovers. Nor was she insensible, it was remarked, to the attentions and manly graces of the handsome Duc de Bellegarde, who,

* L'Estoile; Mathieu; *Mémoires de Sully.*

by the respectful devotedness of his manners, made himself exceedingly agreeable to the new queen. Leonora Galigai was also in her suite, and there were several Florentine attendants, male and female. From Toulon she proceeded by way of Marseilles and Avignon to Lyons, where she arrived on the 8th of December, having been welcomed throughout her journey with much noise, endless harangues and discourses, but little enthusiasm, — the people, like the king, feeling more dread of the Medici than love for them.

While the bridal arrangements were proceeding in Florence, the war between France and Savoy continued. The duke, starved in his camp by the master of all his strong places, had reëntered Piedmont with the remnant of his army, who had suffered greatly from heavy snow-storms and tempestuous weather in the mountains. He had lost all his possessions in Bresse and Savoy. The discontented nobles had not stirred in his favour, and Biron, baffled in his schemes to bring either the king or the grand master unawares under the fire of the enemy's guns, could do nothing for Charles Emmanuel but make ineffectual promises.

The success of the campaign is attributed by the contemporary historians, Mathieu and De Thou, mainly to Lesdiguières and the Baron de Rosny. In the determination of the latter to take Montemélian, also Charbonnières, — which appears to have been the more difficult achievement of the two, — he underwent the most extraordinary labour, fatigue, and hardships, exposing himself to extreme personal danger with the utmost *sang-froid*, bent only on succeeding in his purpose, and even more than justifying the praises so liberally and justly bestowed on him. The intervention of the legate had been hitherto wholly without good results. But the duke's pretensions being much abated by his signal defeat, and the Pope more pressingly urgent, while Spain had sent a special envoy, and two agents had arrived on the part of the duke, Henri yielded to the entreaties of the legate, and consented to a conference being held at Lyons on the subject of peace, appointing as his representatives, Cardinal du Perron, Montmorency, the Chancelier de Chiverny, with Villeroy and Jeannin.

Henri of course passed the interval in the society of his mistress, but nothing definitive had been agreed on at the conference, when information was brought to headquarters of the arrival of the bride at Lyons. This must have been an embarrassing moment both for the king and the marquise. Gallantry, however, forbade delay. His mistress mocked; but he, taking a tender leave of her, set out *en poste* with several of his courtiers for Lyons. The *grand-maître* was of the party. Rain, he says, was falling in torrents, and it was eleven o'clock in the evening before the bridge of Lyons was reached.

There, for fully an hour, they waited in tne rain, shivering with cold and their clothing thoroughly drenched. This delay in admitting them into the city was owing to the king's desire to enter it unannounced. He wished to see his bride without being seen by her; to pass in unobserved, and leisurely contemplate her while at supper. She was taking this meal at midnight, and apparently in public, as a great number of people are said to have been present as spectators, who, when the king appeared, not being aware of his desire to remain among them *incognito*, though he was unattended, immediately divided to allow him to pass on. Instead of doing so, he abruptly left the apartment. The queen perceived this movement, but gave no indication of having done so, except that of pushing away all the dishes as they were set before her.

The historian Mathieu, who greatly admired her florid charms, seems to have been quite concerned at the smallness of her appetite. "So little did she eat," he says, "that what she took he thought was merely to keep her in countenance, and not for supper." Supper ended, she left the room. Presently the king reappeared, preceded by Monsieur le Grand, who knocked so loudly at the door that the queen felt assured that it could only be the king. The door being opened, she advanced and fell at his feet. He raised and embraced her, and after many compliments had passed between them, the king mingling therewith many terms of endearment, the queen replying that she had come to France "to obey in all things the king's wishes, as his very humble servant," he took her by the hand and led her towards the fire — for the night was very cold — and conversed with her for more than half an hour.

The king's supper was then announced, and he retired to partake of it.* The marriage was solemnised, with but little pomp, on the 9th of December.

The negotiation of the peace with Savoy was not yet concluded, though Henri had yielded on the question of Saluzzo, and consented to receive in exchange the territorial advantages offered him. He required, therefore, of his plenipotentiaries, being now in Lyons, an account of the articles already agreed to. Finding they had made concessions without consulting him, and had especially promised that Fort Sainte-Catherine, which Charles Emmanuel had erected as a standing menace to the Protestants of Geneva, should not be destroyed, the king, at the risk of breaking up the conference and renewing the war, ordered the grand master immediately to blow up the five bastions of Sainte-Catherine, and to tell the citizens of

* It was then probably that he took the opportunity of sending a line to inform the Baron de Rosny that the bride was terribly strong and robust, for in the half-drowned condition the king and his companions were in, one is surprised that even the king should have been able to present himself that night.

Geneva to come and help in the completion of the work themselves. This was done so speedily and with such hearty good-will that the fortress was soon razed to the ground, and not one stone left on another to mark the place where it stood, all having been carried off in triumph.

The legate was exceedingly annoyed at this act of vigour on the part of the king. The conference was at once put an end to, and the renewal of war seemed imminent. Rosny, about to leave Lyons for Paris, to found more guns and obtain supplies of money, thought it right, under the circumstances, — the king being of the same opinion, — to take leave of the legate. He was booted and spurred, and post-horses waiting on the opposite side of the river, when he entered his eminence's residence. "Where are you going?" he asked, with some surprise; and when Rosny explained, the legate replied: "I beg you rather to remain here, and aid me to renew the negotiation for peace." But the king, mortified that his plenipotentiaries should have departed from his instructions, and apparently, like the rest, have sold themselves to Spain and Savoy, had put aside all thoughts of peace.

Yet Rosny would not positively refuse to assist in renewing the negotiation, though it would be vain to attempt it, he declared, unless his majesty's propositions were fully complied with. These he clearly explained. The legate, after taking a turn or two in his room for reflection, said: "If these proposals are agreed to, will the king consent to yield on other points?" which he named. Rosny thought it likely that he would. "Then go to the king," he said, "at once, and repeat to him our conversation." Rosny did so, and shortly after returned with a *plein-pouvoir* from the king, and the treaty that had languished so long was thus virtually concluded, it being the legate's business to enforce this arrangement on Charles Emmanuel.

Spain sent word to her ambassador to aid the legate in impressing on the duke the necessity of consenting to the king's propositions. Eventually he did so, having also to defray the expenses of the war, and to pay besides 100,000 crowns for permission to use the bridge of Grezin, giving him access to La Franche-Comté. The treaty was published at Paris and Turin on the 17th of January; yet the duke could not reconcile himself to giving effect to the articles of peace he had signed. So many difficulties were raised by him that Henri refrained from disarming while the plenipotentiaries were detained at Lyons, explaining away the frivolous objections suggested by the duke. At last, advised by Rome and Spain, he forbore to again tempt Henri to declare war against him. He had his marquisate, but had paid very dearly for it, "while Bresse, with the rest of the ceded territory, rounded the French frontier very advantageously."

Before leaving Lyons the king had a long conversation with Maréchal de Biron in the cloister of the Cordeliers. The interview was sought by the marshal, who, rather alarmed at finding himself about to be abandoned by the foreigners whose aims on France he had consented to promote to the utmost of his power, thought that the readiest way out of his dilemma was to make a merit of necessity and confess his backslidings to the king. He had been led, he acknowledged, by his vexation and disappointment at being refused the governorship of Bourg to give way to the vehemence of his character, — to ask in marriage, without his consent, one of the daughters of the Duke of Savoy, and to entertain suggestions contrary to the good of his majesty's service.

Ambition for a moment had led him astray; but he now confessed that such conduct was culpable, and implored pardon for it. His eyes were opened, he said. He would sin no more; and with all the appearance of sincerity and deep grief he again entreated the king to pardon him. Biron was not aware that the king knew much more than he had thought it discreet to confess to him, yet he pardoned him, believing in the sincerity of his professed repentance. He even strove to calm his feigned disquietude by proposing to send him on an extraordinary embassy to England, — which at once he did, — and afterwards to Switzerland, thinking to allay the feverish activity of his mind by such honourable employment. Biron had, therefore, succeeded in saving his head for a time. It was terror of death that made him tremble, for, although intrepid on the battle-field, he was in other respects neither a brave nor an honourable man, but a cowardly intriguer.

The great and successful efforts of the Baron de Rosny in this campaign were but slenderly acknowledged by the title of marquis, while at his request a marshal's bâton and the governorship of one of his conquests were awarded to the brave Duc de Lesdiguières.

Henri then proposed to appoint the queen's household. She immediately named as her mistress of the robes Leonora Galigai; but the king objected. He thought her not of sufficiently high rank, and suggested the Duchesse de Richelieu. The queen refused to accept the duchess or any one else he might choose to appoint, at the same time displaying a great deal of temper, and repeating that it must be Leonora or none,—thus giving him notice of what was in store for him, and of the reality of the domestic misery he had foreboded.

Suddenly one night the king and his mistress set off *en poste* for Paris, leaving his bride, it seems, to follow alone, or, at least, unaccompanied by him. His journey to Paris was made by a very circuitous route, and took eight or ten days to accomplish. The queen did not immediately follow him, and then only by very easy stages, her uncle, Don Joãn, attending her. On her arrival at Nemours the king rejoined her, and conducted her to Fontainebleau, whence a few days later she went on to Paris. She was carried in a litter along the fortifications of the city, and passed the first day of her arrival at the Hôtel Gondy, in the Faubourg Saint-Germain, her host as well as Zameti — at whose hôtel in the Marais she remained on the second day — being one of the grand duke's agents, employed in his banking and other monetary transactions. On the third day she took up her residence at the Louvre. As she passed the arsenal the *grand-maître* saluted her with the whole of the cannon of the establishment three times fired.

On the following day the king and queen, with the ladies and gentlemen of the court, dined at the arsenal, the queen being attended by several young Italian ladies as maids of honour, who found the grand master's wine so much to their taste that they partook of it rather too freely. It, however, appears to have been more from mistake than design, the water-jugs having been filled with white wine, described as "clear and bright as water from the rocks." This was supplied to the young ladies, when, finding the burgundy they were sipping too potent for them, they asked for a little water as a corrective. Instead of subduing, it had a contrary effect, and the young ladies began to be more lively and talkative than was considered discreet.

The queen was much annoyed, the king greatly amused, and M. de Rosny severely reprimanded his attendants for their carelessness. However, nothing very shocking to good manners occurred; only a little of the liveliness of the young ladies was imparted to the rest of the company. The queen made no public state entry into Paris. The Parisians expected and wished it; but when Rosny — in virtue of one or other of the offices he held, which really put the whole of the kingdom into his hands — consulted the king on the subject, he replied that "the expense was too great, and the money needed for many things far more useful and necessary." The *grand-maître* appears to have been of the same opinion, consequently the usual ceremony of a public entry was suppressed.

The *grand-maître*, however, gratified himself at the conclusion of the war with Savoy by striking a commemorative medal, following the example of Charles Emmanuel when he seized on Saluzzo — taking advantage of Henri III. being unable to prevent him by the struggle against Guise and the Leaguers. The duke's medal represented a centaur trampling on a royal crown, with this legend, "*Opportunè*" (*à propos*). On Rosny's medal was the figure of Hercules overthrowing a centaur and lifting up a crown, with the legend "*Opportuniùs*" (*plus à propos*).*

* *Mémoires de Sully.*

## CHAPTER XII.

The Peace of Lyons Regarded as a Lasting One. — An Insult to the French at Valladolid. — Satisfaction Obtained. — The Grand Seignior and the Venetian States Congratulate the King on His Marriage. — Henri Being at Calais, Elizabeth Repairs to Dover, Desiring to See Him. — He Fears to Give Umbrage to Spain, Should He Cross the Channel. — Rosny Visits London; Is Received by the Queen at reenwich. — She Explains to Him Her Plan for Curbing the Ambition of Austria. — Rosny Enchanted with Her Wisdom and Prudence. — King Returns to Paris. — The Double *Ménage*. — Maria Furious. — Birth of a Dauphin. — Taken through Paris in His Cradle. — La Rivière's Prediction. — Vague Words. — Queen's Ballet. — The Muses and the Virtues.

THE peace concluded at Lyons between France and Savoy was generally regarded as a solid peace, — one that would permit the king to lay aside helmet and cuirass, at least for some years to come; while, assisted by the Marquis de Rosny, he might devote himself to improving the condition of his kingdom, and assuring the welfare of his subjects. What remained of the winter was, however, to be spent in festivities, in celebration of the king's marriage, — festivities, which, as Madame de Verneuil, with some truth, told him, might be considered as "the funeral rites of his happiness and his life."

An incident that occurred in the course of the summer of this year did indeed seem for a moment to threaten a reopening of the war. It arose from the circumstance of some young Frenchmen at the court of Valladolid, one of whom was the nephew of the French ambassador, the Comte de Rochepot, going out together to bathe. Some Spaniards, observing them, took their clothing and threw it into the river, intending to insult the Frenchmen while amusing themselves. This proceeding naturally roused the anger of the bathers, who, rushing from the water all naked as they were, attacked the Spaniards with their swords — which they seemed to have put into a place of safety — and killed two of them, afterwards seeking refuge at the ambassador's residence.

The relatives of the young men who were slain sought redress from the king, who, disregarding the respect due to the ambassador, ordered the doors of his hôtel to be forced, and his nephew and others to be arrested and imprisoned. When the affair came to Henri's ears he demanded full satisfaction for the indignity put on his ambassador. Neither Philip III. nor his great minister, the Duc de Lerma, was inclined for war, which, with the interference of the Pope, and the disquietude of the Spanish cabinet at the appearance in the western part of the Mediterranean of a Turkish fleet, — sent by the grand seignior to compliment Henri IV. on his marriage, and the probable birth of an heir, — sufficed to obtain for the king all the reparation he demanded. There was no infraction, therefore, of the peace, though for awhile commercial relations had been interrupted. The Turkish ambassadors brought splendid presents to both the king and queen, and two Turkish scimitars of exquisite design and workmanship for the grand master.

The state of Venice also sent a special and magnificent embassy to congratulate the king, who received the ambassadors with great distinction, and entertained them royally. His own service of plate was brought out for their use, and many other attentions marked his sense of the obligations he was under to the first European Power that had recognised his rights, and had thus done him great service. Often the Senate had lent him money, and amongst other sums, a million *livres*, for which he had given an acknowledgment in his own hand. Henri was under the impression that, the public reception being ended, he would be reminded of this debt, and perhaps slightly pressed for payment. He was, however, agreeably surprised when the marriage present, an elegant gold filigree casket, was handed to him, to find the value of the present increased by the munificent gift of a million *livres*, in the shape of his cancelled acknowledgment of that debt, — a generous act, gracefully accomplished, to which, eventually, Henri endeavoured to give suitable recognition.

While the affair with Spain was under consideration, Henri temporarily took up his quarters at Calais, in order to make a survey of his northern frontier. He also thought, by his nearness to them, to encourage the Dutch, who were defending Ostend against Spinola, — the famous Genoese captain in the service of Spain. As soon, however, as Elizabeth heard that Henri was so near a neighbour, she repaired to Dover, and being very desirous of seeing him, sent him word that she had something of great importance to communicate. He would have greatly liked to cross the Channel to confer with his "good friend and sister." But the Spaniards were suspiciously watching his movements, being anxious as to the real motive of his visit to Calais.

The English generals had just victoriously repulsed a descent of the Spaniards on Ireland, and gained some decisive advantages over the insurgent Irish chief O'Neil. The queen was therefore more than ever incensed against Spain; but as Henri had so recently concluded a peace with that country, and satisfaction was already offered for the affront to the ambassador, he thought it unadvisable to give occasion for umbrage to that power, or to the Catholics generally, by visiting England in person. Rosny, therefore, feigning an excursion on his own account, for health or other motive, crossed, in his stead, the Straits of Dover.

His visit was supposed to be strictly private, and he travelling *incognito*. Of course the queen was already informed of the presence of Henri's chief minister in England. He was recognised at once on disembarking at Dover from the ordinary passage boat, in which, with but two or three servants, he had at an early hour left Calais. He, however, protested that he had no letter or instructions from the king, and trusted that his journey to London would not be mentioned to the queen; but in the course of the day a gentleman whom he knew laughingly took him prisoner in her majesty's name, and carried him off to Greenwich. Elizabeth received him with the utmost graciousness, and after many compliments and inquiries concerning "her well-beloved brother," she drew M. de Rosny to the further side of the apartment, that she might converse with him of the unsettled state of affairs in Europe, in greater freedom than when within hearing of the ladies and gentlemen of her court.

She then entered more fully into the subject, and explained her views with so much precision, lucidity, and solid judgment, that Rosny was fain to confess that "this great queen was entirely worthy of the immense reputation she had acquired for wisdom and ability throughout Europe." She held precisely similar views to those of Henri IV. respecting the necessity of curbing the power of the House of Austria, of restraining its ambition within just limits, and rendering the empire elective. It was the king's "grand project" the *grand-maître* was listening to, and it amazed him greatly, as there had been no reciprocal communication of their ideas on this subject.

Her aim at the moment was to induce Henri to infringe the treaty of Vervins, and to join with her in carrying their arms into the Netherlands, but without seeking to profit by it for the extension of the French frontier. This object might have been attained, Rosny thought, had not Clement VIII., dreading the renewal of war, so earnestly insisted on France receiving immediate satisfaction from Philip III. for the affront to the French ambassador. Yet Henri warmly welcomed Elizabeth's overtures, and informed her that they might remain united in their diplomatic views, while waiting for the opportunity of uniting their arms. During his stay in the North the king paid the money owing to the Prince of Orange, and, to aid him as far as he was able, closed his eyes to the fact that a large number of French Huguenots were continually joining the prince's army. This, it appears, was prohibited by treaty, though the prohibition was little regarded.

The king himself had sometimes secretly given

permission to join it, as in the case of the young Comte de Châtillon-Coligny, a very promising young officer who commanded a detachment in the prince's army, and was killed at the siege of Ostend during Rosny's short visit to England. He seems to have regretted him greatly, and to have been much hurt to find Henri so prejudiced against this worthy grandson of the murdered Admiral Coligny, and his whole family, that he refused Rosny's request for a small pension for Coligny's needy mother. Though so young a man, he had already displayed the qualities which form a great general, — valour, prudence, coolness, great intelligence, and the art of making himself beloved both by the men he commanded and his superior officers.

Henri was easily swayed by his Catholic courtiers, and readily gave ear to the paltry gossip and scandal of the court against those who served him best, which one can scarcely believe a really great man would have done. They persuaded him that Coligny sought for his own private aims to put himself at the head of the reformers, both within and without the kingdom; that "his majesty would some day have everything to fear from one who sprang from a stock that had brought so much evil on France and her kings, and in whose steps Coligny confessed himself ambitious of treading." That Henry IV. could listen to such statements against the Coligny family and be influenced by them — and especially against the great Calvinist leader, under whom he had been trained and who had been to him as a father — shows but too clearly his gradual but sure degeneracy since the day of his feigned abjuration of his religion, — a day, as writes a modern historian, to be reckoned amongst the *dies nefasti* of his country.*

The king returned to Paris from inspecting his northern frontier early in September. It was supposed, as France appeared likely to enjoy calm for a time, that besides the inspection of fortresses, the king's journey had a second object in view — escape from the misery of domestic war; for, to use the words of a French writer, "the Louvre had become a hell." It could hardly be otherwise, — a double *ménage*, with wife and mistress under the same roof, was not likely to lead to domestic peace, nor was such an arrangement very creditable to the king.

The Marquise de Verneuil was presented to Maria de' Medici by the Duchesse de Nemours at her first reception in Paris. The position occupied in the establishment by the *belle marquise* was, of course, very soon known to the queen, who became furious, and made free use of her hands and nails on her sovereign's face, and dealt him, with her robust arm, some very heavy blows. The other lady mocked wittily, and made merry

* H. M. Baird, " The Huguenots and Henry of Navarre."

at the queen's expense, and told to all who cared to hear it the story of the marriage promise. "It was she," she said, "who was the rightful queen, not the banker's fat daughter."

Maria de' Medici was then twenty-seven, — short and stout, fair and florid, but without beauty of feature or grace of manner. She had inherited none of the elegance attributed, but with very scant reason, to the Medici, her paternal ancestors, but had more of the qualities of her Austrian mother, though, unlike her, not redeeming her want of beauty and mental endowments by amiability of character. She was jealous, obstinate, irritable, and bigoted. However, it must be allowed that Henri, who was faithful to neither wife nor mistress, gave her very sufficient cause for jealousy; while the great sympathy which, as the wife of so dissolute a man, she at first inspired, was withdrawn when it became known that her own conduct was very equivocal.

In no manner was she drawn into the marriage with Henri by inclination. Concini, young and handsome, had too large a place in her favour, while Virginio Orsini was her devoted slave. Other attachments are said to have been formed after her arrival in France. Her position in relation to her marriage appears to have been similar to Henri's. He was constrained by the importunity of his ministers, and especially by that of the Baron de Rosny; she by the grand duke and

*Concino-Concini, Marquis d' Ancre.*
Photo-Etching. — From Painting by Lecocq.

duchess, but through the agency of Leonora Dori (la Galigaï), who had acquired a great ascendency over her. She could persuade the princess, or almost bid her, to do what she would have entirely refused to the request of the duke or her aunt. Leonora therefore played at once the double part of the duke's faithful agent and Maria de' Medici's guide, philosopher, and friend.

Since her arrival in France there was added to her duties the daily task of endeavouring to reconcile the king and queen after their desperate quarrels, in which Maria, in her rage, would use language quite unfit for lips or ears polite. Often the grand master was summoned to the battle-field to act as peacemaker. He did not always succeed, and, as had occurred more than once when endeavouring to restrain the queen's violence, and to avert the blows from the king, she turned upon him and accused him of striking her. To Henri, in private, he recommended separation from Madame de Verneuil as the most effectual way of dispelling the queen's jealousy, — short of the return of the promise of marriage and its destruction.

The separation from his mistress, he declared, he could not accede to; for when leaving the queen, who in her best and quietest moods was ill-tempered and gloomy, and repulsed with disdain all his attentions, he found, he said, some consolation in the lively, witty chat and merry laughter of the marquise, even when directed against himself and his terrible wife. He should adopt a more decided tone, he was told, — that of master, the despotic "*Je le veux*," or " Such is our good pleasure."

Rosny, who appears to have lived on excellent terms with his wife, yet on one or two occasions when Madame de Rosny expressed herself with a little more energy than he thought becoming, against his harshness — not towards herself, but towards those against whom, as she conceived, he was unjustly prejudiced; the Comte de Soissons, for instance — we hear him saying, as he records in his memoirs : " I imposed silence on my wife." Henri could not have done that. His gallantry led him to regard woman, and lovely woman especially, as an object of adoration. To take the tone of a master to her was not in his nature. He could more readily have taken that of her slave, — and slave he then was of the artful, intriguing Marquise de Verneuil. He inclined rather to sending Maria de' Medici back to Tuscany. He was about to visit Blois and several other places and provinces, for the purpose of dispelling the fears of the inhabitants respecting certain new taxes which discontented and intriguing military men and nobles had reported amongst the people as about to be levied on them in addition to their already too heavy burden.

Maria, suspecting that the marquise was to

accompany him, insisted on going also. The king appealed to the physicians, who told her that travelling about the country was, in her state of health, most undesirable — that, in fact, she must not attempt it, as it would imperil the hopes of the nation. This, and certain information collected for her by Leonora, led her to consent to retire to Fontainebleau, the king accompanying her, and there, some few days after — 27th of September — she gave birth to a son.

Henri's plans were changed by this event; the mother of a dauphin could not be turned out of France. He must try if by patience life might possibly be made tolerable to them. For the moment, there was reconciliation and forgetfulness of the past between Henri and the queen, with general rejoicings and congratulatory addresses from all classes of people. Presents innumerable flowed in from all quarters, with valuable offerings to the dauphin; amongst the latter, the customary "swaddling-clothes blessed by his holiness" were received from Rome, and the municipality of Paris sent the queen a magnificent set of tapestry hangings for her bed. The king added, as *un présent de couches,* poor Gabrielle's favourite residence, the Château de Monceaux.

Henri at first was afraid of the consequences of informing the queen that she had given birth to a son, and it seems that she really fainted with emotion when told that she had fulfilled the hopes of the nation. The king, in his great joy, ran about embracing everybody, — ladies, of course, the most fervently. The château was full of all sorts of people, all, on such an occasion, having a right to press their way even into the queen's apartment if they could. The nurses reproved the king for allowing so many persons to enter and disturb the queen; but he replied: "This child belongs to all the world, and everybody must see him and rejoice!"

Taking the newborn babe in his arms, he asked the blessing of Heaven upon him; then gave him his own benediction. Putting the child's hand on the hilt of his sword, he prayed that he might never draw the sword except for the glory of God and the good of his subjects. All the cannon of the Paris arsenal were fired on this auspicious occasion, and with such good effect that they were distinctly heard at Fontainebleau. Hitherto, all had gone on well. The birth of a dauphin had given general satisfaction, and the king's would also have been complete but for the slight vexation he felt at having forgotten, until nearly a fortnight after the child's birth, to have his horoscope drawn.

Yet he was exceedingly anxious respecting it, and had provided himself with a watch of the most perfect construction obtainable, that there might not be the slightest error in marking the exact moment of the child's entry into the world.

In the general confusion that ensued, it escaped his memory, and only recurred to him when speaking of certain predictions then rumoured about concerning himself and the *grand-maître* — for both were believers in astrology — though the latter did not quite acknowledge it. However, La Rivière, the king's first physician, was immediately sent for. Rosny says of him that "he had no more religion than those who publicly profess to meddle with judicial astrology usually have, though the world did him the honour to say that he concealed a Protestant heart under the exterior of a Catholic."

The king had heard that many of La Rivière's predictions had been fully realised. This made him the more impatient to hear from him the destiny of his son; for it had transpired that La Rivière, for his own satisfaction or amusement, had already drawn the horoscope of the young prince. When the physician arrived, Henri, who allowed only his minister to be present, said to him: "Apropos, M. de la Rivière, you have told me nothing concerning the nativity of M. le Dauphin. What have you discovered?"

"I certainly did commence something about it," he replied, "but I have thrown it aside. In fact, I have given up amusing myself with that science, which I have partly forgotten, have always considered extremely uncertain, and often at fault."

The king saw at once that he was not speaking sincerely, whether from fear of offending his majesty or from bad temper; or that it was the manœuvre of an astrologer who distrusted his secrets.

"I see, M. de la Rivière," said the king, "that you have not given me the real motive for your silence. You are not so scrupulous as you pretend. You are afraid of speaking, lest your prediction should turn out false or should displease me. But whatever it may be, I desire to hear it; and I now command you, under pain of offending me, to speak freely." It was necessary to repeat this command three or four times before he would utter a word. Then, with a sort of mutinous air, real or assumed, he began:

"Sire, your son will live to the age of manhood, and will reign longer than you; but his inclinations, moods, and disposition will differ greatly from yours. He will lean to his own opinions and caprices, but will sometimes yield to those of others. He will accomplish great things, will be successful in his designs, and be much spoken of throughout Christendom. There will be always peace and war. He will leave posterity, and after him things will become worse. Desolation threatens your ancient societies, and all your arrangements will be overthrown or abolished. That is all you will learn from me, and it is more than I intended to tell you."

"I see clearly," rejoined the king, "that you refer to the Huguenots, but that is because you are attached to them."

"I refer to whatever you please," replied La Rivière, sullenly; "but you will learn nothing more from me. He then abruptly left the room. For a considerable time the king and the *grand-maître* remained in the deep embrasure of a window, pondering over and suggesting a meaning to the vague words just uttered, every one of which made a deep impression on the king. The dauphin appears to have been but a weakly child, notwithstanding the robust health of his mother, which Henri again refers to in a letter to Rosny at this time. La Rivière's prediction had reassured him as to the life of his son, but to fortify him constitutionally he determined to have him brought up at Saint-Germain, a more healthy spot, he thought, than even Fontainebleau, and where there was already a nursery of legitimised royal children, to which another son, born some week or two before the dauphin, was about to be added.*

He was, however, anxious that the good city of Paris should be favoured with the sight of the dauphin, and the good citizens bestow their benedictions on him before his removal to Saint-Germain. The king, therefore, ordered the royal

---

* This was the son of the Marquise de Verneuil. He was legitimised, and named, with the king's approval, Henri de Bourbon.

babe to be placed in his cradle and slowly carried through Paris on an uncovered litter, attended by his nurses, and followed by a small military escort. The youthful prince's royal entry appears to have been a great success; Parisians of all classes hailed "the hope of the nation" with enthusiastic blessings and acclamations, the *grand-maître* adding the thunder of his cannon as the tiny babe and his *cortège* passed the arsenal. It was a sort of family *fête* for all France, the hero of it bearing the homage paid him in perfect manly fashion — without shedding a tear or expressing annoyance or dissatisfaction.*

The queen, fresh and blooming, soon reappeared to take her part in the splendid *fêtes* in celebration of the auspicious birth of an heir to the throne. Amongst other festive arrangements was a grand allegorical ballet given by the queen, the idea of which is said to have been both ingenious and moral — a novelty, therefore, at this once more brilliant and dissolute court. The ballet represented the union of the Virtues with the Muses, the result of this alliance being a great deal of graceful dancing by the most beautiful ladies of the court. The king, who was seated by the nuncio during the performance of the ballet, when he saw this bevy of beauties enter, turned to his eminence with the remark that he had never seen a more beautiful squadron, or a more dangerous

* Pierre de l'Estoile; Mathieu; Sully.

one. He was thinking, probably, of Catherine de' Medici's flying squadron, and contrasting them, perhaps unfavourably, with the severer beauties of Maria de' Medici's ladies. What his eminence thought of them is not recorded.

## CHAPTER XIII.

Festivities at Court. — Plots and Intrigues among the Discontented. — Biron Complains of the King's Ingratitude, and Resumes His Intrigues with Spain and Savoy on Returning to His Government of Burgundy. — He Is Betrayed by His Confidant. — The King Promises Pardon if He Confesses His Treason and Abstains from It in Future. — Haughtily Declares Himself Innocent. — He is Arrested, also Comte d'Auvergne. — Confronted with La Fin. — Strange Scene. — Sentence of Death. — Execution. — Congratulations. — Duc de Bouillon Retires to Geneva and Germany. — Visit of Maurice le Savant to Paris. — Henri Confesses Himself Still a Protestant. — Death of Queen Elizabeth.

WHILE all was festivity and rejoicing on the one hand, dark plots and intrigues were rife on the other. Scarcely had Maréchal de Biron made his confession of traitorous conduct towards his sovereign, and been fully and frankly pardoned, when again his arrogance, his dissatisfaction — though so nobly rewarded for his services — broke forth in complaints of the king's ingratitude. But while acknowledging his merits, Henri did not consider that he owed his crown to Biron — as was the marshal's frequent boast, though Biron cared not to remember that he had once in battle owed his life to the king; it was too mortifying to his pride. However,

Henri, unwilling to think ill of an intrepid soldier, for years his companion-in-arms, attributed his discontent to the restlessness of an active mind, and without further delay sent him to England on a confidential mission to the queen.

Before setting out Biron asked the king for 30,000 crowns; his request was immediately complied with, and Rosny was urged, though the recent rejoicings had left him a nearly empty exchequer, not to delay payment, but to find some means of immediately obtaining that amount if he had it not by him.*

Elizabeth received with evident pleasure so distinguished an officer as the Maréchal Duc de Biron; but he, with singular indiscretion, on his first interview with the queen, introduced the sub-

---

* Rosny had recently said that when the cuirass was thrown aside and the sword hung up in its scabbard, his chief care would be to enrich the king without oppressing the people. He oppressed them unwillingly, no doubt; but to raise on the spur of the moment even 30,000 crowns compelled him to oppress a little. But as time ran on and the king became more and more a reckless gambler; the queen more extravagant and a gambler also; the mistresses multiplied, and their demands on the treasury increased in amount and frequency, together with the liberal "gratifications" and pensions to undeserving favourites, and the taste developed by Henri for building, M. de Rosny found himself forced by degrees to forego his benevolent intentions towards the people — by the sweat of whose brows all these expenses were met — and instead of relieving them of their burdens, still further to oppress them. Taxation was less heavy even under the profligate spendthrift Henri III.

ject of the death of the Earl of Essex, and even ventured to express pity for his fate. His services, he said, should have preserved him from so tragic an end. The queen simply replied, without appearing affected by so ill-timed a discourse, that every citizen in serving his country did but fulfil his duty; that, nevertheless, he was recompensed by the glory of it, and the favours accorded by the sovereign. "A rebellious subject ought to be punished," she said, "for the safety of the state. She had heaped benefits on the Earl of Essex, who had been guilty of high treason, and could not deny his crime. Yet," she added, "in spite of his perfidy and ingratitude, he might have obtained pardon had he chosen to ask it; but nothing could touch his feelings or diminish his arrogance, and the royal clemency being repulsed, it was left to justice to decide his fate." *

Rosny was of opinion that the queen, in deigning to give this explanation to Biron, may have seen some traits of resemblance between him and the unfortunate Essex, and thus have sought to suggest the probable results of his own conduct. This she would have learned from her ambassador, who kept her so well informed of all that occurred at the French court. Her words were, indeed, almost prophetic; but Biron was not likely to be impressed by them as a warning to himself. On returning from England, the marshal was des-

* Mathieu, *Histoire de France*.

patched to Switzerland to renew the alliance between France and the Swiss cantons, — a mission accomplished to the king's satisfaction.

Scarcely, however, had he arrived in France when he resumed his intrigues with more persistency than ever, and contracted a closer intimacy with the factious Duc de Bouillon and the Comte d'Auvergne. They were endeavouring, by promising redress of their grievances, to draw the chief men of the Huguenots into favouring their schemes and uniting with them for what they termed their common security "against all and every one *without exception*." But the Huguenot chiefs, in assembly at Châtellerault — Sully as a member of the Synod attending — declared their adhesion to the opinions of D'Aubigné, "that whatever were the grievances of those of 'the religion,' it would be very unwise to rush from the hands of the king into the claws of petty tyrants, who desired to make use of them only for their own advantage." Notwithstanding this decision on the part of their chiefs, many Huguenots were persuaded to join the Catholics in effecting a rising of the people in several towns.

Biron, on retiring from the court to his government of Burgundy, signed a treaty with the Duke of Savoy, who promised him that province, with La Franche-Comté and the Comté of Charolais in independent sovereignty, together with the hand of the duke's third daughter. These arrangements, of course, depended on the success of the conspiracy which was to result in the dismemberment of France, chiefly for the benefit of Spain and Savoy. But failure seems not to have been thought of. This treaty was in the possession of a gentleman, Jacques de La Fin de Beauvais, deep in Biron's confidence, but for some unexplained reason secretly his enemy. Considering the success of the project very doubtful, he sought the king, and revealed the whole of the conspiracy, furnishing him also with substantial proofs of its accuracy, and a list of the names of those engaged in it.

France was in a state of greater disquietude and excitement since peace had been proclaimed than in time of war. The country had so long been as one vast camp, that a difficulty was experienced in settling down to a life of quietude and peace. The men of war felt that their occupation was gone, and found none more congenial to replace it than that of plotting the overthrow of the sovereign whose rights they had hitherto been fighting to maintain.

On receiving La Fin's statement, the king sent to Biron, desiring his attendance at the court, which was then at Fontainebleau. His friend was charged, rather perfidiously, to tell him on his arrival that the king knew nothing whatever of his plans. Biron, therefore, when questioned by Henri respecting the serious rumour afloat of his treasonable acts and intentions, denied positively any complicity in, or knowledge of, the treasonable designs referred to. If anything of that sort had been laid to his charge, he could assign it only to the calumny of spies.

"Biron," replied the king, "you know how highly I have esteemed you; how I have admired your courage as an intrepid soldier, your ability as a general. I now promise fully to pardon those acts of high treason you have been led into against me, if you will acknowledge them and promise to avoid such acts for the future."

"I have nothing to acknowledge," he answered haughtily, "nor do I comprehend why a man of honour should thus be pressed to accuse himself of what he is not guilty of." The king was indignant at his persistence in denying acts of which he held in his own hands the proof that he was guilty. This was the original treaty signed by Biron and the Duke of Savoy, — the latter promising, in the name of Spain, troops and money to effect his purpose. La Fin had persuaded him that such a document was too compromising to be retained in his possession. It would be well to destroy it, as it might be easily renewed when necessary. Biron handed it to La Fin, who adroitly transferred it to his own pocket, throwing a piece of crumpled paper into the fire in its stead. Biron therefore felt very secure that no evidence of that kind could be produced against him.

The marshal had been playing cards with the queen during the evening. In the course of it an officer in attendance on him had contrived to slip into his hand unperceived a paper containing a few words warning him that for safety's sake it was not advisable to remain at the palace a moment longer than was absolutely necessary. But he merely glanced at it contemptuously, then threw it under the table. The king yet hesitated to arrest him; but as on the third interview with him that evening he still persisted in his denial, and assumed an air of bravado, which had served him well on other occasions, Henri became indignant, and, rising to leave the apartment, said as he passed out, " Adieu, *Baron* de Biron." This was indeed a shock to this marshal of France, duke and peer of the realm. It announced a first sentence of degradation.

A few minutes later Biron was arrested by the captain of the king's guards. When asked for his sword: "Take it," he said; "it is a sword that has rendered the king good service." The Comte d'Auvergne, who endeavoured to escape, was stopped by the guard at the gates of the château. On giving up his sword, he said it was "guiltless of shedding any blood but that of wild boars." Both prisoners were sent by water, and strongly guarded, to the Bastille, of which the *grand-maître* had, but a few days before, been appointed governor.

The trial of Biron was confided to the Parliament of Paris. A commission immediately opened the proceedings under the first president, Achille de Harlay. At first Biron persisted in asserting his innocence; but when the treaty and a number of letters to La Fin — which he also thought burnt — were produced, he seemed as if suddenly struck with stupor. He could no longer wholly deny complicity with treason; some things he acknowledged, but the most criminal he would not consent to have attributed to him. He addressed a pathetic request to the king, entreating him to spare his life. He spoke of his many battles and the wounds received in his service; but solicited pardon chiefly, he said, for his aged mother's sake, — the widow of the great marshal who had lost his life on the battle-field in the service of his king.

"It appeared to him impossible," he continued, "that under the reign of the most clement of the kings of France — in fact, of all kings — such barbarity could be perpetrated as that which condemned the aged widow of the hero, killed while sustaining the royal cause, to see her son die on the scaffold." The *noblesse* were twice convoked with the usual formalities; but none appeared to take part in this trial of one of their order. Various excuses were sent for non-attendance, the real ones being inability to declare the marshal innocent, and unwillingness to pronounce him guilty.

This was understood by him as abandonment rather than delicacy of sentiment.

His mother, brothers, and other relatives and friends, earnestly implored the king to regard with leniency the errors which the distinguished son of a great general had unhappily been drawn into. "At least," pleaded the Duc de La Force, "he did not conspire against your majesty's life."

The king, with as much gentleness and pity as was possible, said that the request came too late. The marshal had contemned the royal clemency when open to him, and that for the good of his children and his people he could not now prevent justice from taking its course.

An extraordinary scene ensued when Biron was confronted with his former friend and accomplice who had deceived him and become his denunciator. With the utmost violence and emotion he exclaimed: "It is that sorcerer La Fin who alone has wrought my ruin! It was his reports, his insinuations, his perfidious counsels, his demoniacal arts, that exasperated me against the king and threw me into the arms of Spain and Savoy. It was he who, to draw me deeper into his plots, showed me a waxen figure which had spoken and announced the king's death."

On recovering calmer feelings, he defended himself with much skill, and made a deep and affecting impression on his judges, who — if time had allowed them, while under its influence, to deliberate on the subject — would at least, it was believed, have recommended him to the king's clemency. But his address was long, and the decision in consequence was deferred until the next or following day. The impression made by his defence had then passed away, and Biron was declared guilty of high treason, and condemned to death.

The decree of the judges being made known to the king, he put off the execution of the sentence for a day, which gave a gleam of hope to the condemned man. It, however, brought no change, but that of the substitution of the court of the Bastille for the Place de Grève as the scene of his decapitation. This was reported as a concession to the prayer of his family, but believed to have been determined on rather to avert the probable danger of publicly immolating a distinguished general, whose dauntless bravery had inspired the troops whom he had so often led to victory with feelings of enthusiasm.

On the morning of the 31st of July, when the chancellor, the counsellors of state, and other high officials, entered his prison, he exclaimed, "Is it death?" expecting the answer to be either reprieve or pardon. He could not believe that Henri would prove relentless, and Biron, so intrepid, so defiant of death on the battle-field, when confronted with death on the scaffold became the weakest of men. Yet a short delay is accorded him while the lieutenant of the guard seeks the *grand-maître* to implore him to ask the king to spare the marshal's life, even if for the rest of it he consigns him in chains to a dungeon. Rosny and his wife were much moved by such an appeal from the once haughty Biron, but believing entreaty useless, the *grand-maître* would not venture to comply with it.

It was five o'clock in the afternoon ere Biron's sentence was carried into effect. He had made it more distressing to himself and those who were compelled to be present by his passionate resistance, his explosions of anger, and his vehement curses on the hand that had saved his life, and had "torn from him a glorious death in the hour of victory to inflict on him an ignominious one on the scaffold." " So vehemently did he oppose the carrying out of his sentence that the executioner was obliged to conceal his knife and seize the marshal unawares" (L'Estoile). He was buried at once, without any ceremony, in the church of Saint-Paul, "a weeping crowd following." In the evening of the same day, an immense concourse of people went to the church to throw holy water on his tomb. This homage to the memory of the traitor caused some astonishment, as it was said to be intended as a silent expression of disapproval of the king's rigour.

Greater sympathy was evinced towards the family of the unfortunate, though certainly guilty,

Biron, from the fact that pardon was extended to his accomplices, who were not less guilty than he, — the Comte d'Auvergne, for instance, who placed himself at the king's mercy and was fully and freely pardoned; though it could not be alleged that he had ever rendered the slightest service to either king or country; but he was able to command the all-prevailing intercession of his sister, the Marquise de Verneuil. His pardon could not be attributed to royal clemency, and was thought by the Biron family to demand justification, — this illegitimate scion of the race of Valois being an inveterate intriguer, who was no sooner released and out of danger than he resumed his disloyal practices towards the king.

All the Powers having friendly relations with France hastened warmly to congratulate Henri IV. on the success with which he had broken up the conspiracy against him. The strength of his government was revealed in the example he had given in making it clear to the *haute noblesse* that henceforth they could not with impunity sacrifice the repose of the people to their overweening egotism. Duke Charles Emmanuel and Philip III. were not behind others in offering their felicitations; but Henri made them aware that he was no stranger to the active part they had taken in the affair. They threw the blame of this on their ministers, who had acted, they asserted, without orders or sanction on their part. Nevertheless, those ministers, amongst whom was Maréchal de Fuentés, if reprimanded for form's sake, were not dismissed from their offices.

Biron's death had rendered the conspiracy against king and state for a time at least abortive. There, however, yet remained three powerful and influential men with whom he thought it right to come to an explanation concerning the extent of their complicity in it. They were the Ducs d'Épernon, de La Trémouïlle, and de Bouillon, of whom only the Duc d'Épernon obeyed the king's command to repair to the court. It was known that he professed no friendly feelings towards the king, for "friendship," as he already had told his majesty, "required friendship to sustain it, and was no part of duty." Yet he declared himself one of the most faithful of his subjects, and exonerated himself to Henri's satisfaction, it appears, of any actual participation in Biron's intrigues.

De La Trémouïlle, though dissatisfied, like many others, with the king's evasion of those articles of the Edict of Nantes regarding the eligibility of the Protestants equally with the Catholics to fill the principal offices of state, was yet disinclined to seek redress in rebellion. But the Duc de Bouillon was as guilty as Biron of inciting both Catholics and Huguenots to acts of sedition. When ordered to appear at court, he returned an evasive reply, but protested his innocence of all he was charged with before a numerous assembly of Protestants at Montpellier, and invoked in his favour the intervention of the Reformed Churches.

The king, much irritated at being thus represented as the persecutor of the Protestants, sent a member of the grand council to bring Bouillon to Paris strongly guarded. Fancying that a similar fate to Biron's awaited him, he crossed the Rhône and reached Geneva ere the officer charged with arresting him arrived. Thence he retired to Germany to the court of his brother-in-law, the elector palatine. There he posed as the victim of the Catholic party, sought the aid of the Protestant princes and the protection of Elizabeth of England, thus endeavouring to make his cause appear that of the whole body of the Reformers. Henri had communicated his troubles and vexations to the English queen, who replied that she thought the accusations against the duke very unlikely to be true, "and that instead of overwhelming a probably innocent man, he should seek the source of the evil, and unite with his allies in openly attacking Spain, — the very focus of all the intrigues that troubled France."

The Duc de Bouillon remained several months with his relative, the elector palatine. During that time the Landgrave of Hesse, Maurice *le savant,* visited France *incognito* for the purpose of conferring with Henri on the project of a League of the German Protestant princes under the protectorate of the King of France — the first step towards the realisation of Henri's s heme of wresting the imperial crown from the House of Austria. Henri availed himself of this opportunity of impressing on Maurice that "his sentiments towards the Protestants were unchanged; that in heart he was still devoted to 'the religion;' and further, that it was his intention to renew before his death his public confession of it."

How singularly this assurance contrasts with that of ardent Catholic zeal he was so frequently making to Rome, and with his letter to Épernon expressing his great delight at "the triumph of Évreux over Saumur!" His indifference to both faiths was, however, more generally believed in than his zeal for either, though it is probable that with a view of justifying himself in his own eyes for his feigned denial of his faith, he did sometimes promise his conscience to make amends for that error by publicly declaring himself still a Huguenot. But, as he said, necessity was the law of the times, and made him say first one thing, then another.

Maurice, at all events, had faith in the soundness of Henri's policy as regarded Austria, and with mutual satisfaction they discussed the means of curbing its ever increasing power; first by securing the election of a king of the Romans, as successor to the reigning emperor, who should not be a member of the Austrian family. If the

King of France should aspire to the imperial crown, Maurice assured him that he would be quite disposed to aid him to the full extent of his power. Henri avoided prematurely pledging himself in a matter of so much delicacy; but he and the landgrave separated on terms of perfect friendship, and of agreement in each other's views.

Some troubles and disturbances in Metz, where the lieutenants of the Duc d'Épernon, who was governor of that district, persecuted the principal citizens, had induced the king's proposal to visit that fortress, to place the command in other hands. He was at Nancy when he learnt with much concern that Queen Elizabeth was seriously ill, and declining rapidly, — her physical sufferings being increased by bitter regrets for her rigorous treatment of her favourite Essex. The news of her death on the 4th of April was received a few days later.

The friendship between Henri IV. and Elizabeth had not on the whole been very disinterested. Dark clouds had sometimes overshadowed it, for which he was, in fact, held responsible. But on whichever side the blame lay, Henri now put aside all remembrance of their differences to dwell only on the services she had done him.

"I have lost in her," he wrote to Rosny, "a second self; for the great queen was the irreconcilable enemy of our irreconcilable enemies."

England had made immense progress during Elizabeth's long reign of forty-five years. An energetic spirit of enterprise, both commercial and maritime, had developed itself in the nation, — the result of many years of internal peace, assured by the queen's vigorous government and the able and successful resistance she opposed to the designs of Philip II. So lengthened and prosperous a career dazzled even her enemies, and led them to proclaim her the "most glorious and most fortunate of all the women who had ever worn a crown."

*Elizabeth of England.*

Photo-Etching. —From Painting by Zucchero.

## CHAPTER XIV.

The Landgrave of Hesse Takes Leave of the King. — Henri Sets Out for Metz. — He Is Received with Enthusiasm. — The Despotic Lieutenants Dismissed. — The King Spends His Birthday with His Sister, at Nancy, Where He Receives the News of the Birth of a Daughter, to the Great Disappointment of the Queen, Who Had Expected a Son, as Prophesied by a Nun. — Henri Attempts to Console Her. — The Marquise Bribed to Obtain the King's Consent to Galigai's Marriage with Concini. — Is Invited to the Queen's Ballet. — Consent Obtained. — The Queen Furiously Jealous. — England Expected to Fall Again into the Toils of Rome. — Disappointment. — An Embassy to the English Court.

SOON after the departure of the Landgrave of Hesse the king left Fontainebleau for Metz, for the purpose of quelling a rising of the people against the despotic rule of two lieutenants, whom the Duc d'Épernon, governor of the province, had placed over them during his absence. These officers now set him and his authority at defiance, which compelled him unwillingly to refer the matter to the king; for, like other dissatisfied nobles, Épernon was desirous of holding his government as an hereditary fief, on condition of military service. The king was received at Metz with enthusiasm. After banishing the refractory lieutenants and replacing them by the brothers La Grange de Montigny, men devoted entirely to him, he proceeded to Nancy, at the request of the Duchesse de Bar, who wished him to spend there the 13th of December, his birthday, when she came to meet him, with several members of the Lorraine family.

At Nancy he was greeted by the information that the queen had given birth, on the 22d of November, to a daughter, who had been named Elisabeth. Rosny (who was called away by this event from inspecting a recently purchased domain, where, as was his custom, he was about to build a new château) was charged by the king to "omit no arrangements that could please and amuse the queen and keep her quiet — also, if possible, in a good temper." He, meanwhile, having had some slight quarrel with the marquise, was solacing himself in the society of a new mistress, Mademoiselle Jacqueline de Beuil, whom he had married to a needy gentleman and created Comtesse de Moret, with the gift of a château and estate.

But on this occasion Maria de' Medici was affected far less by the king's infidelities than by her disappointment at the sex of the child she had given birth to. The Pope had recently sent her a nun who was credited with the gift of prophecy, and who had foretold the advent of a son, and in due time two or three more to follow. The failure of the first part of the prophecy sent the queen, who had always an overwhelming deluge of tears at command, into one of her violent fits of weeping, and worse still, induced her to indulge, as she was prone, in very vehement language. The poor erring prophetess fled from her majesty's presence, dismayed by the torrent of invectives so lavishly poured upon her.

Hearing from Rosny of the queen's distress of mind, Henri wrote to console her, telling her in his usual gay manner, "if she had not been of the same sex as her daughter, she would never have been Queen of France," and that the mistake which had been made might yet not improbably be repaired.*

His letters and attempts at consolation met with no gracious reception from the queen, who could not, had she desired, ignore his gallantries, so diligently reported to her by Concini and Leonora. The latter was now very anxious to marry Concini, who, with his royal mistress's consent, had for his own ends made love to her unattractive and deformed favourite. The subject had been mentioned to Henri before leaving for Metz, as his consent must be given before the auspicious union could take place. He, however, curtly refused it, and would have been glad to send both Concini and Leonora out of the country with the rest of the queen's intriguing

* L'Estoile, *Journal de Henri IV.*; Mathieu; *Vie de Maria de' Medici, par* Madame Thioux.

Italian surroundings. But Henri stood greatly in awe of his robust wife, and courage failed him when he strove to make up his mind, as Rosny so often and earnestly advised him, to adopt the tone of a master towards her.

Leonora, too, was not easily discomfited. She had left Tuscany with grand ideas of the wealth and honours awaiting her in France, and had taken the first step towards entering on her new position with suitable dignity. Personally unattractive and of humble birth, her father being a carpenter, her mother a laundress in the royal palace, she yet possessed a certain fascination of manner, with great natural abilities, which, from associating from childhood with the young princess, had been in a measure cultivated by the same professors and governesses as had attended the royal pupil. Leonora had lent an attentive ear to the lessons and general instruction given to the princess, and of the two it was she who derived, it appears, the greater advantage from them. She was, in fact, the superior in talent, and as strong-minded as Maria de' Medici was weak. This the grand duke well knew, and had turned to good account.

Leonora's ambition increased when it was known that the Tuscan princess was to be Queen of France. That she should accompany her was at once decided, also that she should be elevated to the post of *dame d'atour*. To render her more worthy of that and further honour, Leonora discarded her humble patronymic of Dori and assumed that of Galigai, receiving for a considerable sum permission to do so from the needy but very noble Italian family of that name. In this she was assisted both by the influence and the purse of the grand duke and the princess. Great, then, was the disappointment of Leonora Galigai, and greater still the indignation of her mistress, when the king refused to appoint the queen's former waiting-maid to a distinguished post in her household.

However, for peace and quietude's sake, Henri subsequently yielded, and many other concessions he was afterwards constrained to make in order to lull or avert the frequent storms that assailed him in the royal *ménage*. He had yet to be brought to sanction the marriage of Concini and Galigai, and it occurred to the latter to propose to the queen to take advantage of a slight estrangement then existing between the king and the marquise to make some advances to the latter. Leonora, at all events, knew that the moment Madame de Verneuil chose to smile on the king he would be immediately at her feet, anxious to do anything she might require him. That the intriguing marquise loved money was also well known. Like the queen, she was prodigal of it, therefore always in need.

Should Leonora seek an interview and propose

to pay liberally for her influence to obtain the king's consent to her marriage? The queen assented. The proposal was made and accepted, and Leonora conveyed from the queen to the marquise, and *vice versâ*, some words of flattery and compliment. The king was expected shortly in Paris, and in the interval the queen gave a ballet, to which she condescended to invite the marquise.

The king was so much touched by this amiable attention on the queen's part, that on the marquise mentioning how greatly her majesty desired the union of her much attached friends, Concini and the Signora Galigai, he at once gave his consent, and also allowed, which hitherto he had refused, some valuable presents in money and jewels to be made by the queen to her interesting favourites.

Her object attained, Maria de' Medici, while reflecting on the greater influence with the king of a mere word from the marquise, than of prayers and entreaties from herself, became more violently jealous than ever. Galigai could scarcely restrain her from openly insulting Madame de Verneuil. She even vowed she would kill her; for Henri had made his consent to the marriage dependent on his own restoration to his mistress's favour, after one of their frequent lovers' quarrels, and this had duly reached the queen's ears. Rosny was appealed to, but important business of state required his attendance on the king, who had arrived in Paris, but seemed far from inclined to add by his presence fuel to the flames then raging round his domestic hearth at Fontainebleau. Madame de Rosny was therefore despatched to aid Galigai in calming and soothing the queen's perturbed spirit.*

The death of Queen Elizabeth had made it necessary that Henri IV. should send a special embassy to England, to compliment James VI. of Scotland on his accession to the English throne as James I., King of Great Britain. To the extreme disappointment of the Pope and Philip III., no opposition was offered to Elizabeth's successor — named by the great queen herself on her deathbed. Clement VIII. had been so sanguine as to believe that England was destined to fall again under the yoke of the papacy by the rising of the English Catholics in favour of Arabella Stuart, to support whose claims money from Rome and troops from Spain would have been speedily sent. Happily, however, no such calamity occurred.

Failing in their hopes of driving the heretic James from the throne, they changed their tactics and made great advances to him. The Jesuits and priests were strictly prohibited by the Pope from taking any part henceforth in political intrigues. This was with the view of inducing James to tolerate Catholicism for a time, and eventually, it was hoped, of bringing this Prot-

* L'Estoile; Mathieu; Madame Thioux.

estant son of Elizabeth's great Catholic victim to reëstablish his mother's religion throughout England.

But again disappointment ensued, for James lost no time in reprinting the confession of faith of the Anglican Church — referring without scruple to the "Roman Antichrist" in terms of bitter hatred. Even Henri IV. was inclined to look with disfavour on the union of Scotland with England and Ireland under the same sceptre. Scotland had generally proved a ready ally of France against England; but as this would no longer be possible, the king, with better grace than the Pope, submitted to the inevitable.

Rosny, with a numerous and splendid retinue, was charged with conveying the congratulations of the King of France to the King of Great Britain, and of proposing to renew with him the alliance entered into between Henri and the late queen. Of his secret instructions he was to communicate as much as he deemed prudent after forming his judgment of the king's character, and ascertaining his political views.

A better choice for an exponent of his views the king could scarcely have made. Yet the restless, intriguing, and jealous nobility he called to his council blamed the appointment of a heretic ambassador to a heretic king, as likely to raise suspicions as to his motives; to excite the murmurs of the partisans of the Pope and Spain, besides giving occasion to his enemies to declare that he attached importance to no alliance but that with princes of a contrary religion to his own. To send an embassy to the King of Great Britain was in itself injudicious, but to send a Huguenot to treat of the interests of the state with a prince of the same religion was, they argued, to compromise the state, — the more so as the king proposed to give this heretic ambassador a full power to act in his name.

Rosny was unaware, till informed by the king, of the secret efforts of his enemies to displace him. But Henri was not to be turned from his purpose. Rosny was so deep in the king's confidence that there probably was not another man in France to whom this delicate mission could so appropriately have been confided. To add greater *éclat* to his embassy, Henri was desirous of adding to Rosny's honours that of duke and peer of the realm, and inquired from which of his estates he would prefer to derive his title. He replied, "from his recently acquired domain of Sully, when Sully was in a condition to be so honoured;" which would be when his château — whose foundations were only then being laid — and other works in progress were completed. Until then he prayed the king, as already, some year or two before, he had done, to allow him to remain Marquis de Rosny.

The departure of the embassy was delayed by the king being suddenly attacked by a painful malady he was at times subject to, and which, on the occasion in question, appeared likely to have serious results. The king had returned to Fontainebleau, and his sudden illness appears to have subdued the anger of his virago queen, as Rosny, who was immediately summoned at the king's desire, found her sitting composedly at his bedside. The ardour with which the king engaged in the chase was partly the cause of his frequent indisposition, for he was almost as furious a Nimrod as Charles IX., but his physicians remonstrated in vain.

Henri, however, improved the opportunity his illness gave him of gently reproaching her majesty, and of preaching to her of the power of a smiling face and good temper over anger and a gloomy, frowning brow. The mood in which he found the royal pair seemed suitable to M. de Rosny for attempting to bring about a full reconciliation between them. He was so fortunate as to effect it, and, as he afterwards learned, all went smoothly with the royal pair for at least two or three days.

## CHAPTER XV.

Rosny's Special Embassy to James I. — Misunderstanding between the English and French Admirals. — Arrival at Dover. — No Lodgings ; No Coaches. — Governor Weymmes. — From Dover to Canterbury. — Well Received by the Refugees. — The Cathedral. — Bad Treatment at Next Stage, Rochester. — Arrival at Gravesend. — The King's Barges in Waiting. — The Landing at the Tower. — Salute from the Tower Guns. — Arundel House. — Midnight Brawl between Frenchmen and Englishmen. — One of the Latter Killed. — The Assailant Sentenced by Rosny to Death. — Gives up the Prisoner to the Lord Mayor. — Presented to James. — Dinner at Greenwich. — The Grand Project. — James Interested. — Rosny's Return.

N the 12th or 13th of June the Marquis de Rosny set out on his journey to Calais, where he was to embark for England. Upwards of two hundred gentlemen accompanied him, and a numerous train of attendants. Having waited a day or two at Calais for another contingent of gentlemen who did him the honour, he says, to make the journey with him, he embarked, on the 15th, in an English vessel, two of large size being placed at his orders by the English vice-admiral. The French vessel, with Admiral de Vicq in command, in which he had intended to cross the channel, then followed as an

escort. On arriving at Dover, De Vicq, as a farewell salute, hoisted the French ensign, and having lowered it and again raised it, was about to depart with his ensign flying at the fore. But the English vice-admiral brought him to with a bullet, and proceeded to point his guns on him, as though about to give battle. Greatly annoyed that his embassy should begin with so unpleasant an incident, Rosny, with difficulty, he says, persuaded the admiral that De Vicq intended nothing more than to pay a farewell mark of respect to him. To which the arrogant Englishman replied with an oath, that "he would suffer no flag but that of England to be unfurled in that ocean channel." The Frenchman, prevailed on by Rosny, struck his flag and departed, declaring, in terms no less forcible than the Englishman's, that "he would have his revenge when next he met him at sea." *

At Dover the Comte de Beaumont, resident French ambassador at the English court, waited to receive the minister plenipotentiary and suite. With him was a gentleman described as an English officer whose duty it was to provide lodgings, provisions, carriages, horses, etc., for the representatives of foreign powers on their arrival in England. The mayor of Dover also came to compliment and greet the Frenchmen, and a large concourse of people were loud in their acclama-

\* *Mémoires de Sully.*

tions. The governor, confined to his room with gout, sent his nephew to make his excuses and very pressingly to invite the ambassador and suite to inspect the castle.

After the event of the morning, Rosny remarks that he had little faith in English politeness. Yet he considered that he would himself be wanting in courtesy should he leave Dover without acceding to this amiable governor's (Sir Thomas Weymmes) request. Accordingly, he went the next morning with the whole of his retinue, to visit the governor and go over the castle. The object, however, of his civility was soon, he tells us, very clear to him; for all who at that time were led by curiosity to visit Dover Castle were required to pay a ransom ere they quitted it. It was demanded of the Frenchmen in a rough overbearing manner, and was followed by the ceremony of surrendering their swords, Rosny alone being allowed to retain his. The gouty governor was propped up in an easy chair to receive his visitors, and was civil enough until he perceived that some of the officers were chiefly interested in the towers and fortifications. Then he became evidently uneasy, which Rosny remarking, he declined to look further, pretending an unwillingness to give trouble.

Displeased at the manner by which a good round sum had been extracted from them, he impressed on the whole of his retinue the necessity, whatever might be offensively done or said to them, of always bearing in mind the rules of French politeness. Presumably, the numerous party slept on board the two large English vessels while at Dover. But when the time came for setting out for London, "the gentleman" on whom they depended for providing them with conveyances for the journey so utterly failed in his duty that he left them to provide accommodation for themselves, which appears to have been an affair of great difficulty.

Rosny and his secretaries travelled in the Comte de Beaumont's carriage; the rest of the party hired or bought at exorbitant prices any sorry nag or jolting vehicle they could meet with. On reaching Canterbury, matters improved, and they received a most hospitable welcome. But it was not from the English. The small town was densely populated by Walloon and Flemish refugees, who had fled from the persecuting Spaniards, and the cruelties inflicted on them as heretics. Rosny being a Protestant, they naturally treated him with much distinction. Never, he says, was he in any place received with more courtesy and warm-heartedness. He visited Canterbury Cathedral, which he thought a very fine edifice, and attended the service, whose solemnity greatly impressed him.

The next halting-place on this journey to London was Rochester. There again the scene changes. Certain marks, designed to show the travellers where they were to lodge for the night, were placed on the houses engaged to receive them. But the inhabitants so hated the French, that they effaced the marks and would not allow the unwelcome visitors to enter. Luckily for those who could obtain no shelter but that which their clumsy, comfortless vehicles afforded, it was summer, and genial weather prevailed.

The next day they reached Gravesend, where Rosny and his principal gentlemen embarked in the king's barges, and proceeded up the river to the Tower. There a salute in his honour was fired from the Tower guns; so prolonged and loud that it sent back his thoughts to Montemélian and the arsenal, and gladdened the heart of the *grand-maître de l'artillerie*, after the troubles and fatigues of his journey. Yet his troubles can scarcely be said to have ended here; for although a large number of conveyances awaited his landing, and it was decided that for a night or two the ambassador extraordinary should remain at the French Embassy, still no houses were secured for the temporary accommodation of his inconveniently numerous suite.

Arundel House, described as the finest palace in London, was preparing for the ambassador's reception. It contained an immense number of very fine rooms, but they were not yet ready for the guests, who for a fortnight or so disposed of themselves as best they could.

The aversion displayed by the people towards the French was attributed to the arrogance and superciliousness of Biron when on his mission to Queen Elizabeth, as well as to the dissolute conduct, the midnight brawls, and the too free use of the rapier which he tolerated in his cavaliers and very numerous household. The manners of the young Frenchmen of that day, Rosny declared, were very bad. He charges them with frivolity and effrontery, and of being so feather-brained that they were no more capable of circumspection in a foreign country than in their own. He, however, made known to all who accompanied him and were subject to his authority that nothing of the sort would be permitted by him, but that every breach of good manners would be rigorously punished.

A strictly vigilant eye was kept on the younger men of his suite. Notwithstanding, some of the more ardent spirits among them contrived to engage in a quarrel with several young Englishmen; swords were drawn, and one of the Englishmen killed. Rosny, being extremely vexed that his entry into London should be marked by so unpleasant an event, ordered the culprit who had done the deed to be arrested. A council was then assembled of the more elderly men of this retinue, and sentence of death was passed on him.

The young man was a relative of the Comte de Beaumont, who protested loudly against Rosny's proceedings. But he, in his usual high-handed manner, and utter disregard of the opinions of his opponents, ordered the count to leave the room; then despatched a messenger to the lord mayor requesting him to send in the morning six archers to conduct the criminal to the place of execution, and to order the attendance of the functionary whose business it would be to behead him. The lord mayor entreated him to moderate his severity and to impose a less severe punishment on the young man.

He replied that he would not revoke a sentence which no superior authority could prevent him from passing upon such an offender, — a sentence which would prove to the king, his master, and to the English nation, that he had done what duty required of him on so lamentable an occasion. But as he could not carry the sentence into effect, he would leave the matter in the hands of the lord mayor, and give up his prisoner to him, to be punished as he considered he ought to be according to the rules of English justice. It thus became a private affair between the mayor and the young man's relative, the ambassador De Beaumont, who, as Rosny imagined, bribed the lord mayor to liberate his prisoner and allow him to leave England.

The Marquis de Rosny had but a poor opinion of the English generally, "whose intense hatred of the French was the result," he said, " of their pride and presumption, no nation in Europe being more haughty, more disdainful, more deeply imbued with the idea of their own excellence. If you would believe them, intelligence and reason are to be found only in England. They adore their own opinions, and despise those of others, and never does the thought come into their minds either to listen to others or to distrust themselves; their pride inspiring them with the idea that they are in all respects superior to the rest of the nations of Europe."

A series of unpleasant incidents, ill-suited to give him an exalted opinion of England and the English, had certainly attended him from his departure from France to his arrival in London. As a set-off against this he might to a certain extent have placed, with some pride, the success of his mission. He had expected to find the court in mourning; consequently he and the whole of his retinue appeared in sable habiliments. But, to his surprise and even extreme chagrin — for he was an enthusiastic admirer of the great qualities of the late queen — the mourning garb, if not actually forbidden, was viewed with much disfavour. If the name of Elizabeth was ever mentioned, it was with a sort of contempt; and there was a desire, apparently, that, as far as was possible, it should be consigned to oblivion.

On the evening preceding his presentation to the king, Rosny was informed by the Comte de

Beaumont that the courtiers regarded his and his retinue's mourning attire as an affront to them; also that the king, so far from thanking him for the attention, would be extremely annoyed by it, and the negotiation he came to effect prove, from that very circumstance probably, a failure.* The next morning, therefore, the marquis and his suite, with much regret, laid aside their mourning; and later in the day, more brilliantly attired, the king's guards, commanded by the Earl of Derby, escorted him and his hundred and twenty gentlemen, the *élite* of his retinue, from Arundel House to the Thames, where they embarked for Greenwich. There the Earl of Northumberland received them and led the way to the palace through a vast concourse of people.

"Contrary to English custom," — for not even a glass of water, we are told, was ever offered to an ambassador, — "an elegant collation was served to them, and soon after it was announced that his majesty would receive *monsieur l'ambassadeur* in the throne-room." The room was already full,

---

* Though the court refrained from going into mourning, apparently to please James, and the queen's funeral was hastened that he might avoid attending it — lingering meanwhile on his journey and creating a batch of knights at every place he stopped at — yet fifteen hundred persons in deepest mourning voluntarily followed the funeral *cortège* to Westminster Abbey, though the plague was then raging in London. The mark of respect shown by the Marquise de Rosny to Queen Elizabeth's memory, if looked on with disfavour at court, was fully appreciated, he states, by the people.

and became crowded when, preceding him, the marquis's numerous *cortège* entered the apartment, and passed in defile before the king. James was so anxious to see the first minister and confidant of Henri IV. that, as soon as he caught sight of him, he rose and advanced several steps to meet him. This, the master of the ceremonies, in an undertone, hastened to remind him, was contrary to court etiquette.

His majesty then remarked aloud that "although he had received this ambassador in a manner contrary to the customary etiquette of the court, it must not be taken as a precedent for a like reception being given to others. He had a special esteem and regard," he said, "for the Marquis de Rosny, who also was much attached to him. He respected, too, the firmness with which he adhered to his religion, and his fidelity to the interests of his master, the King of France." This was very flattering to the marquis, and gave him hopes of prevailing on James to adopt Henri's views with reference to Spain and an alliance with France. The king afterwards conversed with him in private, making many inquiries concerning Henri's state of health and his passion for the chase, in which he professed himself his rival.

He was also interested in Rosny's religious views, and asked if he would attend the Protestant service in London.

He replied in the affirmative.

"Did he," the king inquired, "when speaking of the Pope, give him the title of his holiness?"

"To conform to the established usage of the court of France, he did so," Rosny rejoined.

James then sought to impress on him that it was a usage offensive to God, to whom alone could the quality of holiness be fitly ascribed.

Rosny answered that "it was not more sinful," he thought, "than that frequent custom of ascribing to kings and princes qualities to which, in truth, they had not the slightest claim."

James seemed to reflect for a moment, but made no reply. The subject was changed, and shortly after, the autograph letters from Henri IV. and his queen to James I. having been delivered and read, Rosny's first interview with the King of Great Britain came to an end.* The letters addressed to the queen were retained by the ambassador, as her majesty had not then left Scotland.

On the following Sunday James invited the marquis's suite of gentlemen to dine at Greenwich, he dining privately with the two ambassadors, who had previously accompanied him to church. There was a magnificent display of gold and silver plate at this private dinner, much of it of exquisite design, and enriched with precious stones.

* His majesty was about to retire to rest for awhile, it being his custom to spend a part of the afternoon in sleep — his siesta sometimes lasting until the evening.

The attendants served everything kneeling, which both surprised and displeased Rosny, who thought it a custom no less inconvenient than degrading, and more honoured in the breach than the observance. The King and Queen of France, the dauphin, the royal family generally, also the ambassador extraordinary and his colleague, were all toasted by James in a very convivial fashion, it being observed that he mingled no water with his bumpers of wine.

In their royal master's name and their own the ambassadors returned the compliment, Rosny not forgetting especially to mention the royal children. On hearing them thus pointedly referred to, James turned towards Rosny and said in a whispering tone, "The next bumper he would drink"—and he held his glass on high—"should be to the double union of the children of the two royal houses." This was one of the proposals Rosny was charged by Henri warily, and in his own name, to make to James; but as it had not yet been brought on the *tapis*, James's confidential whisper took him rather by surprise. He received it with every expression of joy, though he thought the occasion not happily chosen for the introduction of such a topic. He, however, availed himself of this opportunity to ask for a private audience.

Henri IV. had at first proposed to give Rosny a full power to sign a treaty with James I. in his name, but afterwards changed his mind, either at the suggestion of some jealous member of his council, or from an idea — being often very suspicious, even of his friend Rosny — that too much might be risked by it. He had therefore no letter of credence, and none was asked of him; his mission becoming thus ostensibly a mere complimentary one to James on his accession. But whatever he thought might be prudently suggested to the king was to be considered as emanating entirely from himself without any instructions from Henri, yet as representing what he doubtless would readily subscribe to should the king be similarly inclined.

Two or three private interviews, on the subject of an alliance with France against Spain, then took place. But Rosny did not form a high opinion of James. He thought him a man of some erudition, but of more penetration; of extreme pedantry, yet destitute of political wisdom; a lover of peace from indolence and love of ease; likely, therefore, to be governed by others, whether by his wife or "my lord Cecil," whom James had just raised to the peerage, with several of the ministers and a few of his own Scotchmen, after creating knights by the hundred.* But the wily ambassador flattered James, and gained his esteem and confidence.

* In the course of the first three months of his reign James dubbed upwards of 700 knights and created sixty new peerages.

A treaty of alliance between England and France was accordingly drawn up to be submitted to Henri IV., James promising on his royal word of honour to sign it immediately, if returned to him with Henri's signature approving the terms arranged between him and the ambassador Rosny. Although the latter relied but little on James's promise of secrecy, yet after exacting from him his most solemn form of oath ("by the Holy Eucharist") he ventured to impart to him some particulars of Henri's grand project — but feigning that it was entirely his own.

James listened with deepest interest while the French king's plan for abasing the power of Austria and for the readjustment and reorganisation of Europe was unfolded to him. It appealed to his speculative turn of mind as a vast conception, awakening interest, but, from his disinclination to labour or exertion, without leading him to take any active part in its realisation. However, the time had not yet arrived for that, though, as a step towards it, Rosny did induce his Britannic majesty to promise aid to the united provinces in their struggle with Spain. He had hitherto regarded them as in rebellion towards their legitimate sovereign; now, better informed, he declared that neither the provinces nor Ostend should be sacrificed to Spain.

The mission of the ambassador extraordinary now ended. He had succeeded better than he expected with powers so limited, and was anxious to return to France. His enemies were caballing against him in his absence, and Henri had urgently desired him to lose no time in returning. Very valuable presents were then made, first to the king — his queen being still absent — to "my lord Cecil" and other ministers, also to their wives and daughters. Rosny received for Henri IV. and Maria de' Medici portraits of the queen and of James I., King of Great Britain.*

The impatience of his gentlemen to get back to France induced the ambassador to venture on crossing the channel in unfavourable weather, contrary to the advice of the English admiral. A heavy storm placed the vessel in considerable danger; but at last, after tossing about for a day and a half, exposed to the fury of the elements, Rosny and his retinue were safely, but in terrible plight, landed at Boulogne. The king had sent post-horses, which conveyed them to Villers-Coterets, where he was anxiously awaiting the return of his ambassador.

---

* The congratulatory letters and presents to the queen were left with the Comte de Beaumont, to present to her majesty.

## CHAPTER XVI.

The Marquis's Return to France. — Finds the King Occupied with the Question of the Recall of the Jesuits. — The Council Request That Rosny May Join Them. — He Attends at the King's Desire. — Refuses to Take the Lead in the Matter. — Desires to Consult the King. — Discusses with Him the Disadvantages of Recalling so Dangerous a Set of Priests as the Brotherhood of Jesus. — The King's Reason for Allowing Their Return. — Mariana's Treatise on Royalty. — Father Cotton in Paris. — La Flêche Given to Them. — The Pyramid. — Death of Madame Catherine. — The Legate. — Calvin and Luther. — Concessions to Protestants. — Charenton.

HENRI was well satisfied with the result of Rosny's embassy. The terms of the proposed alliance between England and France also met with his full approval, and forthwith a treaty based upon them was drawn up in due form, signed by Henri IV., and despatched to James I. He immediately placed his signature to it, as he had promised the Marquis de Rosny that he would do. He also sent 7,000 Scotch troops to Flanders, to succour Ostend, which had been for upwards of two years besieged, and was still both defended and attacked with great vigour.

Henri now regretted that he had not given his ambassador *carte blanche* to act in his name, as he at first had intended. Greater advantages he perceived might then have been obtained from James.

He, however, declared his conviction that no other man in France would have done so much as Rosny had done with authority so limited. He was very anxious for particulars of the new Scottish court of London; also to hear Rosny's opinion of James I., King of Great Britain. Rosny had been particularly struck by the penetration evinced by the "British Solomon," as well as by his excessive pedantry, and is said to have pronounced him "the wisest fool in Christendom."

The king was amused by Rosny's account of his adventures, and James's evident enjoyment of the change for the better which he found in the comforts and luxuries of his English court, compared with that he had left; but Henri was sincerely grieved to hear that the memory of the great English queen was treated with so little respect that no court mourning was worn for her.

During the Marquis de Rosny's absence the question of the recall of the Jesuits had been under discussion, and was nearly decided in their favour by the king, and, fanatics and extreme zealots excepted, almost by the king only — moderate Catholics and Protestants being alike opposed to it. Clement VIII. was exceedingly anxious for the reëstablishment of the Order of Jesus in France. In 1599, during Henri's short-lived grief for his Gabrielle, the pontiff asked of the king passports for four Italian Jesuits, whose object was urgently to solicit the recall of their order.

The king's heart, if "dead at the root," as he had declared it to be, and incapable of reawakening to the tender emotions of love, might yet be in a condition of partly subdued sorrow favourable to the reception of religious impressions. Such a state of mind these wily priests would know so well how to turn to account — sympathising with the bereaved lover, while gently urging him to resignation and greater reliance in his grief on the consolations afforded by the Church.

When ushered into the king's presence at Fontainebleau, the Jesuits fell on their knees before him; but Henri promptly raised them. He would not allow, he said, the ministers of religion to make their appeal to him in so abject a posture. But whatever benefits the Brotherhood of Jesus may have sought to persuade the king that both he and the nation would derive from their recall to France, Henri was not at that time so completely master of his kingdom as to venture at once on taking decisive steps in a matter naturally so alarming to the Protestants, and sure to call forth very general opposition. Vague promises, therefore, were all they could then obtain from him.

Henceforth, however, Henri was continually beset by pressing entreaties from the court of Rome for the reëstablishment of the Jesuits in France. He was then seeking a divorce from Marguerite of Valois, which would doubtless have been granted with less delay had he then yielded to the prayer of those astute priests. Clement VIII. had been incessantly urged since 1598 to grant the necessary dispensation for legalising the marriage of the Duc de Bar with Madame Catherine. It was still refused; and the marriage, having taken place without it, and some portion of the usual ceremony also omitted, it was annulled by a pontifical brief and the bridegroom excommunicated.

Though this certainly was a far more serious affair than the divorce, yet Henri believed that the Jesuit fathers, so favoured by the Pope above other religious orders, would have overcome Clement's hostility to this mixed marriage, and the dispensation have been forthcoming. Their services, of course, could only be repaid by the extra privileges and increased facilities they would have claimed, in order to extend their influence as preachers, confessors, and teachers of youth. Henri's representative at Rome, as before mentioned, was Cardinal d'Ossat, a rather lukewarm supporter of the king's interests; presenting his requests to his holiness, but often expressing himself unfavourably towards them.

Constantly he advocated the recall of the Jesuits. As constantly the Marquis de Rosny opposed it, and mortified the intriguing cardinal exceedingly by suspending the payment of his pension. Taking advantage of Rosny's embassy to the court of James I., Ossat and his friends, the secretaries of state (Villeroy and Jeannin), urged on the king the advisableness of allowing the French Jesuits to return to their country. La Varenne — the king's confidential agent in his arrangements with his various mistresses, and in the detection and unravelling of political intrigues, schemes of assassination, etc. — especially declared himself the protector of the banished Jesuits.*

He hoped that his zeal on their behalf might eventually be repaid by the elevation of his two young sons to those high dignities in the Church which his ambition led him to covet for them.

When the king, in the early part of this year, was at Metz, four of the Jesuit community of Verdun — where, as also in some few houses in Languedoc and Guyenne, the Jesuits still continued to evade obedience to decrees of banishment — were brought to him by La Varenne, accompanied by their provincial, or superior. Their professed loyalty to the king made them anxious, according to their own report, to avail themselves of the opportunity of paying their court to him, and of supplicating the reëstablishment of their order in France. As usual, when introduced, they threw themselves on their knees at his feet, and he, as usual, would not allow

* La Varenne was also Henri's *maître d'hôtel* and *contrôleur des postes de France.*

these worthy ecclesiastics to assume that humble attitude.

The provincial, however, remained kneeling. He had prepared an address which was ·to be spoken by him as a suppliant in the name of the whole order. It was simply an entreaty that the king would rescind the cruel decree that banished them from their beloved France. When this harangue was concluded, Henri desired that it should be addressed to him in writing. He assured them that, for his own part, he wished them no harm whatever; then entered into familiar conversation with them, and kept them with him the whole day.

In the course of the following (Easter) week they paid him another visit. He then promised to reëstablish them; told the provincial to come to him in Paris, and to bring that famous preacher, Father Cotton, with him.

"I will have you there again," he said; "I esteem your presence useful to the people and advantageous to the state." He then embraced them, and bade them a very friendly adieu.

The Jesuits, of course, went on their way rejoicing, expecting the speedy realisation of his majesty's gracious promises. For the next few months little was heard of the recall of the Jesuits. The king's thoughts were then fully occupied by the change in his political relations with England and Scotland, by the death of his "good sister," Queen Elizabeth, and the accession of James VI. of Scotland to the throne of England; also with the arrangements for Rosny's embassy to the court of London.

This did not prevent their reminding him privately of his promises; but the reinstatement of the order in France was not a pleasant theme to discuss with the Marquis de Rosny. The provincial, however, and that amiable and insinuating *"persona grata,"* Father Cotton, omitted not to avail themselves of Henri's invitation to come to him in Paris, where the wily father, a finished courtier, made himself very agreeable to the king, and sought the favour of as many influential persons of the court as possible to support the aims of his order.

Mariana, a Spanish Jesuit, said to have been the most able man the Order of Jesus had yet produced, had recently published a treatise on Royalty, in which, after expressing himself in deep sympathy with Jacques Clément and his crime, he declared the murder of a usurper to be a perfectly legitimate act; also that if the rightful sovereign by his intolerable vices should imperil the safety of the state, or its religion, he might be declared by the States of the kingdom a common enemy. In which case every private person would have the right of putting him to death, either by open force, by stratagem, or even by poison.

This apology for regicide was published by royal permission, and dedicated to Philip III. It was approved by the royal censor of Spain (a Jesuit), and praised in the highest terms. Henri IV. is supposed to have been acquainted with this work, though it met with but little attention at the time in France, and to have been induced by its influence to recall the Jesuits. On Rosny's return from his embassy he found that the important question was definitely placed before a council nominated by the king for its due discussion, but which he spared the marquis the embarrassment of attending. Rosny therefore, though grieved exceedingly at the decision the dauntless Henri seemed to have arrived at from fear of the Jesuits' knife, was silent on the subject.

Leaving the king at Fontainebleau, he returned to Paris, and retiring again to the arsenal, resumed his duties of grand master of the artillery. He hastened also to inspect the state of the finances, which had been administered very much after the old system during his absence — king, queen, mistress, and others having duly availed themselves of it to put money in their purses. The numerous enemies of the Marquis de Rosny, who could not bring themselves to concur in his strict notions of right and wrong, were ever willing to seize on an opportunity of mortifying and annoying him. Though aware that Henri had fully made up his mind to recall the Jesuits to France, whatever might be the decision of the council, which he had assembled as a mere formality, they yet suggested to him the desirableness of being assisted in their discussion by the experience and opinions of M. de Rosny.

Accordingly, at the king's request, he attended the next meeting; but he declined to take the lead, and give them his views on the subject as they desired. He knew not, he said, what were his majesty's views, but thought it would be well that he should himself take part in the discussion, and explain what advantages he expected to result from the step he proposed to take. Until he knew that, he could give no opinion whatever, and he proposed for that reason at once to seek an interview with the king. This he appears to have done; but only on being commanded to speak his thoughts freely on the subject, would he utter a word of comment upon it.

"If the king had resolved to bring these dangerous priests again into France; to introduce, as might truly be said, an enemy into the country, of what avail was it," he asked, "to suggest arguments against it?"

"I will give all due consideration to your objections," replied the king.

It was evident, however, that Henri's determination to reinstate the Jesuits was irrevocably taken, and that no objections Rosny could offer would change it. He therefore merely said that he was unable to comprehend the king's resolve to receive an order of priests into favour from whom evil can only be looked for, whether as regarded the king personally, or the welfare of the state. He prayed, then, that his majesty would excuse him from taking part in a deliberation so utterly odious to him. He, however, reminded him that his grand project, based on religious tolerance and the concurrence of the Protestant states, would never be consented to by the Jesuits.

The king replied that "to his minister's numerous objections he had two motives to oppose: the first that by recalling the Jesuits, and treating them with the same favour and friendly feeling they had met with in Spain, they would soon forget that country to serve the interests of France. They would even serve her against Spain, as Father Mayus and other principal Frenchmen of the order had confidentially sworn to him — confirming it in the name of the whole society by the most solemn of oaths."

Rosny remained unconvinced. The idea of the Jesuits serving Henri IV. against Spain appeared to him very delusive.

"My second motive," resumed the king, "may perhaps have more weight with you. It concerns my private interests and personal safety, which I am persuaded render the recall of the Jesuits advisable. Should I deprive them of all hope of returning to France, and thus drive them to desperation, there is nothing they would hesitate to put in practice against me, even to the taking of my life. Better to die at once than to live in continual fear or expectation of the poisoned cup or the assassin's knife! I should be miserable!" Rosny made no reply; such a confession from the valiant Henri of Navarre both grieved and silenced him.*

The royal edict recalling the Society of Jesus to France was issued on the 3d of September, and caused general dissatisfaction. The Parliament of Paris declined to register it, and deputed the presidents, De Thou and Harlay, to remonstrate with the king. The latter spoke with considerable vehemence, but entirely in vain. Henri was becoming very despotic; a royal edict must not now be disputed, and its registration forthwith was peremptorily commanded. There were, however, many conditions attached to their recall to France, and all who availed themselves of it must be Frenchmen by birth.

The edict did but authorise them to remain in the cities of the South, where they had continued to reside since 1594, notwithstanding the edicts of expulsion. "They were required to make oath

---

* D'Aubigné also states that "whenever any of his friends privately urged him to reconsider his determination to recall the Society of Jesus to Paris, he would exclaim: 'Will you assure me of my life, and will you guarantee it to me?'" He thinks, he says, "the state of mind of that intrepid monarch most pitiable."

not to engage in anything prejudicial to the king's service or the peace of the kingdom — and this without any exception or mental reservation. They were to be subject to the laws of the realm, and amenable to the officers of the crown in cases similar to those of other ecclesiastics." No complaint of these restrictions was made by the Jesuits. The fact of their recall was sufficient for them; for the rest, the king, at their request, might be relied on to free them from any inconvenient conditions, or from too rigorous restraints being imposed on them, while minor ones they set aside altogether, without scruple.

Generally the interests of the order were greatly served by the wily Father Cotton, who, soon after — on the retirement of the Curé of Saint-Eustache — became confessor to the king, and a very influential favourite. An ecclesiastic better suited for that office could scarcely have been found. He was no rigid casuist, but, on the contrary, was always indulgent towards the weaknesses and frailties of his royal penitent; considerate, too, and sympathetic, — never distressing him by withholding absolution, or inflicting penances too severe.

Grateful for so much consideration, Henri would have obtained a cardinal's hat for his accommodating confessor; but the laws of the society forbade the Jesuits to accept any of the dignities of the Church, unless (and this was a recent innovation) at the express command or with the full sanction of the Pope. This would have, again, been readily granted, had not the reverend father very modestly but firmly declined the honour it was proposed to confer on him; being well aware that, from the weakness of Henri's character, he could, simply as Father Cotton, extract far more benefits for himself and his order than a cardinal's hat would have procured.

This was soon evident. The king authorised them not only to open new colleges at Bourges, Poitiers, Amiens, and other cities against the wish of the people, and contrary to the conditions of their recall, but consented to their reëstablishment in Paris, to the surprise and grief of numerous Catholics as well as Protestants. Many cities would not receive them. The Jesuits then complained to the king, whose intervention on their behalf was not always successful. At Poitiers and Amiens this was especially the case. Determined, however, to give his full support to his new favourites, he made them a present, at the suggestion of his confidential agent, La Varenne, of his château of La Flèche, in Anjou, which was speedily transformed into a very fine college, and most liberally endowed by the king.

One great desire of the Jesuits was to obtain the dismissal and disgrace of the Marquis de Rosny; and it is surprising to find how readily Henri lent an ear to accusations against this long-tried and trusted friend and minister,—accusations he must have known to be false, and having their origin only in the bad feeling of those who concocted them. At times the king would treat him with great coldness, affecting to believe that he was intriguing to obtain a final dismissal of the Jesuits from France. Rosny, however, heeded not the calumny of priests and courtiers, but continued diligently to perform the duties of the various offices he held until it should please his majesty to tire of his assumed restraint towards a minister so invaluable to him, and whose probity, prudence, and ability he knew full well were beyond question.*

* It seems singular that the young pages of the royal household, amongst whom were many youths of noble Protestant families, should have so readily united, notwithstanding their difference of creed, in disliking the Jesuits, and Father Cotton especially. The unpopularity of the Jesuits made it advisable that the reverend father should pay his visits to the Louvre in a coach, where, on his arrival, he was invariably saluted by the mischievous pages with one of the cries of old Paris, "Any old cotton or woollen rags to sell?" "Any old cotton?" "Old cotton!" This was complained of to the king, who ordered some of them to be flogged — probably the Protestants. All of them, however, took offence at it, and beat the Jesuit priest, the next time they met him, with the scabbards of their swords, — not deeming him worthy of chastisement with those dread weapons themselves, which were scarcely less harmless than the scabbards that contained them. No blood, therefore, was shed, nor did the reverend father complain even of a bruise. He indeed magnanimously interceded for his assailants with the king, who had proposed to punish them severely, but contented himself with expelling those daring youngsters from the court. — L'Estoile.

The many favours the king continued to bestow on the Jesuits induced those priests to devise some means of expressing their gratitude towards him. Father Cotton was fully aware that fear of assassination, suggested or encouraged by the Society of Jesus, was the real motive for their recall and the indulgence they now met with. Nothing, therefore, more appropriate, he thought, for their purpose could be devised then a condemnation of Mariana's treatise, "*De la Royauté*". It had been reprinted, and was then exciting much attention in Paris, greatly to the disadvantage of the society, being likely to cause a renewal of the struggle of the Parliament to obtain their expulsion.

In consequence it was decided by the Jesuits of France to condemn the work. While justifying themselves, they would be abating any fresh apprehensions of danger the king might have conceived by the revival of Mariana's regicidal teaching. Aquaviva, general of the Society of Jesus, approved and confirmed its condemnation, and, further, "issued a decree prohibiting henceforth the publishing, teaching, or private advising of anything tending to the detriment or injury of kings and princes.*

\* Aquaviva was the first Italian general of the " Company of Jesus." Mariana, who was a Spaniard, had used his utmost efforts to prevent Aquaviva's election; he therefore the more readily condemned Mariana's regicidal sentiments. Two or three years later Mariana was thrown into prison for publishing a work on the vices in the government of the Company of Jesus.

Notwithstanding this acknowledgment on the part of the Jesuits of the favour and support they had met with from the king, those reverend fathers were not yet wholly satisfied. One thing was wanting to complete their rehabilitation, — the destruction of the pyramid which in 1594 had been erected on the site of the house where the Jesuit student, Jean Chastel, was born. This pyramid, which was twenty-one feet in height, had on it four side-slabs of black marble, on which was engraven a statement of the regicide's deed, with the part that the Jesuit priests were believed to have had in it; also the decree of expulsion.

The removal of the slabs did not satisfy them, and there seems to have been an unwillingness to demolish the pyramid. So much general dissatisfaction was expressed at what the king had already done for the Jesuits that the injured suppliants were entreated by Father Cotton, respecting this pyramid, to be for awhile more patient. Patience had also become necessary on the part of the king, so rapidly did the requests and demands of the Company of Jesus succeed each other. He began also to fear — as, indeed, he told them — that the royal authority would be compromised; the letters he had written at their entreaty respecting the building and endowment of new churches and colleges at Amiens, Poitiers, and other large towns, having in many instances been wholly disregarded.*

In the early part of this year a domestic affliction — the death of his sister, Madame Catherine, Duchesse de Bar — occasioned great grief to the king. Though supposed to be very much attached to his sister, he certainly displayed but little kindness towards her. He was himself very unwell when the news of her death was received, and in consequence it was for some days concealed from him. As soon as it was made known to him, he retired to his private apartments, and declined to receive any visits for eight or ten days. "It was only when alone with God," he said, "that he found any consolation."

All the court went into mourning, including the queen's household and the foreign ambassadors, with the sole exception of the papal nuncio, who excused himself on the ground that the princess had lived and died a Calvinist.

"Tell him," said the king, when informed of it, "that I will not insist on his wearing mourning, but that I shall decline to receive him until the period of mourning is ended."

The nuncio then put himself into mourning, and

---

* The king did not consent to order the destruction of the pyramid until May, 1605. It was then replaced by a handsome fountain. The four statues which had occupied the four corners of that memento of a dastardly crime were deposited in the grottoes of Saint-Germain.

requested an audience of the king, when, instead of the usual complimentary condolences on the death of Madame Catherine, he told the king of the Pope's fear for his sister's salvation, as she had died without the pale of the Church. So ill-timed a communication irritated Henri, and he replied rather warmly:

"To think worthily of God, one must believe it possible that, as the last breath is drawn, some ray of light illumines the mind, and renders the sinner, whoever he may be, in a fit state to enter heaven. I have no doubt of my sister's salvation, and I will not allow it to be doubted in my presence."

The nuncio, perceiving his error, made his excuses, with which the king seemed satisfied.

It was reported that Madame Catherine was "helped to die," and that to the dispensation so long sought and now granted was appended her sentence of death. She had not even the satisfaction of knowing that the Duc de Bar was freed from the persecution he had suffered on account of her heresy, as the dispensation was not received at Nancy until two days after she died.

Her château at Fontainebleau the king gave to Maria de' Medici, that at Saint-Germain to Madame de Verneuil. Her hôtel at Paris, built by Jean Bullant for Catherine de' Medici, who had taken a dislike to the Tuileries (before that edifice was nearly completed), was sold by order of the king, and was bought by the Comte de Soissons.

It was a magnificent residence — one of Bullant's *chefs d'œuvre*. The chapel was of remarkable elegance. After its purchase by the count, it was called l'Hôtel Soissons until the demolition of the building, which took place in 1749. The lofty Doric column — where Catherine de' Medici and her astrologers nightly studied the courses of the stars, seeking to discover by their movements the secret purposes of the Ruler of the universe — was left standing, and still exists.

The princess was buried at Vendôme, by the side of her mother, Queen Jeanne d'Albret.

Pondering in seclusion on the sad end of his sister's melancholy romance, and the part he had had in rendering her life unhappy, may have prompted the wish the king then expressed of making some concessions to the Reformers — of doing something for the benefit of the "people of the religion," to whom she had so steadfastly clung — by way of atonement for the wrong he had done her, for her cruel disappointments and her blighted life. Now that death had irrevocably broken the family tie he had been anxious should unite the Houses of Bourbon and Lorraine, the relations between France and Spain had become more embittered than before, and he was also in fear of a rising of the Huguenots in arms against him.

To this the chroniclers of the period attribute his desire to do something in their favour, rather than to any respect for his sister's memory. They had threatened, on the recall of the Jesuits, to seek the protection of a foreign prince, and but lately, as a preliminary, had held a general synod at Gap to consider once more the question of the possible fusion of Calvinism and Lutheranism. It was earnestly and anxiously discussed, but, as on former occasions, with no successful result. As has been observed, Calvinists and Lutherans came very readily to an agreement when arguing against Rome, but were as far as ever from coming to any satisfactory understanding amongst themselves.

They, however, decided on declaring the maxim, "The Pope is antichrist," an article of faith, — a decision most embarrassing to Henri, who forbade indefinitely the publication of the confession of faith which contained that article. As a compensation very satisfactory to them, but displeasing to the Jesuits and the Catholics generally, he authorised the establishment of a Protestant church or meeting-house at Saint-Maurice, near Charenton. This was annulling the promise made to the Parisians in 1594, and by the Edict of Nantes of 1598, that no public place of worship should be permitted to the Reformers within ten leagues of the capital. Charenton was not more than two leagues distant.

But Henri thought that whatever concession he

made to the Reformers, it must be one of importance, to counterbalance the favours conferred on, and solicited by, the Company of Jesus. The Reformers availed themselves to the full of the king's concession, and Charenton, so conveniently near the capital, became one of the principal centres of Protestantism.

## CHAPTER XVII.

*Henri Surrounded by Traitors. — Nicolas de Hoste Drowned While Escaping. — D'Auvergne Resumes His Intrigues with Spain. — The Marquise Aims at Supplanting the Queen. — She Vows Vengeance on Her Rival. — Scene with the King. — The Marriage Promise Laid at Her Majesty's Feet. — A Brief Space of Tenderness. — Domestic War Renewed with Vigour. — The Marquise Promised an Asylum in Spain. — Henri Entreats Her to Return to Him. — Disdainful Refusal. — A New Mistress Taken. — Arrest of D'Auvergne. — D'Entragues and the Marquise. — Sentence of Death on the Former. — The Marquise Imprisoned in Her Château. — The Queen Pledges the Crown Jewels. — Death of Clement VIII. — Cost of Making a Pope. — Death of Théodore de Bèze. — Marguerite's Return to Paris.*

THE reëstablishment of the Jesuits in France failed either to restore the king's tranquillity of mind, respecting his personal safety, or to release him from the political intrigues of Spain. With almost the sole exception of the Marquis de Rosny, Henri was surrounded by traitors in the pay of Philip III., who bought the secrets of French diplomacy even in the ministerial cabinet, where Villeroy's first secretary, Nicolas de Hoste, sold them to him. When discovered, favoured by Villeroy, he took to flight, and to escape pursuit attempted to swim across the Marne. The river being much swollen and turbulent from recent excessive rain, the disloyal secretary was drowned. If some suspicion rested on Villeroy, nothing was proved against him; he therefore retained his post of chief foreign secretary.

Another traitor was the recently pardoned Comte d'Auvergne, who was plotting against the king and carrying on his intrigues under shelter of the king's own cover. After the free pardon which Henri, at the instance of his mistress, had bestowed on D'Auvergne, the latter had urged, as if to show his gratitude for the favour vouchsafed him, that "by seeming to keep on the same good terms as formerly with the Spanish government, he would be able to warn the king of all their schemes against him, and to facilitate the arrest of the persons concerned in them." But the office of spy which this son of a king was so anxious to assume for Henri's advantage, as he pretended, he continued to pursue for the benefit of the Spanish government and to the detriment of that of France.

He was then concerned, conjointly with his stepfather, the Comte d'Entragues, and in the name of his half-sister, Madame de Verneuil, in a plot which, if unlikely to succeed in its object, — that of supplanting Queen Maria de' Medici and the dauphin by the Marquise de Verneuil and the legitimised Henri de Bourbon, her son, — was at least calculated still further to destroy the domestic peace of the royal household. There was reason also for fearing that it might give rise to much political disquietude, owing to the restless and unsatisfactory state of parties in France, and the general feeling of displeasure created by the ever increasing favour lavished on the unpopular Jesuits.

The marquise's project was received with much favour by the Spanish king. A promise of unstinted support was given to her agents, also an assurance of a safe retreat in Spain, with large pensions both to the marquise and her family, and especially to the asserted heir to the French throne, though he was not the child referred to in the king's eventual promise of marriage. That worthless document appears to have been eagerly seized on by Philip III. and his ministers, as affording, by and by, judiciously managed, an incitement to a war of succession.

The marquise, as a preliminary step, had lately declared in the presence of persons who, as she knew, would repeat it to the Concini, and they again to the queen, her determination of publicly asserting her own and her son's claims to the throne. This so enraged her majesty — between whom and Madame de Verneuil a sort of reconciliation had lately taken place, the queen, to the amazement of many ladies of the court, having received her with far more courtesy than was shown to some of the princesses — that she vowed vengeance on her rival, and again vehemently protested that she would take her life.

When the king made his appearance, the reception accorded him was, if possible, more violent than any he had before encountered. But ere he could escape from the presence of the infuriated queen, she exacted from him, under the pain of appealing to the Pope for redress, the placing in her hands of this marriage promise, which, as she said, served his mistress with a plea for continually insulting her. Henri, whose rage against his mistress was, for the moment, scarcely less than his wife's, vowed, as he left the room, that this promise of marriage, valueless though it was, should be given up to him, if not willingly, then by force.

But when the king demanded this document of Madame de Verneuil, she, in her turn, flew into a rage; declared that she had it not, and that he must seek it elsewhere, accompanying her refusal to obtain it for him with the most aggravating language. The king reproached her with her infidelities, and, as she afterwards herself told the Marquis de Rosny, they "almost came to blows," so extreme was his anger, so tauntingly provoking both her words and manner.

The promise was, however, obtained from the Comte d'Entragues, who was well aware that he could not resist the king's will in this matter, and that even so, the promise was of no value whatever. He therefore generously consented to place it in the king's hands, on condition of receiving from him an acknowledgment that he had done so; in which should be clearly stated — "for the sake of his daughter's honour" — the terms and nature of the promise. Further, that, for this concession, the sum of 20,000 crowns should be immediately paid to the Marquise de Verneuil, and that the king should confer on him (though he had never been in battle) the brevet rank of Marshal of France.

Henri had the complaisance to accede to these terms, and, as soon as the interesting document was restored to him, hastened to lay it at the feet of his queen. His speedy compliance with her wishes appears to have had the effect of putting her into a more amiable mood, and once more Henri IV. and Queen Maria de' Medici were duly reconciled, and past errors mutually pardoned. Even Rosny ventured to hope that the reconciliation now effected would prove of longer duration than former ones, — the queen having written to thank the king "in a letter of much submissiveness, tenderly expressed."

Their reciprocal tender attachment was for several days an edifying spectacle to the whole court, who welcomed this new order of things with great joy and approbation. The queen may, perchance, have hoped to keep the king closely chained to her girdle. But Henri being an unwilling captive, and Maria de' Medici afflicted with an ungovernable temper, their affectionate reunion, from which domestic peace and happiness were augured, came speedily, as on preceding occasions, to an untimely end, — the war in the royal palace being resumed, when the short truce ended, more vigorously than ever.

It seems to have been a custom of the time to have one or more spies attached to the embassies at the various European courts, so that Henri was not wholly dependent on the amateur espionage of the Comte d'Auvergne, of whose treachery he was soon informed, copies of letters from the Marquise de Verneuil showing her complicity in the intrigue carried on by her father and brother with Spain being also forwarded to him. She had feigned alarm at the hatred the queen, she said, bore to her, and requested the king's permission to ensure a retreat for herself and her children out of the country, in case of his death. But instead of endeavouring to secure, as the king supposed was her intention, an asylum in England, he learnt from his private agents that she was in communication with the court of Spain.

Great, then, was the irritation of Madame de Verneuil when, besides the annoyance she felt at the marriage promise having been exacted from her father by the king, she became aware that her intrigue with Spain was discovered, and that the arrangement made with her by Philip III. through the Spanish ambassador, De Taxis, securing her a safe retreat in Spain and the recognition of her son as Dauphin of France, was no longer a secret.

Immediately she broke off all intercourse with the king, and would receive neither letter nor communication of any kind from him. His anger towards her, however, soon abated, anxious fears taking its place, for a report was circulated, intended for the king's ears, that the marquise was about to retire for the rest of her life to a convent. He had then the weakness humbly to appeal to her to return to him. She disdainfully refused.

Thinking to vex her — though she well knew that the lively Comtesse de Moret then reigned supreme — he took another lady companion, to whom he gave a large estate with the title of Comtesse de Romorantin.

The marquise none the less continued to treat the king with haughty disdain, and his efforts to induce her again to smile upon him and return to the court with contemptuous silence. He at length, losing all patience, and finding that her brother and father continued their intrigues, scarcely deeming it worth while to make any secret of it, ordered the arrest of the Comte d'Auvergne, the Comte d'Entragues, and finally of the Marquise de Verneuil herself. D'Auvergne, warned of this, secretly left the court, proposing never to return to it, and announcing that "on the slightest sign of any plot hatching against him he would leave the country altogether." He then shut himself up in an old fort in the Forest of Auvergne, and writing to his wife to send him "a supply of good cheese and mustard, and to trouble herself about nothing more," he prepared to stand a siege. After giving much trouble, he was one day induced by an artifice to leave his stronghold for a few minutes, when he was overpowered by men lying in ambush to seize him, and was conveyed to the Bastille.

Accused of high treason, the marquise and her relatives appeared before the magistrates of the Sovereign Court of Paris appointed by the king to examine the proofs of their crime and to give judgment in the matter. After due consideration the court decided that the crime of high treason was fully proved against the Comte d'Auvergne and the Comte d'Entragues, upon whom sentence of death was passed. The marquise was ordered to be imprisoned until more ample proof against her was forthcoming. The accusation of conspiring to assassinate the king was set aside as untenable, but the council were unanimous in their recommendation that justice should have its course.

But as Henri could not decide on condemning the son of the infamous Charles IX., and the last of his worthless race, to lose his head on the scaffold, he commuted the sentence of death to that of perpetual imprisonment in the Bastille, both to D'Auvergne and D'Entragues, ending soon after by a full pardon to the latter. The marquise had yet to be disposed of; but that no harm could happen to her, whatever might be the sentence of the judges, Henri had taken steps to let her know. He yet hoped that she would be at least so far subdued by what had occurred as to solicit his pardon.

She was a prisoner in her own château, which was vigilantly guarded; but not a word of supplication for release would she utter. Soon, however, she began to weary of her forced seclusion, which Henri, who visited her daily as her chief gaoler, perceiving, proposed as the price of her liberty the renewal of their *liaison*. After considerable hesitation on her part, he succeeded in inducing her to consent, on conditions which she alone dictated, one of them being her father's pardon, another that her innocence of the crime of which she had been accused should be published throughout France.

This great trial, which for some time occupied much of the public attention, was generally believed to have had for its main object the constraining Madame de Verneuil to consent to a reconciliation which the king found he could not otherwise so readily effect. But he did not release or pardon the Comte d'Auvergne. Though he spared his life, he thought him a dangerous character whom, having secured, it would be better to keep from further troubling the state by placing him under lock and key.*

The king was probably the only person to whom the final result of this state trial was wholly satisfactory. The queen was highly indignant at the insult offered to her by the part the king had played in it, and shed a deluge of tears. She complained, too, to the Marquise de Rosny — who on this occasion was deputed to comfort her — that several of the courtiers had been emboldened by the king's neglect to speak to her of love, and that Concini advised her to inform the king. Madame de Rosny excused herself from advising in such a matter. But when Concini, who was present, left the apartment, she told the queen it would be highly imprudent to make such a communication to the king, as he might suppose either that she had given some occasion for such temerity, or that she wished, by wrongfully accusing them, to banish persons whom she disliked from the court.

---

* An attempt was made by D'Entragues in the first year of D'Auvergne's imprisonment to aid his stepson in escaping from the Bastille; but when all preparations were made, the persons in their confidence betrayed them. D'Entragues was interrogated on the subject, but on simply declaring that he knew nothing about it, though it was evident that he knew everything, he was pronounced absolved from all participation in the attempt — the result of having two powerful friends at court. D'Auvergne was more closely confined and was not released until some years after, in the next reign.

Her majesty promised to follow the advice given her; but when Rosny heard of her complaint, he thought it a mere ruse to divert attention from the very confidential terms she appeared to be on with some of the gay cavaliers of the court. For himself, the whole proceeding, he declared, annoyed him, while the king's weakness greatly grieved him. He had recommended that Madame de Verneuil should be sent across the Channel, and the Concini and other Italians over the mountains; but the king was unable to impose any restraint either on himself or the queen.

Again the marquis thought of withdrawing from the court and occupying himself with the superintendence of his buildings and the cultivation of his estates. But the more numerous and important his various offices and charges became, the more unwilling he was to resign them into incompetent or untrustworthy hands, so that, while resolving to give up public life, he still stayed on, for the good, as he hoped, and as it really was, of both the king and the state. As to the king, he began wholly to despair of him, and was himself utterly weary of being continually called upon to attempt the task, under the circumstances, as repugnant to him as in itself it was useless, of interceding with the queen for a reconciliation, rarely fated to endure throughout a second day, unless cemented by a large pecuniary bribe.

Maria de' Medici's prodigality was excessive,

and but recently she had even ventured to dispose of the crown diamonds and other jewels reserved for the use of the queens of France, in order to celebrate with great *éclat* her Italian gardener's wedding, and to make valuable, but very unsuitable, presents to the gardener's bride. Rosny was requested by Henri immediately to redeem them from the hands of the Italian Abbé Rucellai, who had had the audacity to buy them, or to hold them as a pledge for the money advanced — a proceeding which subjected him to severe punishment. But the henpecked royal husband shrank from a scene with the wrathful Maria, and beyond a few words of reproof, the *abbé's* indiscretion passed unnoticed.

By a similar process (an order on the treasury for a large sum of money) were the smiles of the favourite wooed back when she chose to flout and frown on the lover she heartily contemned; while Henri, who became more than ever a reckless gambler, required some thousands of *pistoles* every night to lose at Zameti's. It seemed to have been M. de Rosny's custom to hand him a purse full of gold every evening; but though well filled, it rarely covered his losses, payment then being often made in chains and rings, strings of pearls, and other jewels. In vain the careful minister remonstrated with his extravagant sovereign, and occasionally declined to pay his mistresses, and even the queen, his orders on the treasury — reminding him of the necessity of economy, if the "grand project" was ever to be carried out.

The king would sometimes revert, as an excuse for his mode of life, to the hardships and vexations he had experienced in his early years, when the inadequacy of his means compelled him to forego almost the bare necessaries of existence for the sake of keeping his few troops together. "Surely he might now," he said, "consider himself entitled to take his ease and enjoy some of the pleasures of life." But Rosny could discern no pleasure for a king and valiant soldier in the life he described, and usually led, with occasional fits of devotion to affairs of state.

Affairs of state had been in a measure neglected — at least by the king, though Rosny's vigilance had by no means abated — during the progress of the trial of the marquise and her relatives. While that was occupying public attention, Clement VIII. passed away, — an event of some importance to France, for, partly to gain favour and influence with him, Henri had brought back the Jesuits, and permitted several other religious orders to establish themselves in his kingdom.

Clement VIII. had occupied the chair of Saint Peter thirteen years; but in the last year of his life he may be said to have been Pope in name only, — his nephew, Cardinal Aldobrandino, having then fulfilled the pontiff's duties, he being reduced bodily to a state of utter helplessness, and mentally to imbecility. Great exertions were made to place Cardinal de' Medici, the queen's uncle, on the papal throne, and the news of his election, having taken place on the 1st of April, was received by both king and queen with great satisfaction, though from different motives. The auspicious event was celebrated in France with every demonstration of joy, — *Te Deums*, bonfires, ringing of bells, all the cannon in the grand master's now well-filled magazines being brought into requisition, with a command from the king not to be sparing of gunpowder.

But while the accession of the new Pope, who had taken the name of Leo XI., was being joyously celebrated, the startling news of his death was received. He was taken ill on the 17th on returning from the procession to San-Giovanni Laterano, where the Popes are crowned, and died on the 27th — perhaps poisoned; for there were several disappointed Italian and Spanish candidates for papal honours, and it was well known to Philip III. that France had spared no expense to secure the election of a Pope entirely devoted to French interests. Du Plessis-Mornay states that Leo XI. cost France not less than 300,000 crowns.

Cardinal Borghese was chosen to succeed him, and ascended the papal throne as Paul V.* The

---

\* Clement had left to his successor the decision of the dispute between the Spanish Jesuits, Molinists, and the Dominicans, on the subject of "grace and free-will." Paul merely prohibited same outward demonstrations of joy celebrated the election of Cardinal Borghese as had been ordered by the king for the cardinal's predecessor, except that bonfires were prohibited. Zealous Catholics were anxious to know the reason for this slight, as it was termed, on the new pontiff, and were informed that bonfires were ordered on the previous occasion only because of his holiness, Leo XI., being the queen's near relative.

Maria dè' Medici was, doubtless, much grieved at the unexpected death of her uncle, in whom she had hoped to find a powerful protector and supporter of her queenly rights against the king and his mistresses — while the king had looked forward to usefully employing Leo's restraining influence on the Jesuits, whose encroachments now hampered him exceedingly in his efforts to hold the balance true in his relations towards his Catholic and Huguenot subjects.

The destruction or retention of the Pyramid had again become a subject of angry dispute between Protestants and Catholics who favoured the Jesuits. Henri was besieged by memorialists and petitioners, urging on the one hand the immediate destruction of the offensive and slanderous monument, while on the other were earnest pleadings for its retention as "a souvenir of the

their treating each other as heretics; his care and attention being chiefly given to the improving and embellishing of Rome, and to collecting the finest works in painting and sculpture.

interposition of Heaven in turning aside the assassin's knife when aimed at the heart of their beloved sovereign."

Henri feared the Jesuits too much to give heed to the Huguenots' prayer. His amiable confessor also told him he was partly pledged to the removal of the pillar. Weary of this fertile and ever recurring subject of complaint, he gave immediate orders for the demolition of that memento of the Jesuit student's deed. The people of "the religion" declared that the king's ears were now so stuffed with cotton that the voice of Justice, however loud she cried, could no longer succeed in penetrating it and obtaining a hearing.

In October of this year the Huguenots lost one of their most able and faithful ministers, Théodore de Bèze, who died at Geneva at the patriarchal age of eighty-seven, from sheer exhaustion and decay of nature. From an early age he had accompanied his people through all their wanderings, and had been present at their battles, sharing their hardships and speaking words of comfort and consolation to them when courage began to fail them under affliction and persecution. He appears to have had a great esteem for M. de Rosny, to whom he sent a farewell message with a book, "*Le Trésor de Piété*," which he had dedicated to him.

L'Estoile, referring to the death of the aged Calvinist minister, says it occurred two days after the great eclipse of the sun, a total one, apparently, the darkness being intense, lasting upwards of two hours, and greatly alarming the timid. The astrologers turned it to advantage, and prophesied evils innumerable about to overwhelm France and her king. "The weather," he continues, "was terrific, — raging storms and tempests; many shocks of earthquake were also felt; many dogs went mad, and deaths from hydrophobia were frequent. Every kind of vice and impiety reigned in this extraordinary season. Robberies and assassinations were of daily and nightly occurrence; lackeys were insolent to their masters, and some of them were hanged.

"Several coiners of false money were discovered and arrested, and as regards weather, the new year menaces us with a beginning worse than the ending of the old one. The skies, with their continuous downpour, seem to weep for our sins, and for the absence of the fear of God, which truly is now nowhere found amongst us; while, to complete the general distress, an epidemic rages. It has alarmed the king, for it is not confined to Paris, but extends even to Fontainebleau, where he had his children with him. Without a day's delay they have been removed to Saint-Germain, which he considers a more healthy locale. The whole family has been sent there." *

* L'Estoile, *Journal de Henri IV.*; Mathieu, *Histoire de France.*

In the midst of the series of disasters, storms, tempests, and earthquakes of this eventful or most extraordinary season, as L'Estoile rightly terms the winter of 1605 and 1606, Marguerite de Valois reappeared at the court of France after an absence of twenty-five years. From the time that Clement VIII. pronounced Marguerite and Henri divorced, 1599, permission had been given her to return to the court. She had not availed herself of it, because of her attachment to the old Château d'Usson, and the discreditable kind of life she is reported to have led there. The proposed dismissal of the garrison — maintained there at her expense — with the intended demolition of the fortress, considered in an unsafe condition, probably suggested her return to Paris, instead of accepting another château offered her in lieu of Usson. Some information she was able to give concerning the intrigues of Spain with the Huguenot chiefs in Auvergne obtained for her the confidence and approval of M. de Rosny.

To receive her communication he met her at Cercote, on his way to attend the Huguenot Synod at Châtellerault, taking his wife with him to pay her respects to the ex-queen. The king ordered a distinguished reception to be given her, and sent his eldest son, César de Vendôme, accompanied by the dissolute Duc de Roquelaure, with M. de Château-Vieux representing the queen, to compliment her on arriving at the Château de Madrid, in the Bois de Boulogne, which temporarily she chose for her abode. Thence she removed to the Hôtel de Sens, and afterwards to a house in the Faubourg Saint-Germain.

Personal visits were then exchanged, Marguerite, according to Rosny — whose favour and protection she had adroitly secured — "behaving with perfect dignity and discretion, yet in a manner so gracious and graceful that none would have suspected that the marriage-tie had ever subsisted between her and the king." Truly, in years gone by, they had seen but little of each other, and that little very unwillingly. The king, however, after saluting her with his usual gallantry, made it clearly evident that he knew, or had known, something of her habits, by recommending her to take better care of her health, and not turn night into day and day into night, as of old.

He also spoke freely of the necessity of conducting her household with some regard to economy, and of restraining her tendency to excessive liberality, or rather prodigality. The queen was sufficiently pleased with her predecessor, and on the whole kept on good terms with her; while Marguerite, following the advice earnestly impressed on her by M. de Rosny, wisely abstained from taking any part in the quarrels between king, queen, and mistresses. Maria de' Medici saw that she had now nothing to fear from the youth or beauty of Henri's divorced wife. If Marguerite ever possessed the charms which, like all princesses, she was credited with in her youthful days, no trace of them now remained. She was two years older than Henri — who was then fifty-three — and, like Catherine de' Medici, as she advanced in years, Marguerite's *embonpoint* became excessive.

Her return to the court was hailed by men of letters with much satisfaction. They found in her a munificent patroness, and a liberal entertainer twice a week at her residence in the Faubourg Saint-Germain. On those occasions her hôtel was lighted up by many hundreds of wax candles, which shed their mild radiance over gloomy old Paris, transforming her house into a brilliant beacon, more lustrous from the intensity of the surrounding darkness.*

* Marguerite de Valois survived the assassination of Henri IV. five years, dying in the odour of sanctity, March 27, 1615. She was buried in the church of the Convent of Les Petits Augustins, of which she was the foundress.

## CHAPTER XVIII.

Preparations at the Bastille for Securely Depositing the State's Savings. — A Council Summoned. — Diminution of Taxation Recommended as Preferable to Hoarding. — The Council Dismissed with Thanks. — The Army Reorganised. — Troops in Training. — The Artillery Increased. — Fortifications Erected on a New System. — Bridges Rebuilt. — Marshes Drained. — New Roads Opened and Planted with Elms. — Rosny's Traducers. — The King's Coldness. — Explanations. — Rosny Created Duc de Sully and Peer of the Realm. — Bouillon Refuses to Surrender. — The March on Sedan Prevented by the King's Gout. — Meyrargues and Jean de Lille. — Sully's Reception as Councillor of Honour.

SINCE Henry IV. had given the post of Governor of the Bastille to the Marquis de Rosny, many arrangements had been carried out in that fortress for conveniently and safely depositing the "savings of the state." It was not merely for the security of savings in prospective he was preparing his chests and strong boxes, but for some millions already in hand. So ably had he managed the revenues of France, that, after putting an end to what he termed the organised pillage so long prevailing in that department — from its superintendent to the humblest clerk or messenger employed in it — he had accomplished in five years the amazing result of freeing the king from the thirty-two millions of liabilities he had contracted in payments and pensions promised to princes, governors and captains for their submission to him, and for the subjection of the cities held by the League. In other words, the purchase of the kingdom was completed.

Sixty-seven millions, due to Henri's allies for their assistance in money or troops, were in satisfactory and gradual course of payment. Twenty millions of arrears of taxes had also been remitted to the people, the peasantry especially, who had been brought to deepest poverty by the ravages and miseries of the long-continued civil wars. But fruitful France rapidly recovered herself, and the agricultural districts, under renewed care, again produced the fruits of the earth in abundance.

Many of the nobility, too, finding that war had really given place to peace, and that their occupation was necessarily gone, instead of idling away life at a court scarcely less immoral than that of the Valois, had retired for a time, as the king advised them, to their châteaux to superintend the cultivation of their estates, and thus to retrieve, as many did, a portion of the losses — in some instances almost ruinous — which the late wars had brought on them. Generally, therefore, prosperity had returned to France, and the king, as well as others, or his ministers for him, was putting away, in spite of reckless extravagance, his *économies royales* in the strong boxes of his *château-fort*.

The king's savings consisted of the residue of the quarter's revenue after all charges upon it were defrayed. When sufficient in amount (not less, Rosny calculated, than forty-five millions for a war of three years), and the scheme ripe for execution, then the "grand project" was to be attempted, and the savings employed for its realisation, — the humbling of the power of the House of Austria, and the division of Europe into fifteen states, forming a sort of Christian Republic. The management of this fund, and the manner of transferring the money from the ministry of finance to the coffers of the Bastille and the safe custody of its governor, was privately arranged between the king and his minister.

Yet Henri thought it necessary, though regarding it as a mere formality, and even a condescension on his part, to assemble a council in order to notify the fact to the persons employed to take part in the government of the country, in a manner somewhat less absolute than declaring the resolutions of the sovereign already determined on. He did not tell the council of the grand project, — that was a secret known only to Henry IV. and Rosny, James I. of England, and Maurice of Hesse, *le savant*, — but he reminded them of the inconveniences and hardships his troops had undergone from his frequent want of means to pay them, and the conquest of his kingdom retarded from the same inconvenient circumstance. He had, therefore, resolved, he said, to provide against the recurrence of such a calamity should any war be unexpectedly thrust upon him, while at the same time he proposed to diminish, or, if possible, entirely remove, any tax pressing heavily on the people. With as much sincerity as when he addressed the notables at Rouen, he assured them that when they had deliberated on the matter he would be ready to follow any good counsels they might be prepared to give him. The council, having deliberated, and come to the conclusion that instead of hoarding the surplus revenue it would be better to employ it in diminishing the burden of taxation, suggested as a commencement the abolition of the *gabelle*, or salt-tax, which Rosny himself qualified as "an impost at once cruel and ludicrous." The king thanked the council for their advice; said he would reflect on it, then courteously dismissed them.

The savings would, indeed, have been of larger amount could Henri have been induced to practise the wise economy urged on him by his minister. However, during the five years just elapsed, Rosny had not only brought order out of disorder in the administration of the finances of the state, and put an end to the peculations of the financiers, but in his office of *grand-maître* he had placed the artillery on a footing of efficiency it had not hitherto attained in France. Cannon of larger calibre were founded, rendered necessary by changes and improvements in the art of war, and in the construction of fortifications. Several fortresses were then repaired and furnished with bastions, according to the new system then introduced by Érard de Bar-le-Duc, Marchi, and other engineers of repute.*

The reorganisation of the army occupied both the king and his minister, it being resolved to arm France in a manner formidable both for attack and defence. Its military reputation had declined. Every man was, indeed, supposed to be a soldier, but of good soldiers, amenable to discipline, very few were to be found. Many general officers, also, whose bravery was undoubted, and who were impetuous for the attack, were often destitute of the qualities, so important in war, of vigilance and attention; of the sure eye that decides at a glance on the success of a battle, or of the wisdom of knowing when to defer it.†

The great military renown the Hollanders had recently acquired in their long and desperate struggle against Spain had led to the remark that "the Hollanders made war, while the French only fought." Efforts were therefore to be made to raise the French soldier to the same high level. He was to be highly trained, well equipped, paid

* J. Servan, *Guerres des Français*.   † *Ibid.*

punctually every month, and, if wounded or disabled, pensioned and well cared for. "An army of 15,000 men might have been maintained in this state of efficiency," Rosny asserts, "on the sums the king spent yearly in gambling at Zameti's, Gondy's, or other of the rich financiers, with whom he spent much of his time, and lived on terms of too great familiarity."

During the war with Spain and the League, Henri IV. had several times been prevented from carrying out his plans for besieging the towns that held out against him by the wretched state of the roads. After heavy rains they became impassable either for his cavalry or his often ragged and shoeless troops, who sank at every step a foot deep into the mud baths they attempted to traverse, — as at Doullens, where Henri would have avenged the cruel death of the unfortunate Villars-Brancas, who was horribly mutilated and tortured by the inhuman Spaniards.

Rosny, being chief surveyor of the roads of France, determined to remedy this evil, and at once gave orders for draining the marshes and for the reparation of the principal highways of France, many of which he bordered with plantations of elms.* Many new roads also were

---

* Here and there in the rural districts of France, standing alone on the slopes of the hill, may yet be seen an ancient elm or two yet retaining the name of Rosnys, given to them by the people. They are the remains of the great minister's plantations.

opened where most needed, the work being advanced with great activity. The bridges broken during the war were repaired, and rivers made more navigable, thus opening new means of communication, and facilitating the transport of merchandise. To avoid the necessity of buying horses for the cavalry in Germany, England, or other countries, the foundation of breeding studs was proposed by Rosny, the king fully concurring in his idea of the advantages to be derived from them. Measures were also taken for the regular cleansing of the City of Paris and contributing to its general healthfulness.

While the Marquis de Rosny, with the king's full approval, and often in concert with him, was rendering these services to France, his jealous enemies were insidiously endeavouring to injure him in the king's esteem, by suggesting treasonable motives for his diligence and great exertions in the king's service, and his efforts to promote the well-being of the state. It seems incredible that he should have listened so readily to such accusations against a minister to whom he owed so much, and whom he knew to be almost the only man of incorruptible honour and integrity in his court or his ministry.

Yet the king did frequently give heed and encouragement to the malevolent insinuations against his indefatigable minister, and treated him for a time with a suspicious coldness. Then, suddenly resuming his accustomed freedom and friendliness, he would seek to assure him of his perfect confidence in, and unabated regard for, him, as if to atone for the injustice he had so wantonly done him. Or he may have intended to overwhelm his traducers with confusion by showing them the vanity and futility of their efforts to disparage his long-tried and trusted friend, whose worth he had so well proved.

Something of the sort, but apparently of more seriousness, or, at least, of longer duration than usual, had on the occasion in question recently occurred. Henri was accustomed to converse daily with his minister, when both were in Paris or Fontainebleau, on the business of the latter's various offices, in the most confidential manner. Now, however, he assumed towards him an air of coldness and extreme reserve, to which the impassible Rosny, being no stranger to this kind of caprice, or freak of temper, on the part of the king, gave little heed, conscious, as he was, of neglecting no part of his duty, either to the king or the state. No remark, therefore, or word of complaint, did this change in their usual friendly relations elicit from him.

He waited until it was his majesty's good pleasure to tell him in what he had offended; and as the king began to weary of his self-imposed restraint, and Rosny still gave no sign of seeking enlightenment as to its cause, Henri one morning, after a formal interview at Fontainebleau, and at the moment his minister was leaving his presence, bowing lower than ever, suddenly asked, "Where are you going now?"

"To Paris," replied Rosny. "The business we have been discussing, as your majesty knows, requires that I should lose no time in returning thither."

"But," rejoined the king, "have you nothing to say to me before you leave?"

"Nothing, Sire. I have already said all that occurs to me on the subject you spoke of."

"Then I have much to say to you!" he exclaimed; and, turning to his valet, who was waiting to draw on the king's hunting-boots, "Take those away," he said, "and tell them not to bring out the horses, for I see that the weather is unfavourable for the hunt to-day."

Surprised at this sudden change of purpose, the day being very fine, the valet ventured to say that "the weather seemed to him very favourable for the chase."

"I say it is not," rejoined the king. "Do as I have ordered you."

Several of the courtiers, equipped for the hunt, were waiting his arrival in the avenue of the château when his decree that the weather was bad was announced to them, with the further information that his majesty was closeted with the Marquis de Rosny in his private cabinet. Amongst those gentlemen were some of Rosny's accusers (but he refrains from naming them), who were well aware that the king would report to "the man of the arsenal" — as among themselves they named the *grand-maître* — not only all they had told him, but very much more. For it must be admitted that Henri IV. was no strict adherer to truth, as he acknowledged himself.* The mischief and bad feeling his jesting and tale-bearing sometimes gave rise to in his court were scarcely less productive of danger to himself and the state than the slander, treachery, and discontent of the people around him.

Rosny was accused of employing the great power and influence he possessed in the country, from the many important offices confided to him, in elevating himself to the dignity of a sovereign-prince in Poitou and other governments he held. This was to be done conjointly with the Duc d'Épernon, who, if not his enemy, was scarcely his friend; but this feeling, the king was told, was merely assumed to cover their mutual designs.

---

* On the occasion of some disputed succession in which the king and the Comte de Soissons were concerned, the latter stated that he had been grossly insulted in his honour by falsehood having been imputed to him. "His word," he said, "ought to be sufficient in such a case, as he was not accustomed to lying." "If that were the case, my cousin," replied the king, "you would be unlike the rest of your family, for we all indulge at times in tremendous lying. Your elder brother, the cardinal, was notoriously proficient in it."

Rosny did but vouchsafe a contemptuous smile to charges so absurd, and as Henri complained of being continually annoyed by these slanderous reports against those who served him best, the marquis advised him — the king having assured him that he gave no credence to these slanderous tales — to discountenance them entirely by henceforth refusing to listen to them.*

A conspiracy had indeed been discovered in December of the previous year that, successful, might, like so many similar ones, have led to very serious results for France. The Spaniards, now less disposed to make war than to plot and intrigue against other nations, had persuaded the Baron de Meyrargues to contrive a plan by which Marseilles, so long coveted, and where Meyrargues had considerable influence, should be delivered to them. The secret was divulged to the king, and the baron's guilt being proved, he was arrested while concerting his plans with the Spanish secretary of embassy in the cloisters of one of the churches. His punishment was, as usual in those days, a horrible death. The secretary was liberated by the king's orders, much discussion having taken place respecting the protection secured to ambassadors by the Law of Nations.†

---

\* *L' historiographe* Mathieu, *Histoire de France;* L'Estoile, *Journal de Henri IV.*

† On the evening of the day of Meyrargues's execution the king, while crossing the newly completed Pont Neuf, was sud-

To return to the Marquis de Rosny. On the day following the explanation above referred to — which had compelled him to put off his return to Paris until the morrow — the king very early in the morning sent a message desiring that he would come to him before leaving Fontainebleau. On entering the king's apartment he found the whole court assembled, attending, probably, his majesty's *lever.* Rising and taking Rosny's hand, "*Mon ami!*" he said, "I have had a longer and more refreshing night's rest than I have enjoyed for some time. This I owe to having opened my heart to you, and again made everything clear and satisfactory between us. I trust it has had a like beneficial effect on you." He acknowledged, and truly, no doubt, that it had.

The courtiers then dispersed, the king soon following with his minister, all of them taking, as it seems, a morning stroll in the avenue of mul-

denly attacked by a man, who, rapidly passing the guards, rushed up to the king, seized his mantle, pulled him back on the croup of his horse, and would have killed him had not two of the guards, outstripping the rest, ridden up in time to dash his bayonet to the ground as he was levelling it at the king. After a furious resistance he was secured, and proved to be an escaped maniac. A revolting sentence was passed on him, but the king forbade its execution, and condemned him to perpetual imprisonment, which of course, was but of short duration. Jean de Lille died in prison, and it was better so than that a frenzied mob should twice on the same day witness the brutalising horrors of a public execution, whether inflicted on the guilty or, as no less frequently occurred, the innocent and estimable.

berry-trees.* But M. de Rosny must return to Paris. All pressed round him to offer their congratulations; the king having informed them that the *grand-maître* ("the man of the arsenal") was about to be elevated to the rank — often refused, but now accepted at Henri's earnest request — of duke and peer of France. The mortification must have been extreme when, to the information already given them, the king added that the friendship existing between him and the Duc de Sully was for life and death.

Circumstances having occurred to revive the king's resentment against the Duc de Bouillon, showing that Sedan had become the centre of intrigues and plots against him, he had determined to compel him to submit or to crush him. Deputations from all parts interceding for the duke flowed in upon the king, who was inexorable, and proposed to take the command of his army and march on Sedan in person. A fit of gout intervened before preparations for this expedition were much advanced. In the event of the continuance or return of the gout he desired to transfer the command to the *grand-maître*. But for so distinguished an honour as that of supplying the place of the king as commander-in-chief of the

* These trees had been lately planted with a view to the breeding of silkworms and the establishing of silk manufactories in France, in which the king took great interest. Rosny discouraged the idea under the mistaken notion that the climate was unsuited to such an enterprise.

army, "it was imperative," he said, "that suitable dignity should be combined with the necessary authority." He therefore was anxious that the letters-patent conferring on the Marquis de Rosny the style and title of Maximilian de Béthune, Duc de Sully, should be prepared, signed, sealed, and registered with as little delay as possible.

As a preliminary, however, Rosny was appointed councillor of honour. Nearly all the grand seigneurs of the kingdom and gentlemen of the court did him the honour, he says, to accompany him when he presented himself before the Parliament for the ceremony of his reception. All the princes of the blood, with the one exception of the Comte de Soissons, also attended. The Grande Chambre, the Hall of Séance, even the courts were so crowded that it was difficult to move about.

At the conclusion of the ceremony sixty of the principal nobility returned with the new duke to the arsenal, where a splendid banquet awaited them. It was probably a fast-day, as dishes of the most *recherché* kind were provided, to suit both the Catholics and the Protestants. A gratifying surprise to M. de Sully on returning from the ceremony was to find the king at the arsenal. He had given him no notice of his intention to honour him with his company to dinner, but had slipped away unperceived towards the close of the ceremony of the reception and had installed himself at the arsenal to await the duke's arrival.

*Duc de Sully.*

**Photo-Etching.** — From Painting by F. Porbus.

"*M. le Grand-maître!*" exclaimed the king, as soon as he entered, "I have come to the feast, though not invited. Shall I dine well or ill, do you think?"

"Your majesty would probably have dined better," replied Sully, "had you given me notice of the honour you proposed to do me."

"I know then," rejoined the king, interrupting Sully's expressions of gratitude for his majesty's condescension, "that I shall dine well. For, weary of waiting for you, I paid a visit to your kitchens, where I saw some very fine fish, and several ragoûts, which I expect to find excellent, and, as you were tardy in returning, I ate a few of those small fresh oysters, and drank a glass or two of your famous *vin* d'Arbois, — certainly the best I have ever drunk."

The king appears to have been in his liveliest mood. His gaiety, remarks Sully, had the effect of putting everybody into good humour — enlivening the repast, and adding to the pleasures of the table by flashes of wit and continual laughter. The rest of the day, he says, was passed in a manner that gave perfect satisfaction to the king and all who honoured the new duke with their presence at his table.

It was for this occasion that Sully prepared the gold and jewelled chain of SS. to which was attached a portrait of Henri IV. engraved in relief.

Some few days after the above events, another attempt was made by the king, through the intervention of the Princess of Orange, for whom he had a great esteem, to come to a friendly understanding with the Duc de Bouillon. He, however, proved obstinately averse to any arrangement involving acknowledgment of error on his part, or the throwing himself on the mercy of the king. He feared the fate of Biron, and therefore declined to appear at the court of France as invited by his majesty. Consequently the preparations for taking Sedan were resumed. Henri was assured by many of those who favoured De Bouillon that Sedan would rival Ostend and maintain a three years' siege. But the king, who was not unacquainted with the fortress of Sedan, laughed at the prophecy.

## CHAPTER XIX.

The March on Limousin. — Henri's Ardour Revives on Resuming the Cuirass and Helmet. — Hunting *en route* from Fontainebleau to the Gates of Sedan. — The Gates Thrown Open. — Bouillon Owns His Errors. — Acknowledges the King's Protectorate. — Sedan Given to the King for Four Years. — Bouillon Pardoned. — His Duchy Returned to Him. — He Resumes His Former Position at Court. — Domestic Misery. — The King's Ailments. — Canals Projected. — Olivier de Serres. — Mulberry Trees and Silkworms. — The Gout Again. — Ladies Sit Round the King's Bed to Amuse Him with Lively Talk. — D'Urfe's "Astrée." — Royal Christening. — A Chevalier de Malthe.

WHILE the ineffectual attempt to negotiate with the Duc de Bouillon was proceeding, Sully secretly employed the engineer Érard to make exact plans of the supposed redoubtable fortress of Sedan, which the endless communications received on the subject sought to persuade the king could be reduced only by a long-protracted siege, or by famine. Sully, however, pointed out its weak places, and assured him that eight days would be amply sufficient to compel surrender. Henri had long suspected that even the invincible Duc de Lesdiguières gave his support to Bouillon; yet not for his defence only, but with the view of establishing a pact among the leading men of the party for their mutual protection.

But although the reports of the confidential agents of the Duc de Sully were reassuring to the king, so far as they concerned the loyalty of the principal Huguenot nobility, "it yet appeared that Spanish gold had succeeded in fomenting dissatisfaction and considerable agitation among the Huguenots of those parts of the kingdom where De Bouillon and the family of the unfortunate Biron exercised a sort of feudal influence." The king, therefore, thought it advisable to show himself in person in those parts, and as a prelude to the siege of Sedan — which he had determined on, if milder means should fail to bring the Duc de Bouillon to his senses — he marched on Limousin at the head of a small *corps d'armée* towards the close of 1605.

As soon as news of this expedition was brought to the duke, he sent orders to his officers to open the gates of Turenne and his other fortresses to Henri IV., and to offer no resistance. In spite of this ready submission, several magistrates of the Parliament of Paris soon after arrived to hold their *séances* in that town, and five persons accused of high treason were beheaded. Six others were executed in effigy, and several gentlemen of distinguished family in Languedoc and Provence were sentenced to death.

The king was again free from gout, and unless

another attack should compel him to put the *grand-maître* in his place, he announced to Sully that he should be prepared in the spring to take the command of his army, and to march on that centre of sedition which disquieted the whole of the northern frontier. Sully's formidable artillery, conducted by the *grand-maître* in person, was in readiness to join the army on its march. At the beginning of April Henri left Fontainebleau to besiege Sedan with an army of 15,000 men, in all respects efficiently equipped, as no troops he had hitherto commanded had been. Fifty of Sully's great guns accompanied them.

The king was again in his element, and Sully, who loved war no less than his royal master, says one could see by the exhilaration of his spirits how his heart expanded with joy on resuming his old profession of arms. The ardour of other days seemed to revive, his countenance brightened up with animation, and the weight of years, brought on him in appearance by domestic worry and misery, vanished now, temporarily free from them. He seems to have advanced on his march very leisurely, as he writes to Sully of having amused himself *en route* with hunting. He had missed, he said, capturing the stag, but had taken two wolves, which he thought was of favourable augury for the result of the expedition.

At Rheims, too, where he was joined by many of the nobility, he waited to perform his Easter devotions. The Duc de Bouillon had therefore abundant time to prepare for resistance had he desired it; but yielding to the entreaties of the deputies from the Protestant churches, who were endeavouring to effect some satisfactory arrangements for him with the king, he consented to acknowledge in general terms that he had been in fault, and to request his majesty to grant him "letters of abolition." This did not satisfy the king; he required that Sedan should be given up to him, which Bouillon refused. Henri, therefore, with a division of his army and a train of artillery, advanced to the gates of Sedan.

Having but a few hundred troops to oppose the king's army, and, like Biron, disappointed at finding no disposition on the part of those who had interceded for him to take up arms in his favour, he determined to capitulate at once, recognising the king's protectorate of Sedan, and placing that fortress in his hands for four years. On those terms Henri absolved all past offences, and received him at Donchery — where the duke made his submission to him — with all the cordiality of an old friend, giving him the usual three embraces.

The king wrote to the Princess of Orange, who had endeavoured to mediate between him and the duke: "My cousin, I may now say with Cæsar, '*Veni, vidi, vici,*' and you will be able to judge whether I was not better informed of the real strength and resources of Sedan than those who were anxious to persuade me that I was about to bring ruin on my kingdom by undertaking the siege of a second Ostend."

Bouillon then quietly returned to the court and resumed his former position there, together with the charges and dignities he had been for a time deprived of. Henri confided the care of Sedan to a Protestant officer, but, in his rather extreme generosity, a month had scarcely elapsed ere Sedan was restored to the Duc de Bouillon. Sully would have preferred the transfer of the principality to the crown at that opportune moment, and while the heads of those partisans whose rebellion Bouillon had encouraged, and who had suffered in his stead, were still exposed as traitors on the gates of the cities of Limousin. But to those who, like Sully, disapproved the extreme confidence placed by the king in the Duc de Bouillon, he replied, shrewdly: "I would rather that the duke should be in his own principality than a wanderer in the German courts."

This affair, which had threatened to embroil the kingdom with further intrigues of both Catholics and Protestants, was finally settled without drawing the sword or firing a single cannon. The *grand-maître* returned to Paris, not too well pleased that such an army and such a train of artillery had been brought together without achieving the triumph he had expected. The king, however, had a fancy, or his courtiers urged it upon him, to reënter Paris in triumph, and La Varenne was sent to overtake Sully and to inform him of it.

"Eh! M. de La Varenne," exclaimed the *grand-maître* in amazement, "what is the king thinking of? Have we given a single blow with either sword or pique, or fired a shot from either cannon or arquebuse, that we should play the victorious, when, in fact, we are the vanquished, — having bought with credulity what the king should have owed to his courage? Tell him that every one says so, and that entering the capital in triumph will but bring upon us mockery and derision."

Henri heard this message with emotions of anger he found difficult to conceal, and Sully confesses that he perhaps had spoken too frankly in his extreme vexation at what had occurred. But presently came a second message, brought by his brother, De Béthune, and the Duc de Praslin, whom the king had deputed to tell him, in terms as deferential as possible, that there was nothing unreasonable in what he exacted of him. Sully endeavoured to convince them to the contrary. Unable to persuade him to take a different view of the matter, they returned to the king, whom this second refusal put into a violent rage, and occasioned some very harsh epithets to be bestowed on his resistance to the king's will.

"This abominable man," he exclaimed, "with

his arrogance and obstinacy, thwarts me in everything; but, by Heaven, he shall obey me!"

A third message was despatched, with a command from the king, requiring him in very absolute terms to do as he was ordered without further delay or demur. A little piqued by the style of Henri's message, Sully hastened to do his bidding, and announced from the arsenal and the Bastille his approach with his army to Paris with a promptitude that surprised the king, following it up by several salvoes from the fifty cannon he had brought back from Sedan, astonishing the Parisians with an uproar more violently and tumultuously startling than that with which he had received the Pope's legate at Montemélian.

Henri laughed heartily, and the people gave him so enthusiastic a reception that it banished all traces of his anger against Sully. When, some hours after, they again met — slapping Sully on the shoulder, as was his undignified custom — "*Grand-maître*," he said, "you have proved yourself worthy of the office you hold; I must embrace you."

The interior of the kingdom was now considered tranquillised, resistance to the king's authority subdued, and the public welfare, under the wise administration of the finances, well assured. The burden of taxation was lessened where possible, and although many abuses and hardships doubtless had still to be borne, yet, with peace, both within and without the kingdom, commerce promising to become flourishing, and the king and his first minister both bent on the thorough reorganisation of the state, their removal at an early period might be reasonably looked for.

Soon after the peaceful settlement of the affair of Sedan, the king, desiring still further to increase the influence and power of the Duc de Sully by heaping honours upon him, which, indeed, tended rather to add to the malevolence and slanderous attacks of his jealous enemies, proposed to ensure to him and his sons the survivorship of the high office of Constable of France; also the government of Normandy, on the death of the Duc de Montpensier (who was then dangerously ill), with the post of grand master of the king's household, of which he was the titular occupant. To Sully's son, the Marquis de Rosny, he offered the hand of one of his daughters with a large dowry and pension; the governorship of Berry and survivorship of that of Bourbonnais.

The price to be paid for these lucrative honours was that Sully and son, with the rest of the family, of course, should renounce "the religion" and enter the fold of the faithful.

"I entreat you," said the king, "not to refuse me this satisfaction; it is for the good of my service and for the full and assured establishment of your house."

"Your majesty," replied Sully, "does me far

more honour than I merit, have hoped for, or desired. As regards my son, I can decide nothing respecting your proposals in his favour. He is of an age to choose his religion, and capable of making the necessary reflections before taking so serious a step. For myself, the case is different. I should be grieved exceedingly to receive an increase of honour, wealth, or dignity at the expense of my conscience. Should I ever change my religion, it would be from internal conviction only; neither avarice, vanity, nor ambition would ever lead me to do so. Were I to do otherwise, I should give your majesty good reason for suspecting the sincerity of a heart I could not guard faithfully for God."

"Why should I suspect you," rejoined the king, "for doing what I have already done myself, and what you counselled me to do when I proposed the question to you? Think well of it, and gratify me in yielding to my earnest request. I give you a month to reflect on it."

"I desire, Sire," replied Sully, "nothing more ardently than to obey your wishes in whatever is in my power. I promise to think seriously on all you have been pleased to propose to me, and have hope of satisfying your majesty, though it may not be in the manner you expect."

Great was the alarm of the Huguenots when these flattering proposals to Sully became known to them. His Protestantism was not regarded as very rigorous, or likely to withstand the strong temptation placed before him. Yet his influence with the king, and his retention of his various offices, in spite of the unceasing efforts of the Catholics to displace him, led the Huguenots to look on Sully as a sort of security to them against oppression and persecution, which the king, now surrounded by Jesuits, might, under a Catholic minister, be induced, to show his zeal for the Church, to inflict upon them. Their alarm was intensified by the report that the marriage of Sully's eldest son with Mademoiselle de Créquy, daughter of the Protestant Duc de Lesdiguières, had been broken off at the king's command, that he might marry him to Henriette de Vendôme, his and the Duchesse de Beaufort's daughter.

During the month in which Sully was to decide on accepting or rejecting the wealth and dignities offered him, and which he passed at his estate of Sully, in retirement, every means was brought to bear, by cardinals, bishops, and other ecclesiastics — the atheist Du Perron especially — on his supposed love of riches and honours in order to prevail on him to cast aside his heresy and enter the "pale of the true Church." Even Paul V. sent him a flattering letter, full of professions of the highest esteem for his character, and anxiety for his soul's salvation; declaring also that "the extreme interest he took in the matter would induce him to leave Rome for Paris to add his supplications to those of his other friends, were he not prevented by the rules of his office of supreme head of the Church."

With much impatience Henri waited Sully's reply. Villeroy was sent to receive it, but to him he merely said that "he humbly thanked the king for the honours he had proposed to confer on him; but that on no account could he accept offices which were already filled, or even enter upon them should they become vacant; being fully occupied by the duties of those with which he was already charged. For the rest, Cardinal du Perron would convey his answer to his majesty."

This gave great hopes to the king, — to the cardinal also, it may be inferred, as he at once hastened to the arsenal, expecting to hear the gratifying announcement that the stern Huguenot *grand-maître* consented to be converted. But he was soon convinced of his error. Neither his learning nor his eloquence touched Sully's stony heart, and Du Perron departed to inform the king that the "man of the arsenal" was inflexible. One last effort to shake his resolution Henri then determined to make. It proved as ineffectual as the efforts and arguments which had preceded it.

As he had replied to James I., who questioned him on his attachment to his religion, Sully now answered Henri IV., to the effect that, although he might seem to be almost exclusively occupied with worldly cares and worldly grandeur, and wholly indifferent as he apparently thought him on the subject of religion, it was none the less true that he was so much attached to his, as to place it before fortune, family, country, and even the king, to whose service he had so long devoted himself. The king had no reply to make to this, and as the son seems to have emulated his father's firmness in his faith, Henriette de Vendôme was given in marriage to the son of the Connétable de Montmorency.

No estrangement between Henri IV., and the Duc de Sully followed the refusal of the latter to abandon his religion. It is even suggested that the request that he would do so originated less with the king than with Sully's enemies, who urged on Henri IV. that so valuable a public servant was but insufficiently rewarded; but that if he would abjure his errors, the Pope, who esteemed him, would readily give him absolution, and the king, unfettered by his minister's heresy, might more suitably honour him. Yet it could scarcely be expected that Sully would renounce his opinions with regard to religion more readily than was customary with him on subjects far less important.

The slanderers of the court had already on more than one occasion very nearly induced the king to disgrace him; his resistance, therefore, in this matter to the entreaties of king, Pope, cardinals, etc., would probably so incense him that the desired downfall of this able and favourite minister might be thus accomplished. Being reminded that he had urgently recommended the king to renounce heresy and embrace Catholicism, he replied that it was as a sacrifice to the welfare of the nation, then deluged with the blood of her people, half depopulated by years of civil warfare, and on the very brink of ruin. In his own case it would have no higher motive than the mere selfish ends of his own individual elevation.*

Henri IV. was then leading a life of domestic misery, so much so that Sully speaks of him even with compassion, and laments the change in him, observable in his careworn appearance and loss of gaiety of temper. It was his hope that a short war, "by way of recreation," would restore him in some degree to his former self. But the signs of improvement which the march on Limousin and the projected siege of Sedan produced vanished when the result of those warlike preparations was for the army a mere march there and back again, and for the king a return to his life of hunting, gambling, and quarrelling with his wife and mistresses.

Frequent attacks of gout, often combined with another malady to which he was subject, at times compelled him to remain for days together in bed.

* *Mémoires de Sully;* L'Estoile, *Journal de Henri IV.;* *Mercure Française.*

He would then discuss with Sully his plans for connecting the rivers by means of canals. That of Briare, which was to unite the Loire to the Seine, was already begun. The more important proposal to unite the Mediterranean with the ocean, by the Aude and the Garonne, which was first suggested in the reign of François I., was now laid before Henri IV. in a well-devised plan, and was under consideration. But this, like many other lesser schemes for promoting the prosperity of the kingdom, was destined to wait yet many years for its realisation.

Olivier de Serres, a Huguenot gentleman of Languedoc, who has been named the "father of French agriculture," warmly seconded the views of Henri IV. and Sully in their endeavour to introduce a better and more profitable system of tilling and cultivating the long-neglected land, and improving husbandry generally. De Serres possessed, at his manor of Pradel, a sort of model farm of great extent, where the most perfect system of agriculture was practised, new plants, etc., were introduced, and new experiments in their culture. He had written a very able work on the subject "*Théâtre d'Agriculture*," and dedicated it to the king.

From it, and conversations with its author, Henri had derived the knowledge which led him to persist, in opposition to his minister, in planting the gardens of Fontainebleau, of the Tuileries, of his château of Saint-Germain, and the centre of his new square of Place Royale (one of the greatest improvements he made in Paris) with avenues of mulberry-trees, and constructing " magnaneries," or places for the rearing of silkworms. But Sully's opinion that the climate of France was suited neither to mulberry-trees nor silkworms afterwards yielded to the assurance of Olivier de Serres that both would speedily become acclimatised and flourishing.

The grounds of Sully, Rosny, and Moret, to please the king, were soon after planted with the mulberry-tree. But one of Sully's chief objections to the introduction of manufactories into agricultural France was the "fear that a sedentary life in the close, impure atmosphere of a manufactory would soon damp the spirits of the French and unfit them for that life of movement, of fatigue, of activity in the open air, that made the agricultural people a nursery of good soldiers."

De Serres's agricultural work was rather a ponderous volume, but the king made a point of attentively perusing it for an hour every day. When he was unwell it was read to him; but if he could not give due attention to it, then the ladies of the court (we do not hear of the queen being at any time among them) would often sit around his bed and enliven him by their presence and conversation. Or on sleepless nights, another work, also dedicated to him, and of which the first only of its five volumes was then printed — a written copy of the remaining four being sent to the king — was read to him in turns by his three favourite companions, M. le Grand (Bellegarde), Bassompierre, and Grammont.

The work in question was the Marquis d'Urfé's pastoral romance of "*Astrée.*" D'Urfé had been a Leaguer, though not one of the most violent. He had made his peace with the king; had retired to his estate, and there met a lady with whom he fell desperately in love. Unfortunately, it happened that the lady's affections were engaged, and M. le Marquis, taking his disappointment much to heart, secluded himself in his château, and to soothe the pangs of unrequited love wrote this tender romantic tale of the griefs and joys of a party of lady and gentlemen shepherds and shepherdesses.

D'Urfé's romance had a far more happy effect than De Serres's agriculture in wiling away the weary hours of the king's illness; so deeply was he interested in and pleased with it, that no twinge of gout disturbed him while listening to the story of the platonic amours of those lovely Phyllises and gentle Strephons, as they reclined on mossy banks, their pet lambs beside them, decked with ribands of rosy hue, or led by silken cords. He even imagined that something of the kind might be realisable for him, to gently cheer him in his declining years. From what eventually took place it may be inferred that it was not a mere passing idea, but one he kept well in view.

D'Urfé's "*Astrée*" had an immense success, and although the five volumes, or parts, as they were called, were published only at intervals of two or three years, the interest in the work was so well sustained that their appearance was looked forward to with amazing anxiety. It created almost as great a sensation as the ten-volume romance of Mdlle. de Scudéry, "*Artemène; ou, Le Grand Cyrus*," published twenty-five or thirty years later — *le grand Cyrus* supposed to represent Henri IV., Artemène, the beautiful Duchesse de Longueville, daughter of Charlotte de Montmorency, Princesse de Condé.

The king being once more free from the attacks of his enemy, the gout, determined to christen M. le Dauphin and the two Mesdames de France, — the queen having lost her second son and given birth to another daughter. It was proposed that the ceremony should be of great magnificence, for Maria de' Medici had heard wondrously exaggerated accounts of the splendour with which the children of the Duchesse de Beaufort had been christened, and was anxious that the christening of M. le Dauphin and sisters should throw into the shade all royal christenings which had preceded it.

The ceremony was to have taken place in Paris; but, as usual, the plague, or some similar epidemic, was raging in that city. L'Estoile, however, says that the death-rate did not exceed the usual number, which he gives at eight persons daily. He attributes the change to a desperate quarrel between the king and queen, the latter insisting, and the king in the end yielding to her wishes, that her sister, the Duchess of Mantua, who with the reigning Duc de Lorraine was to be present as one of the sponsors, should take precedence, not only of the foreign princes expected to be present at the ceremony, but even of the princes and princesses of the blood; while Concini and wife were to be assigned a distinguished place among the nobility of France.

So indignant were the royal princes that they determined to absent themselves. Many of the *haute noblesse* also declined to obey the king's command to attend, while he reproached his wife — "*triste femme*," as Dupuy calls her, "who brought him neither beauty, esprit, nor good temper." Sully was sent for, but his intervention did not improve matters. He would have said in the tone of master, "*Je le veux*," or "*Je ne le veux pas*," and have settled the difference at once. But the king could not be brought to adopt his minister's advice, and as Maria de' Medici continued inflexible in her demands, Sully withdrew in despair. His conscience probably reproached him, — he having been the principal agent in inflicting this *triste femme* on the unwilling king.

*Madame Royale, Daughter of Henri IV.*
Photo-Etching. — From Painting by Harding.

The Duchess of Mantua was received with great distinction; splendid *fêtes*, banquets, and balls followed the pompous ceremony, though shorn of a part of their brilliancy by the absence of the princes. The queen, for the occasion, threw off her usual air of gloom and disdain, and was full of mirth and gaiety as none before had beheld her. The ballets and Italian comedies were of her invention, and were pronounced highly entertaining and successful. All the king's children were present — amongst whom the little Duc Alexandre de Beaufort, Gabrielle's second son, was conspicuous in his costume of a Knight of Malta, into which order he had been received three years before.*

* The ceremony took place in the nave of the Temple Church, when the little duke, being unable to repeat the vows proposed to him, the king hastily left the throne prepared for him to witness his son's installation, and made the vows himself in the hands of the grand prior, promising that they should be ratified by the child on attaining his sixteenth year. — DE THOU.

## CHAPTER XX.

**Mediation of France between Paul V. and the Venetian Republic.
— Jesuits Expelled from Venice. — Long and Difficult Negotiation between Spain and the United Provinces. — France and England Intervene and Guarantee the Observance of the Twelve Years' Truce. — Arrival of Don Pedro de Toledo. — The Queen's Intrigues with the Jesuits and the Court of Spain. — Proposals for a Family Alliance. — Vivacious Scenes. — Don Pedro Boasts of Spain. — Henri Compares Spain to the Statue of Nebuchadnezzar. — Preparations for War on a Grand Scale. — The *Fêtes* at the Arsenal. — Profligacy of the Court. — Laws against Duelling, etc.**

THE ascendency which France at this time had acquired in Europe is evident from the mediation of Henri IV. being accepted by both Rome and Venice in the dispute that arose between Paul V. and the Venetian Republic. Paul had signalised his elevation to the papal throne by arbitrarily casting aside all those restraints which the Italian governments had imposed on the pontifical authority in the relations of Church and state. Generally, where they did not yield entirely, concessions were made; but Venice resisted, and the republic was placed by his holiness under an edict. The Senate, notwithstanding, ordered the clergy to resume their functions. They obeyed, with the exception of the Jesuits, Théatins, and Capuchins, whom forthwith the Senate expelled.

Paul, who was despotically inclined, was greatly enraged, and threatened, "if the spiritual sword was disregarded, to employ the material one." Venice replied by menacing an appeal for aid to the Protestant Powers. To prevent so great a calamity as the introduction of reform into Italy, the intervention of France was sought. Rome was represented by the powerful Jesuit preacher, Bellarmin, who supported Paul's extremest pretensions. He, however, met with a formidable opponent in Frà Paolo Sarpi, one of the Venetian Council of Ten, "a profound scholar, polemic, and eloquent historian, and regarded by many as a Protestant in the disguise of a monk."

The contest was long and excited, frequently suspended and renewed. Attempts were made to assassinate Frà Paolo, but he escaped the assassin's poniard, and renewed his defence of Venice with more vigour than before. At last Paul V. yielded on the most important points of the discussion; while Venice, reserving on principle all her rights, refused, even at the entreaty of France, to allow the Jesuits to return (September, 1607).\*

Scarcely was this dispute ended when the intervention of the French government was sought for

---

\* They were not again permitted to establish themselves in the Venetian territory until 1690, under Pope Alexander III.

another, yet more complicated and difficult, — a satisfactory settlement of the contest between Spain and the United Provinces of the Netherlands. Since the taking of Ostend (September 22, 1604), after a siege of three years and two months, the Spaniards, thoroughly exhausted by the long and arduous struggle, maintained on both sides with unflinching obstinacy, made very feeble attempts to continue the war. The United Provinces, on the contrary, renewed hostilities with great vigour by sea, harassing the Spaniards by their successful maritime expeditions, taking their vessels, invading their coasts, and finally, in April, 1607, after a brilliant naval victory, gaining possession of Gibraltar.

This was a great humiliation to the Spaniards, while the Netherlanders, after this exploit, were also, both by sea and land, at the end of their resources. They were divided, too, among themselves. Maurice of Nassau, with the army and those whose interests it served that the war should go on, was for resuming hostilities; while the chief citizens, headed by the famous Olden-Barneveldt, were disposed for peace. A suspension of arms was at last agreed to, and Henri IV. sent his minister Jeannin to assist in the negotiation, which lasted many months, the truce of twelve years with which it concluded not being finally accepted and signed until 1609.

Even then neither the peace nor the war party

was fully satisfied, there being nothing definite in the arrangement. Yet the archdukes * renounced all pretensions to the United Provinces, and declared them free states over which they claimed no authority. But it was difficult to place faith in the Spaniards, who might, when it suited them, invent some pretext for breaking the truce. Henri IV., to reassure them, then signed a treaty binding him to afford powerful aid to the United Provinces in case of any infraction of the truce on the part of the Spaniards.

James I. also took upon himself a similar obligation. Spain had made great efforts and proposed substantial advantages to induce James to conclude a treaty with them, offensive and defensive, tempting him with the promise of opening the trade of the Indies to him. But he repelled all their advances. The troubles which their intrigues, or imputed intrigues, with the Jesuits had occasioned in his kingdom, together with the danger he and his Parliament had incurred from the Gunpowder Plot scheme, had made the King of Great Britain wholly averse to any nearer alliance with Philip III.

James even availed himself of the opportunity, as Sully states, of reminding Henri of the "grand project," and had determined, while awaiting its realisation, to enter into a closer alliance with

\* The infanta and her husband, Albert of Austria, as joint rulers of the Netherlands, were so termed.

France. Henri himself appears to have thought that political events were gradually leading to the fuller development of his project, but that Europe was not yet sufficiently prepared for the general and ready adoption of his views; while any step prematurely taken might greatly imperil the eventual successful establishment of the great "Christian Republic," or "fraternal association of the independent nationalities."

While the negotiation between Spain and the United Provinces of the Netherlands was proceeding, efforts were secretly made to induce Henri to abandon the cause of his allies. No immediate reply having been given to the proposals addressed to him, it was inferred by the queen, her Italian favourites, and the Jesuits (the assurances of the king's confessor, Father Cotton, confirming them in their error), that Henri was favourably disposed towards them. Shortly after the signing of the twelve years' truce by Spain and Holland, Henri IV. and James I. having become guarantees for its due observance, Don Pedro de Toledo arrived in Paris, avowedly to discuss officially with the king the proposed secret treaty to the prejudice of the Netherlanders, of which he had received from Spain the preliminary articles.

Some warmly vivacious scenes occurred between the king and Don Pedro, who was a grandee of Spain, the Governor of Castille, and a relative of Maria de' Medici. The queen, besides her unceasing quarrels with the king and his mistresses, had lately become a political *intrigante*, adopting a policy entirely opposed to Henri's, and caballing against him in concert with the Spaniards. She had given birth on April 26th to a third son (Gaston d'Orléans), whose advent was celebrated with a splendour and *éclat* rivalling that of the dauphin. The latter was a sickly child, frequently ill, in spite of the king's anxious care that he and the rest of his children should be kept far away from pestiferous Paris, — not even passing near it when on their way to healthier spots. He dreaded the loss of any of his children; they "delighted him so much," he said, "and were the prettiest in the world."

With this latest addition to the number the queen was also delighted; for she had set her heart on a double marriage with Spain, while Henri was partly pledged to a similar engagement with England. But the haughty Don Pedro addressed the king as though he had proposed this family alliance of his own children with those of Philip III., and for the honour of the Catholic king's accession to it was prepared to abandon Holland, on condition of Philip's second son succeeding to the governorship of the Netherlands and marrying a daughter of the Most Christian king.

Henry listened with indignation. "No alliance," he replied, "had been proposed by him, and as to consenting to abandon his allies, he would prefer that they should cut off his head." Angry disputation was the only result of their interviews. The Spaniard on one occasion was vauntingly declaiming on the greatness, the wealth, the power of Spain, when Henri, losing patience, exclaimed: "Spain is like the statue of Nebuchadnezzar, composed of various metals, but having feet of clay."

Don Pedro was greatly annoyed; and the king, again addressing him, said: "*Monsieur l'ambassadeur*, you are a Spaniard, I am a Gascon; let us no more excite or aggravate each other." But — according to Péréfixe — this haughty Spanish grandee was so enthusiastic an admirer of Henri IV. that when, walking one day in the gallery of Fontainebleau, an officer was passing him with the king's sword on a velvet cushion, Don Pedro stopped him, and, dropping on one knee, respectfully kissed the sword, "thus," as he said, "rendering honour to the most valiant and glorious sword of Christendom." The ambassador lingered in France much longer than his special mission to the French king seemed to warrant. He had hoped that his Jesuit confessor would have used his influence with greater success; but all that Father Cotton had recently obtained from his penitent was the promise to leave his heart to La Flèche, and to make him a present of thirty thousand crowns.

The still protracted residence of Don Pedro at

the French court began to annoy the king, who was well aware of the intrigues it fostered, and of the part taken therein by the queen and her Italian counsellors, supported at Madrid by the agent of the Duke of Tuscany, her uncle. It was time, the Spaniard perceived, to withdraw. He had failed in coming to any satisfactory arrangements to deprive the Netherlands of the friendly support of France, and in his extreme vexation he, at one of his interviews with Henri IV., exclaimed that "the King of Spain, his master, was as well able to uphold the factious subjects of the King of France as he to encourage the rebels of the Netherlands."

"Let him beware of attempting it," replied Henri, "for I shall be in the saddle before his foot is in the stirrup."

This was probably the leave-taking. But although the ambassador took back to Spain no treaty, he might truly report to his master that France was becoming a formidable neighbour. He had observed her with a vigilant eye, and could not fail noting the signs of growing prosperity, or that Sully was preparing for the possibility of war on a grand scale, and that in spite of the king's really culpable prodigality, the government had a great command of money, — paying all salaries, pensions, and other expenses, within and without the kingdom, with strictest punctuality.

Manufactories of gold and silver brocades and other rich fabrics, with carpets and fine linen, were already established, aid being given where pecuniary loss was at first sustained by the persons who had undertaken their direction. "Let them not lose, but let them not get too rich," was the king's recommendation to Sully. A large sum was set aside yearly for building. The Place Royale, the Place and the Rue Dauphine were completed. The gallery connecting the Tuileries with the Louvre was in progress, also the Pavillon de Flore, with the château at Saint-Germain-en-laye, its terraces, grottoes, and gardens.

The Pont Neuf was finished and opened, also the Pont Marchand, built by the king's permission by Charles Le Marchand — captain of the City Archers — entirely at his expense, but on certain conditions which were granted — one being that it should bear his name.* It replaced a bridge that was carried away by an inundation, and which was called the Millers' Bridge, from having a mill on each arch. Several new quays were also in course of construction. The royal palaces were kept in good repair, additions being sometimes made to them, or alterations to suit the convenience of king or queen. It was the custom of the former to make the round of these residences in the course of the year — rarely

---

* L'Estoile describes it as "an exquisite work of singular excellence, enriched by very fine buildings, serving as ornament, convenience, and embellishment to the great city of Paris — the first and most beautiful in Europe."

with the queen, generally, indeed, to fly from her reproaches and ill-temper.* Chantilly, Compiègne, and Fontainebleau were refurnishing, and Monceaux, for the queen's pleasure, was being enlarged.

The productions of the manufactories of tapestry at Arras, so long admired, and in great request in the preceding century, were quite thrown into the shade, and eventually lost favour and vogue when the magnificent specimens of the tapestry of the Gobelins and Savonnerie, which date from this time, were first seen draping the walls and windows of the principal rooms of the royal residences and châteaux of the nobility.

With the view probably of increasing the number of his places of refuge, the king had lately desired Sully to have quarters prepared for his occasional stay at the arsenal, when he visited Paris and cared not to encounter the Italian clique at the Louvre. He felt more at home there, he said, than elsewhere, more free from the restraints of his usually numerous suite of

* One of his mistresses on those occasions usually accompanied or followed him — the chief favourite at this time being the lively, spirituelle Comtesse de Moret, whose temper appears to have been as amiable as that of the marquise was malicious. The queen tolerated the countess, though she had her apartments also at the Louvre, but did not obtrude herself on her majesty. Against the marquise and her son — the possible future queen and dauphin — Maria was as furious as ever.

attendants. For the extra expense this arrangement would entail on Sully the king proposed an addition of six thousand crowns yearly to the salary of his office of *grand-maître de l'artillérie*. Sully encouraged the king's idea of becoming an occasional lodger at the arsenal. He hoped then to induce him to give more of his personal attention to the direction of public affairs, and to certain branches of industry in which the king took greater interest than his minister.

But especially he desired to detach him, if possible, from his life of ignoble pleasures, which was unfitting him, he conceived, for the realisation of his grand political views, when opportunity should offer to take the first step for the abasement of Austria, which, from the general restlessness prevailing in Europe, he thought near at hand.* During the greater part of the years 1607 and 1608 the king had been chiefly occupied with the settlement of the differences between the Pope and the Republic of Venice, and the less satisfactory negotiation with Spain on behalf of the Hollanders. Thus his attention had been in a measure diverted from the administration of the affairs of his own kingdom.

There had been, however, rather an increase than a relaxation of vigilance on the part of the Duc de Sully in his efforts to thoroughly reorganise those branches of the government the

* *Mémoires de Sully;* Mathieu ; *Mémoires de Bassompierre.*

management of which devolved on him. From the numerous offices he held, this might be said to embrace almost the entire superintendence of every important executive part of the administration.

The arsenal residence appears to have been of vast extent, and since the *grand-maître* had become Duc de Sully the principal *fêtes* of the carnival — masquerades, Italian comedies, and ballets, frequently of the queen's invention — were often given there. Though Sully himself was little prone to waste the hours, so precious to him, in frivolous entertainments, yet his new dignity imposed on him the duty, he conceived, of contributing to the general hilarity of the carnival, which the king declared afforded him more amusement at the arsenal than at the Louvre, or even at the hôtel of Queen Marguerite in the Faubourg Saint-Germain, where "a sumptuous collation was always provided, costing not less than 4,000 crowns" (L'Estoile always ascertains the cost of the extravagant banquets of the period). The *grand-maître's* collations were not less sumptuous. But after assisting at the reception of the guests by the Duchesse de Sully, he generally sought an opportunity of quietly withdrawing to his study.

There, accompanied by three or four of his favourite companions, the king would sometimes surprise his indefatigable, hard-working minister. The attendants' invariable reply to the king's inquiry, "Where is the *grand-maître?*" was, "*Monsieur le duc,* Sire, is in his *cabinet d' affaires.*" Turning to his companions, the king would laughingly ask them "if they had not rather expected to hear that M. le duc was out hunting, was engaged with his hair-dresser, or amusing a party of lively young ladies."

Then, hastening to the study and knocking loudly at the door, a voice within would ask, "Who's there?" "The king," was the reply; and forthwith the door flew open, — Henri much amused, Sully not always so. He did not like these interruptions, and scarcely felt flattered — though the king may have intended to commend the *grand-maître's* devotion to his service — when, to his question, "For how much would you live the life that he does?" Bassompierre would reply, "*Par ma foi,* Sire, not for all the gold in your majesty's treasury."

The extraordinary superstition of the day converted the events of 1608 into omens of the most dismal and threatening kind. The Loire had overflowed its banks to an alarming extent, owing to the sudden melting of immense masses of snow on the mountains of Auvergne. But for the breaking up of the embankments, the city of Tours would have been submerged. Blois also ran great risk of a similar catastrophe. Sully, who was then at his duchy, very narrowly escaped drowning, and much damage was done to his estate.

The *Mercure Français* speaks of the loss of life — men, women, and children — as very considerable; also of cattle, houses, windmills, and every description of property. Not a bridge on the Loire but was either swept away or the arches broken by the force of the torrent; while large tracts of land were for a time rendered sterile by the masses of sand and stones hurled from the mountains. The peasantry were reduced to extreme poverty and misery, and Henri, as was his custom, made great professions of his love for his people, and desired Sully to extend to them such relief as he was able. But he abated not one jot of his own reckless expenditure to enable his minister to relieve their wants effectually, any more than he had done to give the peasant that long-promised weekly *poule-au-pot*, which a little discretion at the gambling-table might years before have allowed him the satisfaction of doing.

A comet made its appearance in 1608, betokening, it was said, woe to France and her king. Monsters — of what kind not reported — were born, it was announced, in various parts of the world. An enormous fish of an unknown species was caught on the coast of Holland. Again, rabid priests denounced from their pulpits the heretics and their protector. Shocks of earthquake were reported, and pestilential Paris was once more afflicted with the plague; while, to usher in 1609, the astrologers prophesied that Henri IV. would not survive his fifty-eighth year.* "Yet," exclaims L'Estoile, after enumerating the many evils which astrologers, in whom he evidently believes a little, though treating them with superb contempt, declared were about to fall on the devoted city — "yet the profligacy of the court is increased. Piety and the fear of God are extinct; blasphemy is authorised, and gambling, its companion, is in greater vogue and credit than ever."

Since the civil wars were ended, duelling, though expressly prohibited by severe enactments in 1602, had yet so greatly increased that Sully called the king's attention to the necessity of putting a stop to this "epidemic of folly" — it being computed that upwards of two thousand gentlemen had been slain in duels since the termination of the wars. Henri's own habits and temperament, however, gave countenance to these combats, and favour had been shown to those who displayed great bravery in them.

Had he not been king he would have fought many duels himself. But as his confessor — who on this subject happened to be in agreement with his minister — told him "he was responsible before God for all the blood shed in these encounters," they were more stringently forbidden. But should honour be in any way compromised by refraining to accept a challenge, the question was to be referred to the constable and the marshals

* L'Estoile, *Journal de Henri IV.*; Mathieu; Péréfixe.

of France, who would decide if a duel was necessary.

While the infraction of this edict was treated with greater severity than before, Sully, who never accompanied the king in hunting the stag, wolves, or wild boars, would have mitigated the stringency of the cruel laws then in force relating to the chase, and which have generally been considered a blot on Henri's character for humanity — so remarkable for the age in which he lived. Simultaneously, however, with the issuing of the new code concerning duelling, the lieutenant of police was desired to print and post as a placard at the corners of the streets and public places of Paris, orders for the punishment of blasphemers of the name of God, gamblers, and drunkards; also the "importunate homeless vagabonds who called themselves soldiers, and infested the streets in large numbers." A strict prohibition, with a fine for its infringement, forbade the Parisians to keep pigs, pigeons, or rabbits in their houses — the police being warned to bear in mind that these orders were not for the summer season only, but were to remain in full force throughout the year.

"Very good ordinances," remarked some of the people who stopped to read them; "but will they be carried out?" To which the reply, when it met with one, was an expressive shrug of the shoulders, which each one interpreted according to his interests or fancy.

## CHAPTER XXI.

The Marriage of César de Vendôme and Françoise de Lorraine Opposed by the Duchesse de Mercœur. — The Young Lady Abhors Her *Fiancé*. — The Marriage Proposed by the Duke and Accepted by Henri in 1598. (The Duke Served in the Hungarian Army and Died of His Wounds in 1602.) — Father Cotton Employed and Succeeds in Removing Scruples. — Henri Meanwhile Falls in Love with the Beautiful Daughter of the Connétable de Montmorency, Promised to Bassompierre, Who, to Gratify the King, Resigns His Claim to Her. — The King Marries Her to Prince de Condé. — Sully Uselessly Implores the King to Give His Attention to Public Affairs.

TWO royal marriages — or, more correctly perhaps, semi-royal — were on the *tapis* at the French court early in 1609, affording much speculative gossip amongst the ladies and the cavaliers as to whether they really would or would not take place. Obstacles had arisen to both, and the plotters and intriguers — now more numerous about the court than ever — watched with vigilant eye the course, not of true love — of that there was little, if any — but of events, in hopes of turning them to some account as aids to the furtherance of their own schemes.

The first of these marriages the king was most anxious to celebrate was that of his and Gabrielle d'Estrées' eldest legitimised son, — César Monsieur,

Duc de Vendôme, with Françoise de Lorraine, only daughter and heiress of Philippe Emanuel, Duc de Mercœur. The duke had offered his daughter to Henri's son on making his submission to the king and restoring Brittany, of which province he had for ten years usurped the government. The king acceding to the proposal and accepting the conditions, the marriage was arranged at Angers, where in 1598 the betrothal took place with much pomp and ceremony. After his surrender the duke asked and obtained permission of Henri IV. to enter the military service of Hungary, then at war with the Turks.

In 1602 he died at Nuremberg, while returning with the army, having in more than one battle greatly distinguished himself. His widow — Marie de Luxembourg, Duchesse de Mercœur — and her mother then expressed great disapproval of the marriage, and so influenced the mind of the young princess that her aversion to her youthful *fiancé* became so intense that she could not endure even to hear him named, and prayed that she might be allowed to enter a Capuchine convent, and devote her life to God rather than be compelled to marry César de Vendôme. This youth had just completed his fifteenth year; the princess was entering her seventeenth. Her family would have preferred that Prince Henri de Condé should take the place of Vendôme. The prince was about twenty or twenty-one, a more suitable age certainly; but the prince is described as "a young man without youth, false and cunning, and already leading a vicious kind of life." The king, however, had other views for him.

Judicial proceedings were threatened by the king, which were expected, with fines, etc., to cost the duchess ruinous sums. But so immense was the wealth of this family that she declared the cost of the proceedings to be a matter of utter indifference to her. The king had recourse to Sully, who declined to interfere. His majesty must be aware, he said, from his ill-success in keeping peace between him and the queen, how incapable he was of conciliating or soothing the wounded feelings of angry ladies, — how destitute of the power of persuasion, so necessary for bringing such matters to a satisfactory issue. He advised him rather to avail himself of the "honeyed eloquence" of Father Cotton.

This was a new and bright idea to Henri. He knew how irresistibly tender and entreating the good father could be when he had a point to gain. To him, therefore, was confided the task of bringing the Duchesse de Mercœur, her mother, and her daughter to a sense of their duty, — that of fulfilling the engagement made by the late duke with the king, to which at the time they were consenting parties, together with Queen Louise, the duke's sister, also since deceased.

The second marriage, which was destined to

create much scandal, was that of the above-mentioned Prince de Condé, the reputed son of Henri II., Prince de Condé, poisoned in 1588, and Charlotte de la Trémouille, accused of poisoning him.

In February, during the carnival *fêtes* of this year, there appeared at court for the first time a brilliant young beauty of sixteen, Charlotte de Montmorency, the youngest daughter of the Connétable de Montmorency. She was already promised to the Maréchal Comte de Bassompierre, who declared that "beneath the heavens nothing so lovely, so full of grace and graciousness, so utterly perfect, existed." Yet he was induced by the king, who at first sight fell passionately in love with the beautiful Charlotte, to renounce his claim to her.

The marshal relates, when referring in his "*Mémoires*" to this matter: "After a deep sigh, the king said to me: 'Bassompierre, I will speak to you as a friend. I am not only in love, but intensely, madly enamoured of Mademoiselle de Montmorency. If you marry her and she should love you, I should hate and abhor you. Should she love me, then I shall incur your hatred. It is better that such a matter should not be the means of putting an end to the good feeling existing between us. I should regret it, having a sincere regard and affection for you.'"

He had already questioned the young lady

respecting her marriage. She replied that "her father desired it, and that she believed she should be very happy with M. de Bassompierre." Henri was piqued by her declared expectation of happiness that did not include him, and was jealous of the gallant and elegant cavalier of twenty-nine. Their marriage was broken off, the Connétable de Montmorency having actually no voice in the matter; for the sons and daughters of the nobility appear to have been disposed of according to the whim or good pleasure of the monarch.

But Henri informed his friend Bassompierre, for his consolation, that he proposed to marry the fair young bride he had deprived him of to his cousin of Condé — or nephew, as he preferred to call him — first prince of the blood. This, as he told him, was that Charlotte might be near him, as one of his family, to soothe and amuse him in that dreary period, the autumn of life, which he was about to enter. He would give his nephew, who was then but scantily provided for, and who was far more attached, he believed, to hunting than to the society of ladies, 100,000 crowns yearly to spend according to his own pleasure or fancy; while of the princess he would ask, pretending certainly to nothing more, only filial regard and affection.

The king had taken to wandering alone in the gardens of the arsenal, for at the Louvre or Fontainebleau the royal *ménage* was in a furious state of commotion, the queen very naturally witnessing the progress of this new intrigue with extreme vexation. So entirely did Henri seem to have given the reins to this absorbing new passion, that he was unable to dissemble or conceal it, thus giving occasion for fresh scandal where already there was too much talk of his depravity and the licentiousness of his court.

The Concini party persuaded the queen that Henri was seeking to divorce her, that he himself might marry this youthful beauty and place the crown on her brows. They implored her also to touch no food sent to her from the king's table (for she seems to have frequently dined alone, the king sending such dishes as he thought would best please her taste), or which came directly from the hands of the king's chief cook, insinuating an intention on the king's part of removing her out of his way after a manner in which her uncle Ferdinand of Tuscany was accused of disposing of troublesome individuals who proved obstacles to his plans — poor Gabrielle d'Estrées, for instance.

Yet once more, at his urgent request, Sully endeavoured to come to an arrangement with Maria de' Medici. The king would promise, he told her, to entirely give up his various mistresses if she would consent to the dismissal of Concini and his wife, with three or four other Italians in her confidence, and at once send them back to

Italy. It was but fair, he said, if he renounced the society of his mistresses to gratify her wishes, that she should yield in some things to gratify his. The proposal put Maria into a great rage. She positively refused to part with her friends, and as Henri declined to use his authority to order their expulsion, domestic life at the palace became more troubled and stormy than before. These Florentine favourites, brought up in a court familiar with every crime, put no bounds to their suspicions, while they encouraged and increased those of their mistress.

Though Henri made Sully his confidant, and even visited him in the dead of the night, awaking the surprised *grand-maître* from his slumbers to hear him descant on the perfections of the fair Charlotte de Montmorency and his all-absorbing, passionate love for her, he yet turned a deaf ear to his sage Mentor's prudent counsels. The "grand project" had lost all its attractions, and the evils which Sully foresaw and strove to impress on him as the certain results of this unseemly infatuation he heeded not, professing to seek in this attachment, as he had already told Bassompierre, nothing more than consolation for his declining years in the society and filial affection as of a loved daughter.

But neither Bassompierre nor Sully believed this. The former says "he wished to marry her to the prince, whom, from his comparative poverty and devotion to the pleasures of the wild life of the period, he expected to find submissive and supple in the furtherance of his views." Sully remarks that he did not, in this affair, look for that generous resolution in Henri, of which some lovers of honourable principles have been capable : that of imposing on themselves the necessity of relinquishing a beloved object by her marriage with another.

What he apprehended was an entirely contrary course. He foresaw on the part of the outraged young prince, of the parents of the princess, and of that of the offended queen, only resentment and fury. He therefore implored the king, as he never before, he says, implored or importuned any one, to give up the pursuit of this young girl and attend to the pressing affairs of his kingdom, that he might dismiss from his mind those reprehensible thoughts which should never have found entrance there. But, in spite of all the *grand-maître's* prayers and entreaties, the fatal marriage, not many days after, took place.

It was celebrated at Chantilly on the 3d of April, almost privately, which may have been owing to the severe attack of gout which for several days confined the king to his bed. The constable gave his daughter 100,000 crowns and the estate of Isle-Adam. The king promised to increase the prince's pension, and to raise Isle-Adam to the rank of a *duché-pairie*. The king also presented the bride with 2,000 crowns for her wedding dress, jewelry to the amount of 18,000 *livres*, with several smaller presents and a large sum of money to the prince.

The princess's portrait was painted at this time, with her hair, which was very abundant and of a bright golden colour, flowing over her shoulders. When shown to his majesty, the enamoured monarch gazed long upon it, as though enraptured; this silent sort of adoration being followed by ecstasy so extreme that the princess could not refrain from laughter, and turning to the prince, said, in an undertone, "*Jésus, qu'il est fou!*" Henri had become more madly in love than ever, and gave way to his passion without measure or decency. The young princess was amused by the king's folly, and coquetted with her royal lover. "*Jésus, qu'il est fou!*" was constantly on her lips, the prince, at first, appearing to be utterly indifferent to the king's mad folly.

Soon after he became very jealous, and is said to have ill-treated the princess, declaring that she lent herself to the carrying on of this intrigue with the king. There was even a question of a divorce; Maria de' Medici, however, foolishly believing that she would be included in it, interfered to prevent it. But so ardently continued was the king's pursuit of the young princess that with the greatest alacrity he would change his usual dress, alter the fashion of his beard, and disguise his countenance on the chance of seeing her for a few minutes in private or even of kissing his hand to her from a distance.

The prince considered that the king's conduct gave him just cause for complaint; he therefore, in order to avoid the usual results of these fancies of his majesty falling on him, requested permission to retire for a time with his wife to one of his estates. The absence of the princess, he thought, would be the mildest and surest means of obviating the inconveniences of the king's mad love, and of mitigating its ardour. This request was very ill received by his majesty, and as the prince was bent on urging it, while Henri felt that he could not, for however short a time, support the *ennui* of the princess's absence, he not only harshly refused to grant his request, but launched forth into menace and insult.

The prince replied rather haughtily, using amongst other terms that of tyranny, as if to tax the king with it. Very angrily taking up this word, he rejoined that "the only act of tyranny with which he could justly charge himself was that of recognising the prince for what he was not, and that whenever he chose he would show him his father in Paris." This was acknowledging what indeed few persons of the court and many others ever doubted. But they were cruel words, which greatly grieved the heart of the young prince. Knowing that his mother had been employed to corrupt the mind of his young wife, he lavished on her epithets of the grossest kind, and said that she had painted shame on his brow.

"Here," exclaims that diligent chronicler of the events of his times, L'Estoile, "is a brief specimen of the deeds and words of daily occurrence at our court."

The prince, however, secretly took his wife to Muret, the king, for some time without success, assuming various disguises to discover the place of her concealment. An event which Sully hoped would turn the king's thoughts into another channel occurred at this time — the death of Jean Guillaume Duc de Cleves, who was said to have left all Europe, if not all the world, his heirs. A general war therefore seemed imminent.

The principality of Cleves and Juliers had become wealthy and of importance by the marriage of several of its dukes with heiresses, whose dowries, chiefly small fiefs with the title of principalities, had added to its extent and power, but to which, at the late duke's death, there was no direct heir, male or female. Spinola at once took possession of Cleves and its fiefs, in the name of the Emperor Leopold; while almost all the German states claimed at least a share of them, and called on Henri IV. for his promised aid to enforce their rights against Spain and Austria. The moment seemed to have arrived for taking the first step — the abasement of the latter power —

towards the realisation of Henri's "grand project" of the establishment of a Christian republic, hitherto regarded, perhaps, but as a vague idea, but to which events were gradually giving form and substance.

But while Sully was enrolling troops and preparing for the departure of his formidable artillery and other material of war,—the young nobility also rejoicing in the near prospect of again unsheathing the sword,—the Duchesse de Mercœur and family yielded to the persuasive tongue of "Father Cotton," and consented to the marriage of the heiress of their house with César de Vendôme, notwithstanding the young lady's aversion towards him.

The marriage was celebrated with great magnificence on the 7th of July. The bride's dress of rich white satin, with the *fleur-de-lys* woven in silver, gave great offence to M. de Soissons, who, more severe in such matters, it appears, than the rest of the princes of the blood and *haute noblesse*, declared that M. de Vendôme, being only a legitimised scion of royalty, his bride, though of the royal House of Lorraine, was not entitled to the *fleur-de-lys* of the Bourbons. The place assigned him at the ceremony also was not exactly, he thought, the prominent one that should have been his; he therefore determined henceforth to deprive the court of his presence.

But the king heeded not the pleasure or displeasure of M. de Soissons; for on that occasion he was, as it were, in Elysium. The Prince de Condé had brought back his "*bel ange*," that he might not be said to have failed in his duty, — court etiquette requiring that he and the princess should be present at the grand court ceremonies. Usually the king piqued himself on the plainness of his dress. He now wore a wedding garment of extreme brilliancy, and though all around him sparkled and glittered, his majesty, covered with pearls and diamonds and other dazzling gems, shone like a sun amongst the stars, his refulgence overpowering the milder radiance of those lesser lights.

The queen, having no quarrel with, or complaint against, M. de Vendôme and his bride, arranged a new ballet for the festivities following their marriage. In this ballet, gracefully yet scantily arrayed as a nymph, appeared the lovely Charlotte; her long, fair hair falling around her, and in her hand a javelin, which, brandishing as she danced, sank deeper and deeper into the already rankling wound in the king's heart. He gazed on her wholly entranced, and for some time after, so strange were his acts, and so madly did this gray-bearded, weather-worn lover of fifty-seven conduct himself, that, as was truly said, he seemed to have lost his reason.

Sully was in despair. "Yet it was remarked that he carried things before him with a very high hand, — braving the first in the land, without permitting them to brave him." But the king, it was said, was weary of being governed, lectured, and opposed by his minister; and, had he really been so, it would not have been surprising — as "he daily became more depraved, more oppressive in imposing new taxes, or desiring Sully to do so; more lavish in gifts to his mistresses; more addicted to furious gambling, and if not more, certainly not less, dissolute than any King of France before him." *

After the marriage of César de Vendôme, the Prince de Condé took his wife to Bréteuil, which the king having ascertained, in order to speak with her while the prince was out hunting, he left the town in disguise with six or seven of his servants, disguised like himself, and wearing false beards. When passing the ferry at Saint-Leu they were taken for robbers, and the Provost des Marechaux sent after them. Being informed, by a person who had recognised Henri, notwithstanding his disguise, that the king was among them, the provost very discreetly turned his horse's head, and without seeming to notice the suspicious-looking party, rode leisurely back again.

The prince was informed of this act of folly on the king's part, and at once returned to his home; but his majesty had disappeared, the people he had on the watch having given him

* L'Estoile, *Journal de Henri IV.*; Mathieu.

notice of the prince's movements. The king's proceedings were now the common talk of Paris, but generally in an undertone, because of the danger of openly referring to them. The christening of Henri's youngest son was about to take place, which gave the king hope of again seeing and conversing with his "*bel ange.*" To his great disappointment, neither she nor the prince appeared, and he learned from Sully that the latter had been with him bitterly to complain of the king's conduct.

He could no longer doubt, he said, of his passion for his wife, and the further injury he sought to inflict on him; he proposed, therefore, to leave the country. Whither he should take the princess he scarcely yet knew, — perhaps to Spain, whence offers had been made to him. Soon after the king was informed that the prince and princess were on their way to Flanders. He had carried her off in the night, not too willingly on her part, it appeared; for she was believed to have been amused, if not flattered, by the king's secret homage, and to have coquetted with him, rather than repelled him, often exclaiming, with much laughter, "*Jésus, qu'il est fou!*"

When Henri heard that the prince had eloped with his wife, taking her *en croupe* behind him, and proposing to reach the court of the archdukes, he was angered and troubled immensely — much more than he liked to appear to be.

Their journey proved a most unpleasant and fatiguing one, and they were compelled, having wandered from the right road, to seek rest and shelter for the night in a miller's hut, where they had neither bed, fire, nor food. The rain was falling in torrents when, on the morrow, they arrived at Landrecies, where they obtained provisions and some better accommodation. It was November, and the princess, owing to the soaking rain and bitter cold of the night, was unable to draw off her gloves without taking the skin from her hands with them. Balagny, sent by the king in pursuit of the fugitives, endeavoured to enter their apartment to arrest the prince, and to take both him and the princess back to Paris; but Condé laughed at his pretensions.

The Duc de Praslin was also despatched by Henri IV. to Brussels to require the archdukes to give up the prince and his wife. His mission was, however, as unsuccessful as Balagny's, the Archduke Albert replying that he had never yet violated the law of nations in the person of any individual who sought refuge in his domains, and certainly would not begin to do so in the case of the first prince of the blood of France. He immediately after sent a sum of money to the prince, and an escort of troops to conduct him and his wife to Brussels.

The constable, confined to his bed by illness, was much troubled and scandalised by the king's and the prince's proceedings, as were, indeed, the nobility of the court generally; but none presumed to speak his thoughts on the subject openly. The constable, at the king's request, demanded his daughter of the archdukes. "His son-in-law," he said, "had greatly offended him, and had ill-treated his wife." A divorce was spoken of, and the prince partly assented to it, but took no steps towards obtaining it. He, however, wrote to the king, expressing "regret at leaving the court. Only to save his honour had he done so, and by no means with the intention of being other than his majesty's very humble relative, faithful subject and servant." He returned Sully's letters, and declined to receive any further communications except from the king.

All through the autumn and winter warlike preparations were hurrying forward, that everything might be in readiness for the king to take the command of his army, as he had announced his intention of doing, early in the spring. But these arrangements devolved chiefly on Sully, for the king was by no means cured of his insane passion. He was then employing the poet most in vogue, François de Malherbe, to write tender ditties in praise of his mistress's perfections, or touching laments over his own miserable condition and the sorrows of separation.

If now he spoke of war, it was of carrying fire and sword into Belgium; of marching to the rescue of his mistress at the head of 25,000 men. "Never," says Bassompierre, "did I see a man so distracted, yet so passionate. He was dying with love for the fugitive princess, and could not live if his eyes were not sometimes gladdened with the sight of her." By keeping several people continually travelling between Paris and Brussels, and on the watch to discover the movements of the princess, he frequently contrived to have the tender missives he wrote to her expressive of his ardent and undying love delivered into her own fair hands.

It is not surprising that the royal household should have become, under such circumstances, a den of greater misery than ever. Plotting and intriguing were carried on there with feelings more embittered against the king than elsewhere. The French ambassador at Madrid, Count Vaucelas de Cochefilet, was surprised to find that the queen and Concini were in active correspondence with the court of Spain — Villeroy and Épernon being also concerned in it, and a system of policy adopted entirely opposed to that he had received instructions to enforce. This was so openly done that Vaucelas believed that the king must be aware of it, but did not care at once to reveal the change in his views. At all events, he fancied that the king had withdrawn his confidence from him, and appealed to Sully, who was his brother-in-law, to tell him in what he had unconsciously displeased his majesty.

Glad to awaken the king from his amorous dream, Sully laid the ambassador's information before him. Henri was greatly mortified. "This intrigue," he exclaimed, "can only be founded on the expectation of my death being near at hand." He knew that several soothsayers had announced that he would not survive his fifty-eighth year; but the originator of the prophecy was a crazy nun named Pasithée, who pretended to Divine inspiration, and was greatly in the queen's confidence, willingly aiding in the pernicious designs of the factious Italians and others who surrounded Maria de' Medici, and whose aim was doubtless not only to circulate an evil prophecy, but to ensure its fulfilment.

## CHAPTER XXII.

Martial Ardour Reawakens when Sully Lays before Henri His Ambassador's Report of the Intrigues of the Italians with Spain. — The Peace Party Recommend Him to Reject War and Live a Life of Ease. — Henri Inclined to Acquiesce in Their Views, for His Passion for the Princesse de Condé is Not Abated. — The Nun Pasithée. — The Army Begins to Defile towards Cleves; but Henri Lingers, though Sully Urges Departure. — The Queen Crowned at Saint-Denis. — Henri Full of Sad Forebodings. — Leaves the Louvre for the Arsenal. — Stabbed by the Assassin Ravaillac. — The Royal Widow. — Lying in State. — Funeral of the Two Kings.

SULLY'S communication, while occasioning much bitterness of spirit, yet seemed to have the good effect of rousing Henri from his lethargy, and reawakening the martial ardour of other days. Turning to account this, perhaps, merely transitory state of feeling, the minister sought to impress on the king that, having opened his heart to projects so noble, he should now close it to a taste for frivolous pleasures and amusements, and cease to lavish immense sums on unsatisfactory objects unworthy of a great king who had at heart the prosperity of his kingdom and welfare of his people.

Sully urged him the more earnestly because there were amongst his courtiers some who, in opposition to the war party, sought to persuade the king that he, who had spent so many years amidst the din of war and its fatigues and hardships, should now think of enjoying the repose and pleasures of a life of ease. Since his passion for Charlotte de Montmorency had so greatly occupied him, he seemed at times to acquiesce in these views, which Sully's aim was to discountenance.

He proposed to nominate the queen regent during his absence, but with a council of regency to direct her, as he had no confidence in her ability or wisdom. She, however, was dissatisfied with being controlled by a council, but as the king insisted, the Concini and others urged her to propose her coronation, in order to strengthen her claim to continue her office of regent " should anything happen to the king." He was decidedly averse to it, and the prophecies of the epileptic nun did not incline him to be more yielding. Pasithée had left France for awhile for her Italian convent, whence she sent the queen Divine messages concerning the destiny of the king, translated for her by her confessor. Henri declared she should no more enter France; also he determined that there should be no coronation; but his irresolution was so extreme that no dependence could be placed on these promises. What he resolved to do one moment the next he resolved not to do. But the queen was more persistent, and in spite of all that Sully could do to keep the king firm in his resolve, or to induce Maria de' Medici to change hers, the latter triumphed, and orders were given to prepare for the event with all due magnificence and *éclat*, though both Sully and Henri pleaded, vainly. indeed, for some mitigation of its proposed pomp and splendour, because of the expenses of a great war at hand.

The threatening storm was to begin on the side of Germany, and Henri had asked permission of the archdukes "to pass through a part of their domains as a friend, and of course with the promise to abstain from any act of hostility."* The grand army destined to occupy Cleves numbered 20,000 infantry, 4,000 cavalry, and 6,000 Swiss troops. The equipage consisted of not less than fifty cannon, chariots, horses, mules, baggage wagons, and the rest of the material of war in proportion, — all, Sully remarks with some pride, in a condition of great efficiency and amply provided for.

Being in readiness, the army began to defile towards Cleves, though war was not yet declared. The question even was asked, "Who is the enemy? Is this army destined to begin the abasement of Austria, or to rescue another Helen?" The king had unwillingly deferred his departure for a fortnight to be present at the queen's coronation, at which he assisted as a spectator only,

* The answer arrived the day after his death.

an astrologer having warned him that his life would be imperilled by taking part in any great public spectacle; also that misfortune would happen to him when in a carriage. He laughed at the prediction, though in reality he took it greatly to heart, knowing probably that, as in many similar instances, it was made with a view of preparing for its realisation when opportunity offered.

The coronation was an affair of great splendour, which on that bright May morning drew towards Saint-Denis a vast concourse of people from all parts. Henri was anxiously watched and guarded by many friends, whom his constant repetition of his belief that he was not destined to leave Paris had similarly affected and occasioned them great anxiety. "They will kill me. I perceive plainly," he said, "that my death is their only means of successfully carrying out their own designs." Sully, who was suffering from the reopening of the wound in the nape of his neck, strongly urged him to leave Paris for the army. But the queen was to make her public entry into the capital on the following Sunday, May 16th, and for that he had promised to remain.

On the 14th Sully was still confined to his bed. The king sent him word that he would go the next day to the arsenal, then threw himself on his couch to endeavour in sleep to put aside the sad thoughts that oppressed him. His confessor, Cotton, had told him within the last day or two of ten plots against his life, but seems to have omitted the one so near its accomplishment, and in which he and other Jesuits were believed to be implicated.

Henri, not succeeding in casting off his sad forebodings, the captain of his guards (Vitry) recommended him to take a drive, thinking the air would do him good. Unhappily, or perhaps it only hastened the deed by a few hours, the king followed the officer's advice. "He would go then," he said, "to see Sully, instead of the next day." But, alas! he never reached the arsenal. The infamous Ravaillac had been watching for him the whole day, and would have despatched him in the morning had he not been joined by his son Vendôme. In his capacious coach, with leathern curtains, seven of his friends, to cheer him, accompanied him. One of these seven friends, or comforters, was really his declared enemy.

The only escort was a company of five or six cavaliers and a few *valets de pied*. A stoppage at the corner of the narrow-winding Rue de la Ferroniere arrested the progress of the royal carriage, of which Ravaillac availing himself, hastily mounted the steps of the vehicle, and with a poniard he had concealed in his dress stabbed the king in the heart. He fell back in his seat, and said softly: "*Ce n'est rien*" (It is nothing). In some of the greatly varying accounts of this deed, it is reported that the "friendly hand" of the Duc d'Épernon, to put an end to possible suffering, as the king did not appear to be dead, plunged a dagger he had also very strangely concealed into Henri's heart. Blood flowed from his mouth; he breathed a heavy sigh, and all was over. Others relate that the second blow was given by Ravaillac, and even a third, at a sign from the duke.

The murderer was seized and conveyed from the spot, or the people in their rage would have torn him to pieces. The leathern curtains were closed, and the anxious people informed that the king was only wounded. He was then conveyed to the Louvre, and only two hours after Maria de' Medici appeared in widow's dress in the hall of the Sovereign Court of Paris, where the presidents and magistrates had been hastily assembled. She led by the hand her little son, Louis XIII., then eight years old. They were escorted by the Duc d'Épernon, who claimed on her behalf her right to the regency, which scarcely could be doubted. The queen's tears, meanwhile, rolled as usual from her eyes in a torrent, resembling an impetuous cascade.

When Ravaillac was questioned, he declared that he had no accomplices, and had been influenced only by Jesuit teaching to do a deed which he thought would rejoice the nation. He would have done it before, he said, but waited until the queen was crowned and could take the king's place. The poor creature, who appeared to be a religious maniac, was punished, tortured, after the manner of those times. The blood runs cold when attempting to relate the horrors of a death so revolting.

The next day — 15th — the king's heart was placed in a silver casket, and, instead of being sent to Notre-Dame, was given to the Jesuits, who deposited it in their church of La Flèche. Numberless persons were accused of complicity in Henri's assassination, especially Madame de Verneuil, the Duc d'Épernon, and the Concini. The queen herself did not escape suspicion of having at least not dissented from the proposal to remove an obstacle to her plans, if she did not actually consent.

"It still remains doubtful," says a modern writer, "whether the war Henri IV. was about to undertake when stopped by the poniard of Ravaillac, was the adventure of a chevalier, or the expedition of a conqueror. Was it Amadis de Gaule or Alexander the Great whom the king then took for his model?"

The king lay in state for some days, but was not buried for nearly six weeks after — June 19th. Six days later the body of Henri III. was brought from Compiègne by the Duc d'Épernon, to be placed in the royal vaults of Saint-Denis. But the great magnificence of the funeral of the first of the Bourbons strikingly contrasted with that of the last of the Valois. The body of Henri III.

waited for the hour fixed for the funeral ceremony in a common auberge, or tavern. The monks of Saint-Denis refused to enter so profane a place, consequently some half-drunken men from the tavern were employed to carry the body into the abbey, where, before they had reached the middle, they let the coffin fall. The next day the tomb closed over Henri IV. and his imputed grand designs.

**THE END.**

# INDEX

Aiguillon, Duc d', I., 234.
Albert of Austria, I., 33; II., 40.
Amiens, captured by Spaniards, II., 85, siege of, 96.
Amours, Gabriel d', I., 75, 238.
Angoulême, Comte d', I., 324.
Anhalt, Prince of, I., 175.
Arques, attack of, I., 46.
Arras, manufactories of, II., 349.
Assembly of Notables, convocation of, II., 57, meeting of, 68.
Aumale, Chevalier d', I., 76, 79, 89, 101, 103, 146, 266, 334 et seq.
Aumont, Duc d', I., 28, 30, 38 et seq., 50, 76 et seq., 96, 321.
Auverne, Comte d', II., 163, 185, 225, 228, 233, 286, 290 et seq.
Bar, Duc de, II., 137, 140, 174, 267, 280.
Beaufort, Duchesse de (See Gabrielle d'Estrées).
Beuil, Mdlle. de, II., 240.
Biron, Maréchal de (elder), I., 28 et seq., 44, 54, 76, 80, 92, 123, 141, 146, 176, 181 et seq., 197 et seq., 204.
Biron, Maréchal de (younger), I., 128, 205, 236, 314, 320, 323, 333 et seq.; II., 4, 7 et seq, 94, 100, 119, 184, 188, 199 et seq., 222 et seq.
Bouillon, Duc de (see Turenne).
Bourbon, Cardinal de (elder), I., 1, 34 et seq., 41, 60 et seq., 69, 102, 304.
Bourbon, Cardinal de (younger), I., 41, 56, 147 et seq., 154, 232 et seq., 243, 248 et seq., 326 et seq.
Bourgoing, I., 55.
Brissac, I., 70, 287, 290 et seq.
Brisson, I., 67, 168.
Bussy-Leclerc, I., 169, 172.

Caëtano, Cardinal, I., 60, 65 et seq., 94, 99 et seq.
Calais, siege of, II., 38.
Cambray, surrender of, II., 19.
Carlovingian crown, destruction of, I., 266.
Catherine, Madame, de Navarre, I., 41, 93, 148, 239, 273, 331;
    II., 72 et seq., 130, 137 et seq., 174, 240, 267, 280 et seq.
César Monsieur, I., 330; II., 5, 39, 111 et seq., 357 et seq., 367.
Chambéry, siege of, II., 190.
Champagne, subjugation of, I., 338.
Charles X. (see Cardinal de Bourbon, elder).
Charles Emmanuel, at Fontainebleau, II., 175, defeat of, 194.
Chartres, siege of, I., 14, taking of, 144.
Chastel, Jean, attempts to assassinate Henri IV., I., 345, execution of, 346; II., 1.
Château-Dun, taking of, I., 55.
Châtillon-Coligny, II., 210.
Châtillon, Comte de, I., 6, 46 et seq., 53, 112, 144, 164 et seq.
Clement, Jacques, I., 16 et seq.; II., 26.
Clément VIII., I., 212 et seq., 218, 251 et seq., 260 et seq., 316 et seq., 325; II., 11 et seq., 18, 62 et seq., 108, 161, 170, 174 et seq., 265, 297 et seq.
Concini, II., 193, 211, 241 et seq., 287, 294.
Condé, Prince de, II., 13, 63, 357 et seq., 368 et seq.
Conti, Prince de, I., 39, 112.
Corisande (see Grammont).
Cotton, Father, II., 268, 275 et seq., 344, 367.
Courtenay, Mdlle. de, I., 160 et seq.
Dombes, Prince de (see Duc de Montpensier, younger).
Dreux, capture of, I., 95, siege of, 235.
Du Perron, characterisation of, I., 150, interview with Rosny, 278; attack on Du Plessis-Mornay, II., 186.
Du Plessis-Mornay, I., 8, 41, 113, 187, 255; attack upon by Du Perron, II., 186.
D'Urfé, publication of his "Astrée," II., 337.
Edict, granted by Henri III., II., 2.
Edict of Nantes, II., 115, registration of, 146.
Egmont, I., 72 et seq., 76 et seq.
Elizabeth, of England, I., 50, 175, 187, 310; II., 20, 36, 38 et seq., 93, 207 et seq., 223 et seq., 227, 237.

# INDEX 385

Entragues, M. d', I., 324, 327; II., 163 et seq., 291 et seq.
Entragues, Mdlle. d', II., 162 et seq., 189, 195 et seq., 211, 287, 291 et seq., 381.
Épernon, Duc d', I., 30, 41, 205; II., 32 et seq., 187, 234, 236 et seq., 239, 314, 380 et seq.
Essex, Earl of, I., 175, 187; II., 38.
Estrées, Antoine d', I., 138; II., 105 et seq., 179 et seq.
Estrées, Gabrielle d', I., 134 et seq., marriage of, 139, becomes mistress of Henri IV., 140, 156, influence upon Henri, 208 et seq., baptism of son of, 330, at Amiens, 337; Mayenne's promises to, II., 29, narrow escape from accident of, 44, baptism of daughter of, 83, 98, at Paris, 103, at Brittany, 117, christening of second son of, 130, letter from Henri to, 135, at Fontainebleau, 150, death of, 153, funeral of, 158.
Falaise, siege of, I., 71.
Feria, Duc de, I., 220, 224 et seq, proposition of, 227 et seq., 293, 298, 322; II., 16.
Finances in France, condition of the, II., 58.
Franche-Comté, taking of towns of, II., 6.
Fuentés, military exploits of, II., 10.
Galigai, Leonora, II., 201, 241 et seq.
Givry, Baron de, I., 28, 96, 101, 128, 191, 335.
Gondy, Cardinal de, I., 213.
Grammont, Comtesse de, I., 140, 148, 151 et seq., 167, 276, 278 et seq.
Gregory XIV., I., 133, 140, 147, 151 et seq., 167.
Guise, Charles, Duc de, I., 1, 32, 165 et seq., 170, 189, 233, 265, 338 et seq.; II., 30, 32 et seq., 94.
Guise, Henri, Duc de, I., 1.
Harley, I., 67; II., 2, 92.
Henri III., I., 2 et seq., 18 et seq.
Henri IV., at Tours, I., 3 et seq., 12, attitude of Parisians toward, 23, enemies of, 28, promises of, 29, leaves Paris, 38, takes Clermont, 39, acquires Dieppe, 39, at Arques, 47, attack on Paris, 53, victories of army of, 55, acknowledgment of claims by Venice, 57, at Tours, 58, attitude toward Cardinal Caëtano, 68, at Falaise, 71, at Ivry, 72, 78, takes Mantes, 89, indecision of, 91, admiration for Antoinette de Pons, 93, takes Dreux, 95, military tactics of, 96, his efforts toward

conciliation, 106, clemency of, 110, assault of the faubourgs, 113, retreat from Paris, 120, his letter to Madame de La Roche-Guyon, 122, at Lagny, 125, his regret at the death of Sixtus V., 133, meets Gabrielle d'Estrées, 134, renewed attempt to take Paris, 142, takes Chartres, 144, takes Noyon, 146, intrigues against, 152, convokes assembly at Mantes, 152, goes to Compiègne, 156, projects of, 177, in camp at Darnetal, 181, at Aumale, 193, takes Yvetot, 200, takes Caudebec, 204, takes Épernay, *ib.*, at Mantes, 208, poverty of, 210, message to States General, 218, besieges Dreux, 236, his lack of firmness, 240, becomes catechumen, 243, abjures Protestantism, 249, his truce with Mayenne, *ib.*, terms to States General, 254, attempted assassination of, 260, surrender of various towns to, 264, preparations for his coronation, 265, his interview with Queen Louise, 269, his projects for marriage of Catherine, 276, coronation of, 283, proposals of peace offered by, 288, his negotiations with Brissac, 291, his entry into Paris, 293, his proposition to Duke of Feria, 298, appeals to foreign powers for funds, 310, receives allegiance of various cities, 314, at siege of La Capelle, 321, at Laon, 322, 333, at Amiens, 336, victories of. 338, reformations instigated by, 344, attempted assassination of, 345; at Chauny, II., 3, policy toward Spain, 4, at La Franche-Comté, 9, receives public absolution, 11, appeals for aid, 20, signs treaty with Mayenne, 22, his efforts at Calais, 38, pecuniary embarrassment of, 42, convokes Assembly of Notables, 56, his approbation of Rosny, 62, oration by, 66, at Saint-Ouen, 68, *fêtes* of, 81, begins siege of Amiens, 96, victory over Spanish, 101, concessions made to Duc de Moncœur, 111, at Brittany, 117, signs treaty with Spain, 119, matrimonial projects of, 128, at Fontainebleau, 150, his grief at death of Gabrielle, 153, procures a new mistress, 164, his negotiations for marriage, 171, his former marriage annulled, 174, declares war against Charles Emmanuel, 185, at Chambéry, 190, his marriage by proxy, 192, his victory in Savoy, 194, meets Maria de' Medici at Lyons, 190, his treaty with Charles Emmanuel, 199, marriage festivities of, 206, trials of his private life, 213, his joy at birth of dauphin, 216, his interview with Biron, 227, his communication with Maurice, 236, at Metz, 237, birth of daughter of, 240, sends embassy to England, 245, his interview with Jesuits, 269, his concessions to Jesuits, 276, reorganises army, 309, his suspicions against Rosny, 315, prepares to attack Sedan, 320, victory at Sedan, 323, his proposition to Rosny, 329, christening of royal children of, 337, mediates between Paul V. and Venice, 340, negotiates between Spain and Netherlanders, 342, his interview with Don Pedro, 345, his ordinances, 355, projects for marriage of César de Vendôme, 358, plans concerning marriage of Charlotte de Montmorency, 360, proposal to Maria, 362, infatuation of, 369, makes preparations for war, 377, assassination of, 379, funeral obsequies of, 381.

Holland, military renown of, II., 309.
Huguenots, their sentiments toward Henri IV., I., 256; dissatisfaction of, II., 1.
Ibarra, Diego d', I., 171, 294, 322.
Infanta, Clara Eugenia, I., 61, 132, 170, 227.
Innocent IX., I., 198.
Ivry, siege of, I., 72, 78.
James VI., II., 20, 245, 258 et seq., 343.
Janville, taking of, I., 55.
Jesuits, recalled to France, II., 275.
Joyeuse, Henri, Duc de, II., 30 et seq.
La Capelle, siege of, I., 321.
La Fère, capitulation of, II., 40.
La Fin, II., 226 et seq.
La Franche-Comté, siege of, II., 9.
La Fond, I., 159 et seq.
Landriano, I., 140.
La Noue, I., 6, 14, 50, 96 et seq., 164.
League, councils of, I., 31, decrees of, 69, army of at Meulan, 70, consternation of, 86, proclamation of, 95, hatred toward Sixtus V., 130, machinations of, 167, effect of death of Prince of Parma upon, 206, renewed vigour of, 287, takes oath of allegiance, 302, strongholds of, 338; submission to Henri of, II., 30.
Leo XI., II., 298.
Leonora, ambition of, II., 42.

Lesdiguières, Duc de, I., 59, 205; II., 188 et seq., 194, 321.
Liancourt, Sieur de, I., 139 et seq.
Longueville, Duc de, I., 25, 28, 38, 40, 50, 96; II., 19 (note).
Lorraine, Cardinal de, I., 1.
Lorraine, Duc de, I., 32; II., 143.
Lorraine, Françoise de, II., 111 et seq., 357, 367.
Louise, Queen of France, I., 38, 269; II., 25, 118.
Lyons, Archbishop of, I., 63, 86, 212.
Maignan, at Ivry, I., 80.
Malherbe, François de, poems of, II., 372.
Mansfeldt, Comte de, I., 225 et seq, 288 et seq., 323.
Mantes, surrender of, I., 89, Rosny's attack of, 158.
Marck, Charlotte de la, I., 176 et seq., 283.
Marguerite de Valois, I., 139; II., 29, 103, 117, 124 et seq., 129, 135 et seq., 160 et seq., 174, 266, 302 et seq.
Marseilles, victory at, II., 34.
Mayenne, Duc de, I., 4, 8 et seq., 32, 40 et seq., 46, retreat of, 50, ambition of, 61, at Ivry, 72, military tactics of, 79, at Saint-Denis, 89, anger of Parisians against, 117, reception at Paris of, 127, 160, his treatment of the League, 167, policy of, 172, signs truce, 249, anger of people against, 262, 286 et seq., obstinacy of, 343; in Franche-Comté, II., 9, 16 et seq., Henri's concessions to, 27, at Amiens, 100.
Meaux, Bishop of, I., 63.
Meaux, surrender of keys of, I., 263.
Medici, Alexandro de', II., 62 et seq., 83, 298.
Medici, Catherine de', I., 13, 32, 158, 296; II., 141.
Medici, Maria de', II., 147, 169 et seq., 175, 193 et seq., 203, 211 et seq., 215, 240, 345, 378, 380.
Mendoza, I., 14 et seq., 34, 61 et seq., 106, 117, 228.
Mercœur, Duc de, II., 36, 108, 110.
Mercœur, Duchesse de, II., 111.
Monceaux, Marquise de (see Gabrielle d'Estrées).
Moncenigo, I., 56.
Monks, demonstration by, I., 98.
Montemélian, attack at, II., 191.
Montholon, Comte de, resignation of, I., 35.
Montmorency, Charlotte de, II., 359 et seq., 368 et seq.
Montmorency, Damville, I., 59; II., 22, 82, 185.

Montmorency, Duchesse de, I., 9.
Montpensier, Duc de (elder), I., 39, 52, 76.
Montpensier, Duc de (younger), I., 28, 76, 117, 177 et seq., 268, 271 et seq., 282, 283, 320; II., 32, 47 et seq., 72, 185.
Montpensier, Duchesse de, I., 17, 21, 89, 103, 300; II., 26.
Morosini, I., 6.
Mourad, Sultan, letter to Henri IV., I., 57.
Nassau, Prince Maurice of, I., 176.
Nemours, Duc de, I., 79, 89, 103, 116, 263.
Nevers, Duc de, I., 6, 9, 113, 251, 261; II., 20 et seq, 42.
Noyon, capture of, I., 146.
O, François d', I., 25, 91, 110, 221, 309, 328 et seq.; II., 41.
Ornano, Alphonso d', I., 59.
Paris, attack of, I., 53, hatred of people of, toward Henri, 103, famine in, 104, siege of, raised, 120.
Parliament, decree of, I., 69, steps taken by, 305.
Parma, Prince of, I., 15, 71, 88, 95, 97, 116 et seq., 119, 123 et seq., 187 et seq., 198 et seq., 205 et seq.; II., 100.
Paul V., II., 298 et seq., 330, 340.
Perron, Jacques de, I., 148 et seq.
Philip II., I., 5, 22, his pretensions to throne of France, 33, designs of, 61 et seq., his gift to Mayenne, 72, suspicions concerning, 132, policy of, 231, his promises to Mayenne, 288 et seq.; declaration of war against, II., 6, defeat of his troops at Marseilles, 34, death of, 121.
Picardy, subjugation of, I., 338.
Pisani, Marquis de, I., 214.
Placentia, Bishop of, I., 217.
Pons, Antoinette de, I., 93, 94, 96, 123.
Pont, Marquis de, I., 51.
Pontoise, surrender of, I., 15.
Porto-Carrero, death of, II., 99.
Processions in Paris, I., 109.
Rambouillet, Marquis de, I., 4 et seq.
Ravaillac, assassinates Henri IV., II., 379.
Rochefoucauld, De la, I., 90.
Rome, festivities at public absolution of Henri at, II., 11.
Rosny, Baron de, influence of, I., 4 et seq., 39 et seq., at Arques, 47, at Paris, 54, at siege of Meulan, 70, 72 et seq.,

anecdote of, 87, made chevalier, 87, at the attack of the faubourgs, 114, attacked at Mantes, 158, anecdote of, 159, at siege of Rouen, 183, 236 et seq., Henri's reliance upon, 270, diplomacy of, 278, his interview with Villars, 312, his efforts to obtain funds, 329, at Laon, 333; anecdote of, II., 44, Henri's projects concerning, 54, his efforts to adjust the finances, 59, his interview with Catherine, 77, at Amiens, 97, obtains governorship of Mantes, 107, remonstrates with Henri concerning Gabrielle, 132, salary of, 148, new appointment of, 180, his preparations for siege, 188, new title of, 201, his visit to England, 208, his embassy to England, 246, promises made to him by James VI., 262, his career as financier, 306, accusations of Henri against, 315, new honors of, 318, at Sedan, 323, proposition of Henri to, 329, refuses to abandon his religion, 332.

Rosny, Madame de (see Mdlle. de Courtenay).
Saint-Denis, ceremony at, I., 249.
Saint-Mesmin, Mdlle. de, I., 159 et seq.
Sancy, I., 27; II., 5, 6, 10, 38, 92 et seq.
*Satire Menipée*, circulation of the, I., 222.
Savoie, Duc de, his pretensions to the throne, I., 33; II., 16, 120, 175 et seq., 181 et seq., 188 et seq.
Schomberg, Colonel, anecdote of, I., 74.
Senlis, siege of, I., 14.
Sixtus V., I., 60 et seq., 66, 89, 100 et seq., 129 et seq.
Soissons, Comte de, I., 41, 50, 93, 148, 266, 271 et seq., 345; II., 75 et seq., 130, 138, 140, 185, 282, 318.
Spaniards, entrance into Paris of, I., 144, march on Picardy of, 189; defeat of, II., 40, take Amiens, 85.
Spinola, II., 207.
States General, convocation of, I., 206, opening of first session of, 215, second session of, 273.
Sully, Duc de (see Rosny).
Suresne, conference of, I., 226.
Toledo, Don Pedro de, II., 343 et seq.
Tours, meeting of two sovereigns at, I., 11.
Treaty between Henri III. and Henri of Navarre, I., 8.
Treaty between James VI. and Henri IV., II., 264.
Treaty of peace with Spain, II., 119.

Treaty signed by Henri IV. at Château de Folembray, II., 22.
Treaty signed by Henri IV. at Tours, I., 30.
Treaty signed by Henri IV. with Mercœur, II., 111.
Treaty with Duke of Savoy, II., 199.
Trémouïlle, Duc de La, I., 26; II., 9, 49, 234.
Truce, signed between Mayenne and Henri IV., I., 250.
Turenne, Vicomte de, I., 112, 154, 175 et seq.; II., 3, 4, 10, 49, 53, 94, 225, 234 et seq., 317, 320 et seq.
Urban VII., I., 133.
Velasco, Fernando, II., 6 et seq.
Vendôme, Cardinal de (see Bourbon, Cardinal de, younger).
Vendôme, Duc de (see César Monsieur).
Verneuil, Madame de (see Mdlle. d'Entragues).
Vilette, De la, I., 205.
Villars, I., 182 et seq., 197, 218, 270, 273, 274, 282, 291, 311 et seq., 317 et seq.; II., 10.
Villeroy, I., 36, 94, 212, 218, 286, 288.
Vitry, surrenders keys of Meaux, I., 263.
Yvetot, capture of, I., 200.

www.ingramcontent.com/pod-product-compliance
Lightning Source LLC
Chambersburg PA
CBHW030213170426
43201CB00006B/71